THE SALES COMPENSATION HANDBOOK, SECOND EDITION

THE SALES COMPENSATION HANDBOOK, SECOND EDITION

Stockton B. Colt, Jr., Editor
Towers Perrin

AMACOM

American Management Association

New York · Atlanta · Boston · Chicago · Kansas City · San Francisco · Washington, D.C.
Brussels · Mexico City · Tokyo · Toronto

This book is available at a special
discount when ordered in bulk quantities.
For information, contact Special Sales Department,
AMACOM, a division of American Management Association International,
1601 Broadway, New York, NY 10019.

This publication is designed to provide accurate and authoritative
information in regard to the subject matter covered. It is sold with the
understanding that the publisher is not engaged in rendering legal,
accounting, or other professional service. If legal advice or other expert
assistance is required, the services of a competent professional person
should be sought.

Library of Congress Cataloging-in-Publication Data

The sales compensation handbook. — 2nd ed. / Stockton B. Colt. editor.
        p.   cm.
    Includes index.
    ISBN 0-8144-0411-1
    1. Sales personnel—Salaries, etc.   2. Incentives in
industry.   3. Compensation management.   I. Colt, Stockton B., 1946–   .
HF5439.7.S24 1998
658.3'22—dc21   98-13160
                                                                    CIP

Printing number

10 9 8 7 6 5 4 3 2

Contents

Preface

Some business meetings drive me up a wall.

I'll admit it. Maybe I'm getting older—or just more impatient—as time goes by. My mind drifts to the Caribbean, or Santa Fe's mountains, or anywhere but where it should be: focused on the words and expression of the executive in front of me.

Forgive me, but I've heard it too often. The poor sales compensation plan gets blamed for everything up to and including the state of the coffee harvest in Colombia! "Salespeople are doing strange things, the business is in disarray, and our customers are bolting at the mere sight of our name. It's got to be the incentive plan! We've got to fix it now!"

"And," says the executive, "it'll be tough to fix. Our company is unique; no one can match us." (Given their recent performance, few would want to!) "Besides, our industry is so highly specialized that common practice has no meaning here. Which means, of course, we can't look to others for guidance, inspiration, or knowledge. But what's important is to replace that incentive plan; that'll fix everything." Right.

Hoping to keep you from indulging in such flights of fancy, we have prepared this second edition of *The Sales Compensation Handbook*. We hope you're interested.

You should be. Properly understood, sales incentive compensation can be a valuable tool, allowing you to execute a sound marketing strategy, create loyal customers, and excite employees. As you read this handbook, my colleagues and I will try to impress on you some core lessons from our consulting work. For example, we believe that problems with sales incentive pay usually are symptoms of much larger weaknesses in sales management processes. Fixing the incentive plan may not even put a dent in the real problem! So, in this handbook, we discuss the other factors that must be considered. Companies—and their management teams—can learn enormous lessons in incentive design from others. In fact, several chapters of the book detail common incentive design principles—principles that apply to all sales forces, industries, and companies. And, yes, there is a unique aspect to every company; its culture and that of its management affect incentive design, as you will learn in this book. But as an excuse for poor performance, uniqueness is a red herring. What *are* unique—and matter—are the company's strategy and its go-to-market approaches; those really drive incentive design.

So stay with us. We'll show you how properly designed and implemented sales incentives, when integrated with business strategy and well-conceived sales management programs, can be effective change agents. That's a tall order, but one that must be filled in the global marketplace of the next century.

With the tools and ideas you'll take away from reading this book, perhaps you won't be saying the same old things.

And it'll be fun to attend your meetings!

Stockton Colt
New Mexico, March 1998

Acknowledgments

In 1990 John K. Moynahan asked several of his colleagues, including me, to contribute to the first edition of this handbook. Little did I realize then how much time and effort were to be required! Apparently having learned little from that experience, I was taken aback at the challenge of developing this second edition, and I am very thankful for the considerable help provided by many. Without them, this edition would still be a glimmer in the eye of Adrienne Hickey, executive editor, at AMACOM. Aside from having the wisdom to suggest *both* the first and second editions, Ms. Hickey showed amazing restraint and patience in dealing with numerous business consultants, who often took on the appearance of human tornadoes.

Twenty-five consultants from Towers Perrin contributed to the development of both *Handbook* editions. They invested their own time to bring these pages to life, I particularly appreciate the recent efforts of the following colleagues, who made the second edition possible: Ron Burke, J. Mark Davis, Philip Davis, Mark Flavin, Kevin Hummel, Gary Lawrence, Chris Lewallyn, Michelle Rogers, Mike Savage, and Tim Weiler. (Gary Lawrence also had the dubious honor of organizing this team, a task much like herding cats.) Not only did the consultants enrich these pages with their experience and knowledge, but they brought enthusiasm and commitment to the creation of the second edition as well.

Producing a 400-page manuscript, as you might imagine, is a challenging effort for which special recognition is due. Amber Black in Atlanta and Janet Colt in Sante Fe made sure all the words reached the page, in the intended order, with the correct spelling, and with the appropriate exhibits. I often marveled at Amber's sense of humor under pressure, especially on New Year's Day. And why my wife Janet stayed married to me during the review process is beyond my understanding—but not my gratitude. Special recognition goes to Nancy Duden, who lent moral support through the entire process; at Towers Perrin, Nancy has kept John Moynahan and me in line for the past eighteen years—no easy task.

Finally, as we did in the first edition, we must acknowledge here the hundreds of business organizations worldwide that provided us the experience that illuminates these pages. Without their request for our consulting help, many lessons might have gone unrecorded. Of course, special thanks go to the thousands of readers who purchased the first edition and gave us the impetus and courage to produce this revision.

1

Sales Compensation—One Component of an Effective Sales Management System

Despite popular opinion, experience tells us that compensation is but one component of an effective sales management system. Yet it is the dial first and most often turned by management when they attempt to tune sales performance. Sales compensation is rarely the sole solution to problems with field performance.

Let's consider some frequently heard symptoms of ailing sales forces and the range of factors to be considered in diagnosing the potential problem, as illustrated in Exhibit 1-1. As we see in this diagnosis, to improve the performance of the sales force substantially, you must look beyond just the pay plan. A well-designed compensation program is a powerful motivational tool, but it is never a surrogate for effective sales management.

To be effective, all of the components of the sales system, including compensation, must be built on a solid foundation. The three drivers that form the foundation for an effective sales system are illustrated in Exhibit 1-2.

1.1 Well-Defined Opportunities

The first step in building an effective sales system boils down to answering one fundamental question: What do our customers need and value? To define these opportunities for the sales force, you must start by segmenting the customer set for your products or services. By analyzing how customers buy, the purchase criteria they use, the size of the opportunity they represent, and the cost to serve each group of customers, you can begin to direct the sales force toward the "sweet spots" in the marketplace. Understanding these dynamics for each customer segment also serves as the starting point for developing a focused and effective sales strategy.

Exhibit 1-3 shows typical sample opportunity identification

Exhibit 1-1. Symptoms of Ailing Sales Forces and Factors in the Diagnostic Process.

Symptom	Potential Diagnosis	
	Pay Plan Issues	*Other Sales System Issues*
Our reps don't bother to sell new products.	▪ Incentive payouts for new products are not sufficient to justify relatively longer sales cycles. ▪ Balanced performance is not required, and reps can choose what they want to sell. ▪ There is a relatively long sell cycle relative to other products of equal value in the pay plan.	▪ Reps lack training on new product: 　—Features, functions 　—Applications 　—Economic justification 　—Installation challenges ▪ The new products are not competitive, readily available, or easy to use.
We're selling ever-increasing volume but not making much profit.	▪ Reps are not measured and paid for their influence on profit margin.	▪ Too much, or too little, control of pricing and other profit drivers is delegated to reps. ▪ Information on which products and which customers are most profitable is either not accessible or not acted on by reps.
We must have bad reps; no one ever makes quota.	▪ Pay plan is either not tied to making quota or does not sufficiently reward for hitting quota.	▪ Quota-setting process is less than rigorous and hence not credible to reps. ▪ Quotas are set at unrealistic stretch levels. ▪ Field staffing is too thin, territories are too large, and assumptions about a rep's ability to sell and service are unrealistic.

Our sales force is costing us a bundle.	▪ The pay plan is too lucrative relative to the level of sales force performance, or relative to prevailing market rates of pay.	▪ The highest-cost channel (direct reps) has been directed to sell to relatively unprofitable (i.e., the wrong) customer segments.
We are constantly recruiting.	▪ Pay levels are not competitive for midlevel and senior sales talent.	▪ Lack of home office support or lack of quality product. ▪ Hostile work environment and weak field management. ▪ Lack of coaching. ▪ Lack of defined career paths. ▪ Quotas that are perceived to be unattainable.
Most of our reps have been with us forever, and our turnover rate is almost zero.	▪ Lack of downside risk in pay plan for poor performance. ▪ Pay/performance equation is heavy on pay and light on required performance.	▪ Lack of focus by field management on addressing performance problems.

questions and how they might affect the formulation of sales strategy—in this example, for a medical products company.

1.2   Clear Strategy

A clear, well-articulated business strategy is the second driver of an effective sales system. It translates both the key elements of the overall company strategy and the customer segmentation analysis results into selling strategy and tactics—a strategy for how the company will go to market.

A clear go-to-market strategy answers four primary questions that ensure the company's business and sales objectives are met:

1. To which customer groups will we sell?
2. Which products or services are these customers likely to buy?
3. Through which channels of distribution should we focus?
4. How will we establish our competitive differentiation?

Exhibit 1-2. Factors of Sales Force Effectiveness.

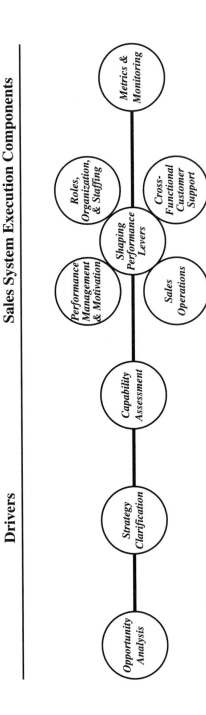

Drivers

Sales System Execution Components

Opportunity Analysis

Strategy Clarification

Capability Assessment

Performance Management & Motivation

Roles, Organization, & Staffing

Shaping Performance Levers

Cross-Functional Customer Support

Sales Operations

Metrics & Monitoring

Exhibit 1-3. Sample Opportunity Identification Questions for a Medical Products Company.

Sample Opportunity Identification Questions	Implications for Sales Strategy and Sales System Design
How should we segment and quantify our marketplace and our existing customer base?	Understanding the size of each segment, and hence its sales potential, by type of product will help us decide: ■ What level of sales coverage might be required for the physician segment versus the surgeon segment. ■ Which products should be sold to physicians versus to nurses. ■ What reasonable sales quotas or objectives might be established given the potential of each segment.
Which customer segments are most lucrative: ■ Financially? ■ Strategically?	Understanding the sweet spots in the marketplace is the first step in deciding: ■ Which segments to pursue, which to serve opportunistically, and which to avoid. (Should we be assigning field reps to cover rural general practitioner physicians, or try to serve them via telesales? Should we be selling to podiatrists at all?)
Which buying criteria are most important?	Understanding the purchase criteria helps us determine where the sales force needs to excel, where it needs to merely be competent, and where it should avoid spending too much time and energy. For example, we might choose to: ■ Invest in demonstrations and training for heart surgeons and a strong service capability for radiologists. ■ Avoid investing in training direct sales reps to sell supplies to nurses when lower-cost telesales reps may deliver higher levels of service.

Exhibit 1-4 illustrates one way to approach clarifying the strategy and the implications the approach has for the levers that will shape how the sales force performs. (This exhibit continues the example of the medical products company.)

In the end, a clear go-to-market strategy provides each channel and each sales position with clear selling priorities: preferred customer segments and preferred mix of product to be sold to each.

Exhibit 1-4. Sample Strategy Clarification for a Medical Products Company.

Sample Strategy Clarification Questions	Implications for Sales System Design
How do customer buying criteria and channel preferences differ by customer segment?	Understanding what will be required to capture a good share of the market for each customer segment will help us decide: • What type of channel (e.g., direct field rep, direct telesales rep, or distributor) will be best suited to meeting customer buying criteria. —Doctors buying expensive ultrasound equipment require product demonstrations and an economic justification, often provided by direct field reps. —Nurses purchasing disposable items like bandages require rapid delivery and replenishment at a good price, often provided by a distributor or a telesales or service rep. • What types and levels of competency will be required for each type of rep. —Heart surgeons may require assistance and training in the operation room (a highly trained and technically competent rep is needed). —Radiologists may require high levels of equipment service (a combination sales and service rep is needed).
How does our cost to serve vary by customer segment and by channel of distribution?	Understanding the true cost to serve has direct implications for: • The primary charter for each channel and each sales job: —What type of distribution should be matched up with each customer segment to maximize customer value and supplier profit? • How to structure the supplier sales organization to serve each customer segment and each indirect channel partner. • How to staff and deploy limited selling and service resources: —How many reps should we have selling to heart surgeons? —How should we assign accounts and territories for the heart surgeon reps?

1.3   Understanding of Company Capabilities

This third driver of an effective sales system involves taking stock of the company's strengths and weaknesses in meeting the needs and wants of preferred customer segments.

In building the first pillar of the system, we identified the most attractive opportunities, and in building the second driver, we created a strategy for capturing those opportunities. Constructing the third pillar involves the sobering work of assessing:

- How well the company and its competitors are meeting the needs and wants of each customer segment—a score card.
- What the company's capabilities and constraints are to improve the score.

Once management develops a sound understanding of the three drivers of sales force effectiveness, it has built the foundation on which the components of the sales system can be evaluated and improved.

1.4   Transforming the Sales Organization

There are four major components of any selling system that can be evaluated and improved to transform the sales organization and shape field performance:

1. Roles, organization, and staffing
2. Cross-functional coordination and customer support activities
3. Sales operations and support activities
4. Performance management and motivation

Within each component are several subcomponents, as shown in Exhibit 1-5.

The four components of the sales system can be viewed as the many dials that can be turned to tune field performance.

Roles, Organization, and Staffing

Determining which type of sales channel to use (e.g., direct versus distributor) and which type of selling or service position to create (e.g., field rep versus channel manager) should reflect the results of the customer segmentation and cost-to-serve analyses.

Exhibit 1-5. Sales System Execution Components.

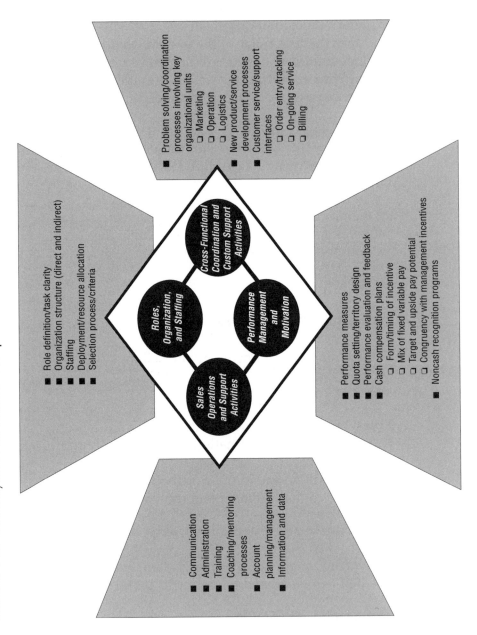

- Role definition/task clarity
- Organization structure (direct and indirect)
- Staffing
- Deployment/resource allocation
- Selection process/criteria

- Problem solving/coordination processes involving key organizational units
  - ❑ Marketing
  - ❑ Operation
  - ❑ Logistics
- New product/service development processes
- Customer service/support interfaces
  - ❑ Order entry/tracking
  - ❑ On-going service
  - ❑ Billing

Roles, Organization, and Staffing

Cross-Functional Coordination and Custom Support Activities

Sales Operations and Support Activities

Performance Management and Motivation

- Communication
- Administration
- Training
- Coaching/mentoring processes
- Account planning/management
- Information and data

- Performance measures
- Quota setting/territory design
- Performance evaluation and feedback
- Cash compensation plans
  - ❑ Form/timing of incentive
  - ❑ Mix of fixed variable pay
  - ❑ Target and upside pay potential
  - ❑ Congruency with management incentives
- Noncash recognition programs

In our example medical products company, if we know which customer segments we want to target (heart surgeons), the particular needs of each segment (high-touch and lots of coaching on product use), and the profit potential of each segment (high due to surgeon focus on product function, not price), we can deduce which channel to use (direct not distribution—to provide high levels of service) and what type of selling position to use (technically competent field rep).

Each sales position or role should be defined across several criteria: customer segment focus, buying process and customer needs during the selling process, product or service focus, type of selling or service proposition, and key account abilities. The objective is to match the different types of selling skills with the differences in customer needs across market segments. Sales force specialization will be discussed in more detail in Chapter 6.

Once roles have been clarified, you can assemble them into a rational sales organization structure (who should report to whom). Information available about the number and size of customers in each market segment can provide crucial insight into sales staffing decisions (How many people do we need in each role?) and deployment (Where should we put all of these people to ensure that we capture the greatest share of the most attractive customer segments?).

Cross-Functional Coordination and Customer Support Activities

Often some of the key customer purchase criteria relate to things not directly controlled by the salesperson. For example, to deliver effectively against customer expectations, a salesperson might be required to build solutions or solve customer problems by working with other supplier functions, such as product development, marketing, customer service, operations, distribution and logistics, order entry and tracking, and billing.

Sales Operations and Support Activities

The third component of the sales system relates to the infrastructure that supports the field. It includes effective communication with the field regarding changing selling priorities, new products, selling techniques, company and individual performance against goals, and competitor intelligence, to name a few. It also includes the various administration and information systems that allow the people in the field to maximize time spent on high-value-added activities (finding, closing, and keeping business) and minimizing the time spent on lower-value-added activities (entering and tracking orders, seeking out information on product availability, and keeping score to ensure that they are paid correctly).

Performance Management and Motivation

There are many aspects to managing performance and motivating a field sales organization. The design of the various programs used to manage and motivate should be aligned with and reinforce the three drivers of the sales system (well-defined opportunities, clear strategy, and a solid understanding of company capabilities).

A holistic view of performance management is required to address the joint needs of the company and the salesperson. Although pay and benefits represent the most significant dollar investments in salespeople, the other levers of performance management should also be recognized and fully optimized. We will discuss managing the other drivers of sales performance in Chapter 22.

In summary, the sales compensation program is but one of the many parts of an effective, integrated sales system. If the other components of the system are not addressed in the diagnostic process, changing the compensation plan in response to concerns over field performance often becomes an exercise in addressing symptoms, not the causes, of the problem.

1.5   Illustrating the Concept of Integration

Sales force compensation is one of a number of interrelated sales management systems. So closely connected are these systems that often what appear to be defects in the sales force compensation system are really symptoms of underlying problems in other sales management systems. When this is the case, strengthening compensation will not in itself improve sales force effectiveness. A number of sales management systems must be properly linked to sales compensation:

- Selection
- Training
- Deployment and role definition
- Sales information systems
- Goal and quota setting

A properly designed sales compensation plan can serve as a powerful medium of organization communication, enabling a company to improve the return on its investment in a most important resource: its sales talent. But if other systems send a conflicting message, a dysfunction occurs, and the sales force will not behave according to management's intentions. This problem frequently develops when related management systems reflect cultural values that are no longer (if they ever were) relevant to contemporary thinking among customers—for example:

Selection	A chemical company had always recruited college graduates with chemistry degrees to staff its industrial sales force. Although the company diversified and acquired a consumer goods business, its selection procedures remained unchanged, despite the fact that a degree in chemistry (and the compensation level that background commanded) was not required in a consumer goods sales force.
Training	A telecommunications company gave its sales reps a three-week training course in basic telephony. Customer needs (and the company product line) later expanded to include far more elaborate systems. Because the training still focused on simple equipment, sales force productivity suffered.
Deployment and role definition	A grocery products company maintained the same organizational structure despite a major change in customer decision-making processes. The company assigned sales reps to geographic territories that could include independent stores, national account headquarters, food brokers, and outlets of national chains. Each distribution channel called for a different level and type of selling skill, yet the sales role, as the company defined it, required that the rep be proficient at a number of difficult—but mutually exclusive—tasks. Thus, because of its traditional geographic-organizational structure, the company wasted much of its skilled reps' selling capacity on relatively mundane activities. The result was unnecessarily high sales costs.
Information systems	An industrial company's strategy called for quickly increasing penetration of the automo-

tive industry. But sales reps preferred to concentrate on industries in which the company was more firmly entrenched. Sales managers' reports identified where products were shipped and whether and how quickly they were paid for but could not differentiate sales by industrial segment. Thus, the company was unable to measure its penetration of its target industry.

Goal and quota setting	A company's sales reps received a salary plus a bonus based on how their sales volume compared to their quotas. Quotas, however, were set arbitrarily and were not based on solid data concerning market potential. Some of the company's best sales reps (in management's judgment) were not even earning the targeted bonus. Management feared losing key contributors and searched for a better compensation plan.

In all of these situations, management perceived a need to improve sales force effectiveness and tried to redesign the compensation program accordingly. Unfortunately, the problems were in sales management systems, not in sales compensation.

2

Cultural Influences on Sales Compensation Strategy

2.1 Corporate Culture

In Chapter 1, we found that compensation is a key element in creating an effective sales organization, but it is not the only one. The four components of the sales system comprise many varied programs and systems, which, when acting in unison, define the performance of a sales organization. Ensuring that these four components (and all their programs, such as pay) are complementary is paramount to a well-oiled, efficient selling process.

Success is also shaped by another factor, often forgotten: corporate culture—the values and beliefs that management brings to the company. The resulting cultures may vary dramatically, as may the sales compensation programs that reinforce them. Time and again we have seen how the beliefs of management can—and should—influence the design of a sales incentive plan. Let's look at some examples.

The vice president of customer service and marketing of a major gas and electric utility pounded his desk and declared:

> "We must change our culture to be more sales oriented for us to be successful in our evolving marketplace. Our industry is being deregulated, and this company must understand the needs of each customer segment. We have to develop a sales mentality to execute our selling strategy of account retention and penetration. This new sales force is the first line of communication with customers, and it must be both efficient and effective."

Sitting in his corner office decorated with golf memorabilia and company-logo-decorated items, the division president of a packaging products company discussed his company's approach to the market this way:

"The majority of our products are highly sophisticated and are sold on their technical strengths. We do not sell the packaging machinery, but we represent manufacturers who make machines that run our materials best. Our role in the marketplace is to assess customer needs, teach customers that our packaging materials are the best from both quality and price perspectives, and deliver on both counts. For example, in the past few years the success of our packaging products has helped revive the fresh pork industry.

"We value knowledge and loyalty among our sales representatives. We treat them like family, and we expect open communications. We hire only the best, provide excellent training, pay above industry levels, and expect that the quality of their performance will reflect the quality of our product. There is little need to spend a great deal on product promotion because the expertise of our sales force sells the products."

Faced with a market with new competitors on all fronts and at the same time developing new markets, the sales and marketing vice president of a telecommunications company contemplates his rapidly changing environment:

"For several years, we have been the only or major provider of telecommunications services in our geographic area. Because of this market advantage, we have done well, but only because our sales force pushes our services into every nook and cranny. We are, of course, concerned with our customers' loyalty and with selling them our traditional services, but our key goal is to ensure profitable revenue flowing from greater use of our new and improved services.

"We must be different from our competitors. They are often more nimble and able to exploit our slow market response. We must get closer to the customers to understand better how they might use our services. Our culture will have to change. That means we might also have to change the type of salespeople we hire and the sales compensation program that motivates them."

These vignettes, about executives of three different companies with different sets of values and markets, demonstrate that corporations have personalities. These personalities, generally referred to as *corporate cultures*, create subcultures for particular functions. In the case of the sales force, such a subculture attempts to align sales actions and behavior with the values of the company. Companies also develop sales management programs, particularly incentive compensation schemes, that support and communicate the corporation's cultural values. But as the examples show, marketplace developments and the resulting evolution in corporate culture suggest that parallel changes are required in the systems that control, monitor, and motivate the sales force.

Examples of factors that might shape a corporate culture include:

1. Internal competition among employees
2. Operating independence
3. Creativity and innovation
4. Respect for the individual
5. Self-confidence
6. Informality
7. Openness of communications
8. Employee and customer participation
9. Customer service orientation
10. Propensity for action and change
11. Decentralization of decision making
12. Orientation to risk
13. Quality emphasis
14. Security and seniority

A company must understand, develop, and communicate its corporate values and beliefs effectively. It must also use these values and beliefs as the foundation for hiring, managing, and shaping the behavior of the sales force. A key vehicle for communicating your company's beliefs to the sales force is the sales incentive compensation program. Its design is critical; it must communicate values and goals accurately and encourage appropriate behavior.

2.2   Corporate Culture and Pay Systems

Let's consider some typical corporate cultures and the sales compensation systems that reinforce them.

Manufacturing or Technology Culture

A company with a strong manufacturing or technology focus normally concentrates on product quality, features, efficiency, and production. The chief executive of such a company is frequently a graduate of the production, research, or engineering function of the company (or one of its competitors), and the style of the organization is characteristically low key, conservative, and participative. Manufacturing- or technology-driven companies often take a somewhat detached view of customers.

Sales reps recognize that nonselling jobs in research or production are frequently more highly valued. For this reason, many often see sales as a place "to do some time" on the way to other positions.

The incentive compensation schemes commonly found in such companies are usually risk adverse. The sales rep generally receives only a base salary or a salary plus a very modest incentive award. (The incentive is usually "backed into" to ensure that the salesperson receives exactly the amount of planned incentive dollars. There is little true variability in the selling situation.) This compensation method does not allow the company to reward specific selling efforts of strategic importance. Consequently, retaining outstanding, high-performing sales reps becomes difficult, especially if competitors are offering variable compensation on top of salary.

Numbers Culture

A numbers-driven company focuses heavily on revenue, profit, and growth. The chief executive usually comes from a finance or engineering background and has a style that is often autocratic, intense, and controlling.

In a numbers-driven culture, the customer takes second place to the internal goal of achieving the numbers, and the sales force is viewed as a cost center rather than an investment. The sales force must create market demand consistent with the company's product goals. Not surprisingly, sales rep behavior reflects the intense pressure to reach management's aggressive financial goals, which are often formulated with little or no counsel from the sales force. This results in turnover, especially among the better salespeople, at the point where experience, industry knowledge, and training begin to pay off.

Pay programs in such companies invariably entail significant risk, often in the form of commission plans whereby the salesperson receives a preestablished percentage of the revenues or profits. Usually the base salary is less than 60 percent of the overall total cash compensation. This scheme reflects the company's philosophy, which says that if the numbers don't come in, sales reps don't get paid market levels of total cash.

This arrangement disposes the sales force to seek quick and easy sales. It is difficult for the company to direct selling efforts toward other strategic goals, such as selling to selected customer groups or pursuing relationship-building activities, that do not result in an immediate sale.

Market Culture

Here the marketing and sales functions are given a high priority, and all senior executives participate actively in formulating strategies. Market-driven companies focus on achieving market-based strategic goals and recognize the importance of knowing their current and potential customers. In the market-based culture, selling is a respected function that carries high stature. In fact, many positions in the company may be involved in the selling activity, and not just the sales force alone. In today's highly competitive environment, where a few large companies often vie for a limited number of customers, many companies are adopting this cultural form.

Pay systems in the market-driven culture tend to be risk oriented, but to a lesser extent than in the numbers culture. The company usually provides a market-competitive base salary supplemented by some form of variable compensation to provide both motivation and direction. The variable component often takes the form of multiple bonuses that vary in proportion to the sales reps' performance against defined, objective goals. These bonuses might concentrate the sales reps' effort on selected customer groups, particularly high-profit product lines, or special selling efforts with long-term significance to the company. Such incentive compensation bonus programs are easier than commission plans to structure in ways that meet the needs of the company's customers as well as the company's strategic and cultural values.

2.3 Reconciling Culture and Market

As the business world grows more competitive, companies increasingly are challenged to ensure greater consistency between the characteristics of their markets and their corporate cultures. They must also ensure that sales management systems focus on customers' needs, not on their own needs.

The first step in strengthening the link between the customer and the company culture is to understand customers' specific needs—for example, delivery speed, availability of terms, technical

Exhibit 2-1. Influence on Sales Management Systems.

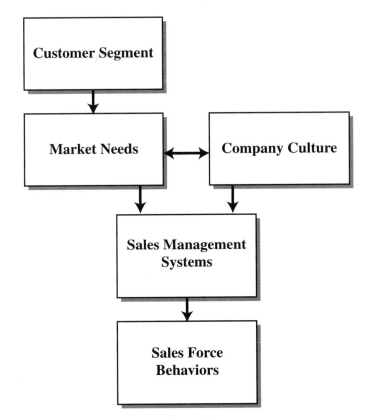

support, on-site repair, and special labeling, as well as customer segmentation and the company's competitive strengths and weaknesses. By analyzing the market, you might learn, for example, that your culture, and therefore your sales management programs, are inconsistent with each other.

The second step, because of this stronger bond between market needs and culture, is to require complementary sales management systems to communicate and reinforce these values, as shown in Exhibit 2-1.

To understand the importance of these relationships, let's return to our three corporate culture models: the manufacturing-driven, numbers-driven, and market-driven companies. By examining the buying habits of their customers, you can learn a great deal about consistency among customer needs, company values, and support programs.

Exhibit 2-2 lists common characteristics shared by the customers served by these companies. Note that their general buying habits vary as widely as the three cultures do from each other.

Exhibit 2-2. Linkages Between Culture and Selling Environment.

Company Culture	Characteristics of Selling Environment
Manufacturing and technology	• There is repetition of sales. • Products are substitutable. • The salesperson's role is minor.
Numbers	• Selling cycles are short. • The incidence of sales is predictable. • There is a high number of transactions.
Market based	• The incidence of sales is unpredictable. • Selling is indirect. • Sales are one of a kind. • Sales situations are multifaceted. • The customer is seeking solutions, not products.

Customers of manufacturing and technology companies require little sales support and buy on the basis of price, quality, or other factors not controlled by the sales rep. Little true interaction with this customer base is required, and, as we have seen, little customer service is provided. Customers in the numbers culture need more attention. Sales calls must be numerous and predictable, but actual demand may be a function of market growth rather than sales rep effort. Customers of the market-based companies require significant sales force support, in such projects as exploring potential applications for products and solving customer problems. The sales force and the anticipatory, strategic activities of management should align with these needs. In summary, a company's success in the marketplace is a function of reconciling its values and systems with the needs and demands of its customers.

Experience has shown that if customer needs and cultural values are not in alignment, sales system components (introduced in Chapter 1) will reinforce values that are inconsistent with those of customers and impair the effectiveness of your sales organization. Indications of sales management programs that are failing to reinforce appropriate values are listed in Exhibit 2-3.

To judge whether your culture and sales system components are complementary, ask yourself the following questions:

☐   Do you set reasonable and equitable goals and judge fairly the sales reps' performance against them? Does the sales force participate in the goal-setting process? Are they a source of information for the process? Do you have

Exhibit 2-3. Indications of Dysfunctional Sales Management Systems.

Indications	Weak System Component
▪ Sets unattainable quotas ▪ Ignores historical sales and market potential ▪ Underemphasizes rep input	Goal and quota setting
▪ Contains little customer-related data ▪ Cannot track desired performance ▪ Fails to identify profitable customers or products	Management information
▪ Applies awards inconsistent with productivity ▪ Provides no motivation to exceed quota ▪ Fails to focus selling activity ▪ Generates uncompetitive earnings	Incentive compensation
▪ Permits weak sales management skills ▪ Produces poor product knowledge ▪ Provides incomplete assistance with customer applications	Training
▪ Fails to distinguish more important prospects ▪ Encourages misuse of selling time ▪ Fails to track how selling time is actually used	Account planning

too many goals that result in small, meaningless incentive payments? How relevant are goals to true market opportunities?

☐ Do your management information systems capture the appropriate information about your customers, their buying habits and practices, and account profitability? Are you able to or do you track the frequency of sales calls and use of selling time for each sales rep? Do your data systems provide information that supports marketing and sales decision making?

☐ Do you recruit and train sales reps whose skills match the needs of your customer base? Do your salespeople have the technical skills necessary to understand customer applications and recommend appropriate company products? Do sales managers receive enough management training to support your selling tactics?

☐ Is your sales force organized to reflect the buying practices and processes of your key customer segments? Is it effective for your salespeople to call on multiple buyers at the same account, or should you specialize the sales force by customer or customer segments? Do your sales managers have the appropriate spans of control and authority to act?

☐   Do you give the sales force a process to classify both prospects and existing customers? Do you help the sales force allocate selling time according to the strategic importance of the prospect or customer, its buying habits, and competitive penetration?

☐   Do you provide the sales force with definitive career paths and the training and knowledge to progress from one level to another?

☐   Does your compensation program reward the achievement of specific strategic goals? Do actual incentive earnings truly reflect sales force productivity and goal achievement? Does the plan design encourage the sale of more strategically important or profitable product lines?

2.4 Cultural Change

As market characteristics change, many companies recognize that their cultures are no longer consistent with their customers' needs. Some of the major external forces driving market changes today are:

- Significant changes in the global competitive environment.
- Consolidation, acquisitions, and mergers of competitive companies seeking scale.
- Rapid evolution of technology.
- Government-directed deregulation, such as the financial services, telecommunications, and utilities industries.

Once your company concludes that cultural change is necessary, you will find that the sales incentive compensation program can be an important agent in affecting that change. With it, the company signals the sales force that certain values and behaviors are required for success and that, by conforming, the force will serve both the customer and the long-term success of the company.

In developing such a reward program, consider the following compensation design issues:

- *Consistency with corporate strategy.* Objectives set for your sales force must be parallel with and communicate the company's marketing and financial goals. To reinforce a cultural change through the compensation program, clearly delineate your goals and incorporate them directly into the compensation program. At issue could be such factors as revenue, market share, or profit growth, team selling activities, specific products or markets, product or customer emphasis, qualitative versus quantitative selling tasks, and selling costs.

- *Defining and balancing performance measures.* Measures might include volume, profit, selling milestones (such as getting a product specified into a customer's engineering drawing), product line activity, customer market share, or customer satisfaction. The company's marketing priorities will dictate the number and balance of these factors. By carefully structuring performance measures, you can focus selling efforts on your competitors' weak spots and shape selling behavior to serve the specific needs of your customers.

- *Variability of the sales force compensation.* How much variable compensation you use in your program will depend on how much your salespeople influence customer buying decisions. A careful study of the interaction between customers and salespeople will reveal the nature of their relationship. Do the salespeople influence only volume, or can they affect other aspects of the sale (e.g., which customer group is targeted or which product lines are sold)? Where it is appropriate, compensation programs should encourage and reward the high-risk selling efforts of highly influential salespeople who have a significant impact on closing the sale. Higher variability in earnings will signal to the sales force the importance of successful proactive selling.

- *Frequency of award calculation and payment.* Customers have a rhythm in their buying, and this pattern should be a key design factor. Some selling situations, such as sales to government entities, require long selling cycles with frequent customer contact that might not result in short-term volume. In the fashion industry, by contrast, the buy decision is made only semiannually or three times a year.

A sales incentive compensation program can act as an agent of change. It directs and molds the actions and attitudes of the sales force through incentive measures. A carefully designed incentive program can ensure proper sales force focus on market needs, successful achievement of company goals, and continual reinforcement of new values.

3

Assessing Sales Effectiveness

3.1 Looking for the Wrong Culprit

The primary reason that management changes sales compensation is to improve the effectiveness of the sales force in meeting business objectives. Management, however, is often disappointed in the performance delivered by a new sales compensation plan as measured from three important perspectives:

1. *Financial.* How well is the sales force meeting the top- and bottom-line objectives?
2. *Customer.* How well is the sales force satisfying the requirements of customers?
3. *People.* How committed, loyal, and motivated is the sales force?

The reason for the disappointment is that before changing sales compensation plan, management usually fails to identify clearly what matters most in improving sales effectiveness. In fact, in case after case, management cites changes in the sale compensation arrangements as the panacea for improving sales effectiveness, usually the wrong place to start.

Consider the prototypical symptoms of ineffective sales forces cited by several executives, shown in Exhibit 3-1. How many of them are truly pay related? These complaints are typical of those heard from many management teams considering a redesign of their sales compensation plan. Frequently management will look to redirect sales representatives' behavior by changing the sales compensation plan, thinking it will increase overall sales effectiveness. In fact, this is often the *wrong* solution because it will not necessarily consider the true causes of reduced effectiveness. Management should conduct a fact-based assessment of the causes of reduced sales effectiveness before prescribing a solution. Such an assessment will not only help determine whether the sales compensation plan needs to be redesigned, but it will also identify the other systems and processes

Exhibit 3-1. Symptoms of Ineffective Sales Forces.

Symptom	Prescription	Challenges
We have developed great new products, but our sales force continues to sell only the old ones.	Let's pay reps only for selling new products.	• Does this involve a new customer segment that reps do not know how to reach? • Do our reps have the technical and selling skills to promote the new products?
Our reps spend almost no time prospecting for new accounts.	Let's pay them a premium for new accounts.	• Do they have time to prospect? • What will happen to existing customer service and management? • Do reps have the required information and competencies to prospect?
Our reps spend less than half their time in contact with customers.	Let's decrease base salaries and increase incentives. That will get them out of the office and in front of customers!	• Do they spend their time servicing accounts due to an ineffective customer service process? • Is the administrative burden too high: too many meetings, call reports, market analyses? • Are reps burdened with operational activities such as expediting orders or order entry?
We are selling high volumes but not making much profit.	Let's base incentives on profitability only.	• Do the reps influence or control profitability levers such as price? • If so, do reps understand the drivers of profitability?
Our sales force is consistently below quota.	Let's put more of their pay at risk to improve results.	• Is the quota-setting process producing unfair and inappropriate goals?
We are not selling enough to our largest key accounts.	Let's increase incentives for key account sales.	• Do reps have the competencies necessary to manage key account relationships? • Do we offer the breadth and depth of product or service necessary? • Do sales, operations, marketing, information systems, and customer service work together well to support these customers?

that must be corrected to derive benefit from a new sales compensation plan. From this assessment, management will develop:

- A clear understanding and ranking of the areas for improving sales effectiveness (which may not involve changes to reward programs).
- A realistic picture of the expected impact that sales compensation changes will have on improving sales effectiveness.
- A context for the extent and timing of required sales compensation changes.

In the first two chapters, we learned that sales effectiveness is driven by several components in the sales process, not by compensation alone. In fact, we saw that even management's beliefs and the resulting corporate culture can affect sales force performance and compensation design. Now we will explore in more detail how to go about assessing ways to improve sales productivity.

3.2   A High-Growth Computer Book Publisher: A Case Example

Background and Problem Statement

The president of the leading publisher of computer books was worried. Revenues had increased by over 80 percent in two years, and the parent company's objectives were to maintain this growth rate for the next two years. Much of the company's success was due to its aggressive sales strategy, which had called for its sales force to double in size in three years. It was now twice as large as its closest competitor. Unfortunately, the company had begun to have problems with this sales force, experiencing declining morale and a 25 percent turnover rate. It became clear that what was once the company's competitive advantage might now be a liability. Improving sales effectiveness was imperative for sustaining the target growth rate.

Management Hypothesis and the Causes

The president and sales management team were quite sure that the sales compensation plan was at the heart of the problem, but they also suspected nonpay-related issues might be contributing factors. Nonetheless, they were convinced they should increase total compensation levels by improving incentive opportunities for the sales force. Once they made a detailed assessment of the situation, however, it became clear that this was not the correct solution. The comprehensive sales effectiveness evaluation resulted in some surprising findings:

- Sales reps were spending only 17 percent of their time on direct sales activities and 35 percent of their time on operational and customer service issues.
- They were spending very little time prospecting.
- Sales reps believed that there was no linkage between their performance and their incentive pay.
- Highly paid national account managers were calling on the account's purchasing executive, but not on other functions or levels within the account to build the business relationship.
- Sales managers were spending the majority of their time recruiting, not coaching.

Solutions and Implications for Pay

Using this information, the president launched a major initiative to improve sales effectiveness by redesigning the sales compensation plan and addressing the other priority issues:

- An ineffective customer service function
- Inadequate sales manager coaching and mentoring
- Unclear sales roles
- Inappropriate measures of personal performance
- Inaccurate and inefficient goal-setting processes

In the short term, the selling roles remained high in operational and customer service content, and accurate goal setting would remain an issue. Therefore, the incentive as a percentage of total compensation had to be decreased to reflect the significant operational content of the role, just the opposite of management's original hypothesis.

As the new customer service and goal-setting processes were implemented, new selling roles were designed, and they led to a new sales compensation plan that included an increase in incentive as a percentage of total compensation. Management also added a balanced set of performance measurement criteria with financial (profitability), customer (customer satisfaction), and cost control (product returns) metrics.

3.3   A Global Pharmaceutical Firm: A Case Example

Background and Problem Statement

A major pharmaceutical firm with three large sales forces made a change in its sales strategy to increase market share for its key products. The idea was to have sales reps from all three sales forces work together, rather than independently, to co-promote the same products to targeted physicians. This was accomplished by having sales reps co-promote some common products to select physicians and independently promote other products to different physicians. The new coordinated sales strategy promised several benefits:

- Increased call frequency and market share with key physicians
- Faster and better access to customer information
- Improved leverage of customer relationships
- Better call and program planning
- Improved effectiveness of managed care marketing efforts

The new sales strategy, however, was not delivering the results expected.

Management Hypothesis and the Causes

Management believed that a new sales compensation plan using and emphasizing team-based incentives would change sales rep behaviors and lead to better coordination and results, but they wisely conducted an assessment of the sales force to confirm their suspicions. The assessment revealed a number of nonpay-related obstacles to effective team selling:

- Sales reps did not believe that coordination and team selling would improve results.
- They did not understand the makeup of the team, including its leadership or their roles in the team.
- Sales reps did not believe that being a good team player would lead to additional compensation, recognition, or promotion.
- Sales managers were not coordinating their planning and goal-setting processes.

Behind these perceptions were the following facts:

- Basically, the "lone ranger" sales rep was the success model; promotion continued to be based on individual contributions.
- The sales force organizational structure created silos (that is, independently operating functions) hindering communication, joint planning, coordination, and conflict resolution by the first-level sales managers.
- The sales rep selection profile included such attributes as being highly independent and motivated by individual recognition and money.
- Sales reps could reach their goals and target incentive levels without teaming or coordinating with other reps.

Solution and Implications for Pay

Management came to the realization that making a change to the sales compensation plan in isolation would probably demotivate and demoralize sales reps and actually decrease sales effectiveness. Instead, several initiatives were launched concurrently:

- Senior management became involved in building the case for team selling and articulating its importance to success for both the business and sales reps.
- First-level sales managers from the different sales forces developed their business plans together, clearly articulating the role of the selling teams—the members and the leaders.
- A local market manager position was created to coordinate team activities across sales forces and functions.
- The sales rep selection profiles were revised to emphasize the ability to work in teams.
- Team selling training was developed.

Team incentives were introduced, but initially were designed as secondary to individual incentives in the light of the short-term obstacles to creating high-performing selling teams. A transition plan was developed to increase the emphasis on team incentives as the culture changed, team roles became clearer, and sales reps began to experience the benefit of team selling.

3.4   An Assessment Framework

The causes of reduced sales effectiveness, summarized in Exhibit 3-2, were very different for the two cases profiled. Our research and

Exhibit 3-2. Causes of Reduced Sales Effectiveness.

High-Growth Computer Book Publisher	Global Pharmaceutical Firm
Customer support	Culture
■ Ineffective customer service function	■ Lone ranger sales staff misaligned with need for teams
Sales support	Organization
■ Inadequate sales rep development	■ Unclear team member roles ■ Structural silos impeding coordination
Motivation	Motivation
■ Demotivating goals	■ Misplaced perceptions of management's intent

experience suggest that there are, in fact, many causes of reduced sales effectiveness. As an evaluation tool, we have found the application of a sales effectiveness assessment framework helpful for identifying, categorizing, and ranking the causes in a way that enables management to act on the findings and address ways to begin improvement. Introduced in Chapters 1 and 2, the framework considers the four components of effectiveness as well as the impact of corporate culture. The components are shown in Exhibit 3-3.

To gain an understanding of the areas that need improvement, the five key components of sales effectiveness must be examined:

1. Roles, organization, and staffing
2. Cross-functional coordination and customer support
3. Sales operations and support activities
4. Performance management and motivation
5. Culture

Before applying the sales effectiveness framework, you must have clear business objectives, a clear strategy, and an understanding of the required capabilities to carry out the strategy. The effectiveness of the sales organization is measured by its ability to deliver the required capabilities, carry out the sales strategy, and contribute to meeting the business objectives.

Exhibit 3-3. Sales System Execution Components.

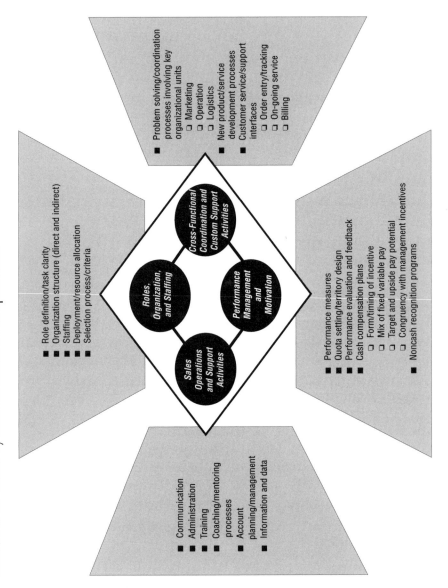

Roles, Organization, and Staffing

As a point of focus in assessing selling effectiveness, organization design encompasses size, structure, territory alignment, and role definition.

- *Are there the right number of people on the sales staff to carry out the sales strategy cost-effectively?* Appropriately sized sales forces maximize the economic return on investment of selling resources. Unfortunately for most organizations and most selling situations, this metric is very difficult to compute. Although determining the marginal cost of a sales rep is usually straightforward, the marginal profitability that they generate is more difficult to determine for two reasons:

1. It is difficult to measure the influence the rep has on the buying decision, relative to other factors.
2. It is difficult to determine the amount of sales effort required on an account or prospect to influence the buying process.

A simpler approach to determining sales force size is to assess if it has the capacity to carry out the sales strategy. That is, is the sales force's capacity (as defined by the aggregate sales rep selling time available) sufficient to enable reps to reach all targeted accounts and prospects the required number of times? Answering this question does not address the economics underlying the sales force size, but it does clarify whether there are enough selling resources to implement the sales strategy. If the answer to this question is no, there are at least three courses of action:

1. Increase the number of sales personnel to the necessary capacity.
2. Redesign the selling roles to increase selling time without increasing the number of reps.
3. Develop a new sales strategy to reach the target markets cost-effectively through alternative means (such as telesales people in lieu of direct sales representatives).

- *Does the organization structure maximize both efficiency and effectiveness?* The best sales force structure balances the need for efficiency, effectiveness, and adaptability. To arrive at the most appropriate structure, several sales organizing principles might be applied: product focused, customer focused, geographic focused, or functional or task focused. Typical selling organizations employ a

Exhibit 3-4. Organization Structures.

Organizing Principle	Critical Capabilities Needed	Attributes
Product focused	• Product expertise • High level of product promotion control	• Complex and varied product line • Relatively homogeneous market
Customer focused	• Deep understanding of customer requirements • Expertise in a facet of the customer's business • Broad product line configurable to specific needs • Long-term customer relationship development	• Sophisticated customer buying processes • Many different customer segments
Geographic focused	• Efficiency • Local market knowledge	• Relatively homogeneous market • Manageable product line
Functional or task focused	• High level of efficiency • High competency level in executing specific steps in the selling process (prospecting, customer service, contracting)	• Varied customer needs over the selling cycle

mix of these structures, as shown in Exhibit 3-4. An assessment of the most appropriate sales force structure requires an understanding of the attributes of the market and the critical capabilities needed for the sales organization.

  • *Are sales territories balanced in workload and potential?* Whether a sales force is deployed geographically, by customer segment, or by product, it is important that territories are designed to enable reps to cover their accounts and prospects efficiently and effectively. Additionally, it is important for territories to be balanced so that individual reps are not advantaged or disadvantaged on the basis of their territories. Well-designed sales territories have the following three characteristics:

1. Balance of workload
2. Balance of potential
3. Reasonably efficient travel to all customers and prospects

- *Are selling roles clear and well aligned with the sales strategy? Are the actual roles being carried out as intended?* If a sales organization design has a clear rationale for its size, structure, and territory alignment, its selling roles are self-evident. Selling roles are clear when they have the following characteristics:

1. Defined account and prospect assignments
2. Clear understanding of decision makers and influencers within accounts
3. Specific products and services offered
4. Specific activities to be accomplished
5. Clear interactions with other parts of the company

Unfortunately selling roles are often ill defined; we will see later in this chapter how this lack of task clarity can negatively affect motivation. Additionally, sales reps often do not allocate their time consistently with the way the role was intended. Asking sales reps to quantify how they spend their time can be extremely useful in determining how the actual selling roles are being executed and in comparing them to the theoretically defined roles. Gaps between the actual and the theoretical roles are common sources of reduced sales effectiveness. For example, senior management of the computer book publisher profiled above was amazed to find that their sales staff spent less than half their time in contact with customers. This revelation was the catalyst for many of the changes implemented.

Further, effective sales forces must have the right people, with the right competencies, with access to timely and accurate market and customer information, operating as efficiently as possible. Effective human resources, communication, and administrative processes support these sales forces.

There are three key questions to consider:

- *Have we clearly articulated the skills and knowledge necessary in the sales force to implement the sales strategy?*
- *Are we selecting sales staff with the required skills and knowledge?*
- *Are we training and developing incumbent sales staff to improve critical skills?*

Effective sales organizations have well-defined competency requirements for each sales role and a strategy to develop and recruit those competencies. Because sales managers tend to be very results oriented, they can lose sight of the importance of developing the competencies that drive results. Competencies and their importance to the organization are discussed in detail in Chapter 22.

In preparation for a deregulated market, an electric utility changed its sales and marketing strategy to improve customer relationships and build barriers to competitive entry. In doing so, it developed a number of energy services products to compete with those provided by energy service and contracting companies. To motivate the sales force, management introduced significant incentive compensation opportunities for selling energy services. It did not work. The sales force was very strong at managing existing customer relationships and offering technical support, but they were not equipped to sell in a competitive market. These relationship-oriented sales reps, who had never been expected to operate in a competitive environment, were completely unequipped. As a result, they were ineffective when matched up against sales reps from companies that had been competing in this arena for years. In retrospect, an assessment of sales effectiveness would have illuminated the need for competencies that supported selling energy services.

The global pharmaceutical firm referred to earlier had a rich tradition of selecting sales reps who were strong individual contributors and were motivated by individual achievement. When the sales strategy changed to emphasize team selling, the collective sales rep competencies were misaligned with the new requirements for the role. Before incorporating team-based incentives into the sales compensation plan, management recognized a need to develop team selling skills.

Finally, two main processes have significant impact on whether your company can organize effectively. They are:

- *Communication processes.* There are two key areas to consider in assessing these processes:

    1. Are the sales strategy and the individual sales rep role in carrying out that strategy clearly articulated?
    2. Do we have the necessary systems for providing the sales staff with timely and accurate customer, market, and internal company information?

- *Administrative processes.* The focus here is on whether the company has adequate administrative resources to ensure that the sales staff is maximizing time spent on value-adding activities.

Cross-Functional Coordination and Sales Operations

There are two key questions to assess these two key areas:

Exhibit 3-5. Requirements vs. Resources.

Complex Customer Requirement	Functions Typically Involved
Timely development of new or customized products or services	Marketing Operations Senior management
Bundling of various products or services to meet specific needs best	Marketing Operations
Integrated logistics	Operations Information systems
Customer service function with a deep understanding of specific customer requirements	Customer service Sales
Co-marketing arrangements	Marketing
Customized pricing and contracts	Sales Marketing Senior management

1. How well are we managing account relationships?
2. How well is our organization supporting the needs of customers?

In the 1990s, managing account relationships and supporting the needs of customers changed dramatically as the nature of buying became increasingly complex. Sales cycles are longer, customers involve more people in the decision process, and customers are becoming more sophisticated and disciplined in managing suppliers. These changes dramatically affect the role of the sales reps, who typically need to manage account relationships diligently and coordinate the efforts of many company resources across different functions to serve their customers' needs. An assessment of customer support and account management effectiveness requires understanding the quality of account relationships and evaluating the effectiveness of your customer support operations.

Examples of typical customer requirements and internal company resources needed to address them are shown in Exhibit 3-5. Coordination among departments such as sales, marketing, operations, information systems (IS), and customer service presents tremendous challenges to traditional functional organizations. Process design and organization structures reflect functional-oriented management philosophies with no way integrated to bring products to market in a tailored manner. Most operations functions are designed to maximize productivity and efficiency. They are typically focused on streamlining and standardizing processes, and are often rewarded for doing so. Any sales function initiative to develop tailored solutions for customers will typically reduce operational efficiency and correspondingly conflict with the priorities (and perhaps the incentives) of the operations staff.

A common cause of reduced sales effectiveness is a lack of clarity of how sales, marketing, operations, IS, and customer service should work together to serve customers. An investigation of why an organization does not coordinate effectively across functions must consider its underlying processes, structure, people, information systems, and culture—for example:

Processes

- Is operations working to optimize process efficiency at the same time that sales is working to develop custom-tailored solutions?
- Is marketing focused on processes to increase margins, while sales focuses on volume?

Structure

- Are the roles of operations and marketing staff in meeting customer needs clear?
- Are organizational silos obstructing cross-functional coordination?

People

- Are the performances of sales, operations, marketing, and customer service measured differently? If so, do the measures conflict? Do these functions have any joint or team measures?
- Are incentive earnings opportunities radically different for sales versus other functions? If so, is the business rationale well articulated and understood?
- Are pay levels of staff from different functions dramatically different, leading to resentment?

Information Systems

- Do we employ the technology necessary to serve our customers' needs?
- Are all members of the customer support team knowledgeable about the customer and the company's sales activity?

Culture

- Do we have inconsistent leadership styles across functions?
- Is decision-making authority different across functions? Does customer service have limited authority to make decisions while the sales staff is fully empowered?
- Does management tend to involve lower-level staff in one function and not another?

In summary, effective account management and customer support organizations usually have the following attributes:

- Excellent relationships with account decision makers at multiple levels and functions
- Highly satisfied accounts
- High account penetration levels
- A wide range of products or services to sell to accounts
- Ability to meet account sales and profitability objectives.

Performance Management and Motivation

While pay is a significant contributor to employee motivation, other factors play a major role. A company's clarity about what it expects the employee to do, how that performance is measured, and how the employee values the result all contribute to motivation.

- *Task clarity.* Research by Stephen X. Doyle and Benson Shapiro of the Harvard Business School has shown that the most important determinant of sales representative motivation is the clarity of the sales task. Two conditions determine sales task clarity:

1. The time span of performance feedback
2. The degree that one can accurately determine the individual results of salespeople

Situations in which there is either a long delay between a sales rep's performance and the measurement of that performance, or when the sales rep's individual results cannot be measured accurately will lead to low task clarity and low motivation. It is imperative that task clarity be high before sales incentive compensation can affect behavior.

The clarity of the sales task is a function of the nature of the role. Long, complex selling involving a team tends to have less clarity than do short sales cycles involving a single sales rep. However, complex sales tasks can be clarified by mapping the sales process and identifying the key milestones that correspond to a major step forward in the process. Given a clear picture of the selling process and the milestones that correspond to each major step forward, timely and accurate performance feedback can be delivered, leading to higher motivation levels.

For example, consider a national account manager (NAM) pursuing a long-term relationship with an original equipment manufacturer. It could take years to convince the account's engineering, production, purchasing, and senior management staff that changing a product's components will improve the quality of the delivered equipment and decrease total production costs. During the selling process, the NAM will involve a host of resources from his company to support this effort, including design engineers, marketing personnel, and even senior management. By mapping the selling process and identifying the key milestones, the NAM's performance can be measured against achievement of milestones, thus increasing task clarity and motivation.

▪ *Performance measurement.* Goal setting is one of the most difficult tasks required of sales management. It is imperative that it is done well. To be motivating, goals must be set as fairly and accurately as possible. For any given sales position within an organization, there will tend to be a normal distribution of performance on any given measure. When setting goals for incentive purposes (minimum, target, and excellent performance levels) many companies set goals to arrive at the following results:

Minimum: 90 percent of incumbents will attain this level
Target: 50 percent to 60 percent of incumbents should attain this level
Excellent: 10 percent of incumbents should attain this level

Analysis of historical goal attainment levels by position as compared to the distribution can be useful for assessing the fairness and accuracy of goal setting. Additionally, it is helpful to collect the opinion of the sales force on the historical accuracy of their goals. If an organization has had chronic difficulties setting goals, the goal-setting process should be examined and reengineered prior to redesigning the sales compensation plan.

▪ *Employee values.* Rewards must be valued to affect behavior. Before designing sales compensation plans, you should understand the relative importance to the sales force of various types of rewards: cash compensation, benefits, recognition, promotion, and job security. This understanding will enable you to craft a comprehensive performance management system that maximizes the return on investment in these programs while providing the employees with a basket of rewards that matches their needs.

Culture

Sales management often initiates tactical changes such as selling role redefinition, performance measurement modifications, or sales compensation redesign without first considering whether the organization's culture will support the change. In fact, many managers will argue that tactical changes can provide the catalyst for desired culture change. However, recommended changes may be completely misaligned with other management systems, creating ambiguity and confusion in the sales force. To make change happen, you must align culture with sales strategy and tactics. Aligned sales organizations have the following attributes:

- Leaders demonstrate the behaviors and performance they expect of employees.
- Sales strategy is reinforced through all management systems, including recruitment, training, promotion, rewards, and recognition.
- Sales staff members feel an appropriate level of involvement in decision-making processes.
- Management span of control is appropriate.
- Information is shared openly.
- Reward and recognition systems consider sales staff values and risk tolerance.

In summary, effective sales compensation plans are aligned with customer needs, the sales strategy, the sales roles, and employee values.

The remainder of this book focuses on assessing and designing effective sales compensation plans. However, before expending time, money, and resources to redesign compensation, you must identify the root causes of reduced sales effectiveness to develop a:

- Clear understanding and ranking of the areas for improvement.
- Realistic assessment of the expected impact sales compensation changes will have on improving sales effectiveness.
- Context for the extent and timing of required sales compensation changes.

4

Checking for Problems

4.1 Why Have Separate Incentive Plans?

Should sales reps be paid differently from the way other employees are paid? If a company gives bonuses to its sales staff, shouldn't it give them to everyone? Human resources specialists, who deal with such issues as compensation equity among employee groups, must frequently respond to these questions. A rational examination of the uses of sales incentive compensation, however, will indicate why a company should pay its salespeople differently from the way it pays other employees.

From the company's point of view, a separate compensation program for sales reps makes sense if one or more of the following conditions is present:

- *The sales management process needs reinforcement.* Compensation serves as a channel of communication between sales management and the field. Without day-to-day supervision, many sales reps will set their own priorities and ignore management's directives to focus on the more difficult tasks (such as securing new accounts and selling profitable products). A compensation plan designed specifically for sales reps provides a strong economic motive to follow the company's priorities.

Sales management—the translation of abstract (usually numeric) goals into account- and market-specific tactics—is an art. It requires skill and hard work on the part of managers, which will be wasted if sales reps disregard the company's wishes. A variable pay system that underscores the message that accomplishing specified performance measures will lead to increased total compensation can strengthen the sales management process in two ways:

1. Recognizing the importance of sales reps in attaining company financial goals and providing the reps with financial rewards for their achievements.
2. Forcing sales managers to improve their goal-setting skills because the achievement of those goals will affect their subordinates' pay.

▪ *Sales reps can create their own value.* In certain businesses, the sales rep's value to the organization resists conventional measurement. The market and the product are such that the sales rep is worth whatever he or she proves to be worth, as measured by some index of productivity (usually volume). The product is indistinguishable from alternatives and the "value-added" that gives competitive advantage derives from the rep's creativity and salesmanship. In such selling situations, the rep's productivity cannot be accurately rewarded through a predetermined salary (although salary may be used for part of the pay package to ensure the steady flow of subsistence-level income). Certain industries, among them door-to-door consumer products, retail stock brokering, and individual life insurance, possess these characteristics and therefore deliver most, if not all, of the sales rep's pay through commission. But in many other industries, sales jobs (or sales roles with particular market segments) may have these same characteristics.

If management is uncertain about whether reps can create their own value in its business, it should consider the following criteria:

1. Does the sales rep have to persuade customers of their need for the product, process, or service?
2. Do numerous, often indistinguishable, alternative sources of the product, process, or service exist?
3. Are these alternative sources formidable competitors that aggressively seek the same business from the same customer or prospect base?

If all three conditions are present, then the sales rep can indeed create value for himself or herself, and the company must offer some form of incentive compensation so that income delivered reflects income deserved on the basis of productivity.

▪ *Incentive compensation is a competitive necessity.* Competition for sales talent includes all organizations that could employ the sales force, without significant retraining, to sell their products or services. Thus, the competition comprises not only direct industry competitors but also other companies whose selling tasks are similar. If competitors characteristically layer an incentive compensation opportunity on top of the sales rep's base salary, then it behooves any competitive sales force to do so as well.

The presence of incentive compensation causes the distribution of earnings to widen. A company that pays salary but no commission in a labor market where its competitors offer both will probably pay salaries that are slightly higher than average, thus ensuring the loyalty of mediocre performers. But such a company will probably not be able to offer salary levels, even to its best performers, that match the total of salary and incentives offered the best salespeople in the labor market. Nor should it want to elevate salaries to such a level, for in our society, it is difficult from a human relations stand-point to rescind a salary increase given in a prior year. Salaries tend to go up, and only up. Because a salary increase is usually perma-nent, its present value (and hence its cost to the company) greatly exceeds that of a comparable payment of incentive compensation, which, to be received in the future, must be re-earned through sus-tained productivity.

▪ *The company has limited resources.* Turning part of sales compen-sation expense into a variable cost is particularly critical to companies that have limited resources. An entrepreneurial start-up venture may not have the capital resources to offer competitive base salaries. In such cases, even if industry practice and management preference are to pay salary alone, economic necessity dictates that sales reps be required to trade off some secure base salary income for the opportu-nity to outearn their salaried peers in other organizations, should their sales performance merit significant commissions or bonuses.

Most organizations find it advantageous to deliver sales force compensation, or a significant portion of it, in variable pay. Only organizations with an exceptionally strong sales management pro-cess and extensive resources, and whose competitors also pay base salary, can safely avoid developing a separate remuneration system for the field sales force. Certain basic industrial sectors such as chemicals, metals, petroleum, steel, and carbon have been able to use salary exclusively. But even in these industries, with the emer-gence of special markets and applications, and as a result of diversi-fication into new ventures, sales incentives are working their way into company compensation packages.

4.2   Matching Plan Design to Company Goals

If sales managers are asked if their compensation plans are effective, some will answer, "Absolutely"; about the same number will re-spond with a no; and most will shrug their shoulders and say, "I'm really not sure. I think it's okay."

"Okay" is not good enough. Sales reps represent an important investment for a company, one that should yield a very favorable return. "Absolutely," on the other hand, sounds a lot more like what most of us would demand if we were paying the sales compensa-tion bill.

What constitutes a sound compensation plan? The first step is to prepare a list of general objectives of a good incentive plan. Most lists would include at least some of the following:

- To reward sales accomplishment.
- To motivate.
- To direct the sales force.
- To make the rep work harder and smarter.
- To attract and retain talented people.
- To encourage poor sales talent to leave the company.
- To create a win-win situation for the company and the sales rep.
- To not overpay for the easy part of the job.
- To pay for more than just current sales (e.g., recognize preparations for future sales, recognize profitable sales, encourage and reward the sale of new products).
- To help sales managers manage.
- To be simple and understandable.
- To remind reps that they are members of a team as well as lone rangers and must help in joint selling and training and be cooperative and do all the reports.

The next step in developing a sound compensation plan is to identify, in as great a degree of specificity as possible, five to ten of the most important objectives for the particular sales organization. Then the current plan can be evaluated by assessing how well it accomplishes each objective very well, moderately well, or little or not at all.

Note that each objective could mean different things to different companies. For example, depending on the situation, "helps sales managers manage" might mean:

- To allow a manager to assign territories or accounts in a way that doesn't have a direct windfall or shortfall effect on the sales rep, so that she can optimize the sales force's use of time.

- To allow a manager to set sales priorities and calibrate plan payouts to recognize the uniqueness of his geographic region—what is easy and what is difficult to sell.

- To keep a rep from becoming indifferent to the difficult aspects of the job after reaching the economic point of indifference (earned plenty) on the easy part of the job (easy customers or market segments).

Focusing on a company's specific sales and marketing objectives permits sound value judgments in the evaluation of a sales compensation plan.

4.3 Looking for Danger Signs

One way of measuring the effectiveness of a sales compensation plan is to examine whether it is accomplishing the company's stated objectives. Searching for specific problems that might indicate a sub-optimal plan represents another approach that allows a more thorough audit of the plan.

After identifying and describing such problems, assess them in the light of improvement opportunities. Any evaluation should proceed on the basis of the following premises:

- No sales compensation plan is perfect, and not all problems are important enough to fix.

- A sales compensation plan should direct the major efforts of the rep and reinforce successes.

- A sales compensation plan should not try to monitor and direct each and every action of a salesperson.

- Sales compensation plan inertia can be a powerful and destructive force that helps preserve inadequate plans. Just as companies regularly revise their sales and marketing strategies to address changes in the marketplace, so too should they review the appropriateness of their compensation plans.

Nevertheless, senior sales management must take care not to appear too impulsive in changing compensation plans, or salespeople may lose confidence in their judgment. A company that has uncovered problems must sense when to overhaul a compensation plan and when to make minor repairs.

Turnover and recruiting problems represent the two most readily quantifiable indicators that a sales compensation plan is in trouble. Several other signs relate to the entire sales management structure.

Perhaps the most important analysis you can perform is also one of the simplest—and often the most overlooked. A central underlying objective of any sales compensation plan is to direct and reinforce the sales force to accomplish those sales-related activities that are called for in the company's strategic sales and marketing

Exhibit 4-1. Sales and Marketing Objectives.

Sales and Marketing Strategy Priorities	Sales Compensation Priorities
Sales volume	Sales volume
Profitability of sales (pricing maximization)	(Covered only to the degree that higher price of selling will cause higher sales revenue)
Product mix	Product mix
New product introduction	(Covered only to the degree that new product selling will result in higher sales volume)

plan. By comparing this strategic plan to the sales incentive plan, significant inconsistencies should become apparent. For companies without a strategic plan, the task is barely any more difficult. The sales managers as a group should chart the sales and marketing objectives that need to be realized, as shown in Exhibit 4-1. In this case, the sales incentive plan neglects to cover pricing decisions or new product introductions, except as they might be reflected in higher sales revenue. Such a sales incentive plan, interestingly enough, might be screaming to the sales rep to do the following:

- Accept lower prices, which, if combined with higher unit sales, would increase total revenue, irrespective of whether this revenue results in lower total profit margins.

- Let other reps introduce new products while he spends his time selling the existing volume product line (which will maximize individual gain compensation today) and selling new products only when they have established market appeal.

Unfortunately, if everyone followed this path, new product introductions might never be successful.

A second possible analysis is to investigate territory assignment and associated compensation opportunity. If there is a mismatch between plan earnings and hours worked, a company is receiving a suboptimal return on its investment in its sales force. Whether your company is using its sales reps' time effectively can be determined as shown in Exhibit 4-2.

This analysis alone may show that rep A is underworked (even though she controls some of the most important accounts) and that rep C is overworked (or at least can't possibly be calling effectively

Exhibit 4-2. Analysis of Use of Sales Rep Time.

Rep	Large Accounts[a]	Medium Accounts[a]	Small Accounts[a]	Travel Time	Total Calling Time
A	$8 \times 24 \times 3 = 576$	$20 \times 12 \times 2 =\ \ 480$	$100 \times 4 \times 1 = 400$	300	1,456 hours
B	$2 \times 24 \times 3 = 144$	$40 \times 12 \times 2 =\ \ 960$	$100 \times 4 \times 1 = 400$	500	2,004 hours
C	_____	$80 \times 12 \times 2 = 1920$	_____	500	2,420 hours

[a]Number of accounts times the required number of calls per year times the number of hours per call.

on all the accounts to which he is assigned). If the sales incentive plan compensated rep A well in excess of competitive levels and compensated rep C well below competitive levels, it would be clear that the company was incurring an opportunity cost. If some of rep C's accounts were transferred to rep A, wouldn't the company achieve better account penetration? Perhaps the sales compensation plan is getting in the way, linking account assignment with resulting pay opportunity. By allocating resources more properly, a manager might, in fact, be raising rep A's "overpaid" status and further deteriorating rep C's "underpaid" status. Such an analysis may reveal a significant inconsistency between the incentive plan and the territory assignment process.

A third analysis revolves around the credibility of goal setting. A sales incentive plan, its earning risk and potential, takes on meaning only when reps know their territory and the goals (quotas) expected of them. Although reps will always complain about their goals, a historical analysis showing what percentage of reps achieved what percentage of goals provides a fair representation of the distribution of results to quotas. You would expect some sort of bell-shaped curve, with perhaps 80 percent of the sales force achieving between 80–85 percent and 115–120 percent of quota.

If the majority of sales reps substantially overshoot quota and the incentive plan is highly leveraged, the plan may be contributing to an overpay problem. If the majority are well under quota and the plan is highly leveraged, then the plan may be underpaying the sales reps. Or, in these same situations, if pay leverage is insufficient, the plan might in fact be acting less as a motivator than as a vehicle to correct (minimize) the ills of the goal-setting process. As far as goal setting is concerned and however it is accomplished, one would hope that 80 to 85 percent of sales reps would qualify for some amount of sales incentive payout. If fewer are qualifying (if the plan threshold is too high), much of the sales force won't be motivated to sell most effectively and intensely. If virtually all reps qualify, payouts may be too easy, with insufficient negative feedback given to the reps who are not really making the grade.

Sales strategy, account assignment, and goal setting all run deeper than sales incentive plan design and, as the primary controls of sales management, must be addressed first. Yet all are inextricably linked with sales incentive plan design. Analysis of these first three should identify significant cracks in the sales management architecture. If the edifice is basically sound, compensation plan design can act as supporting cement. If they are not found to be sound, management must reexamine the foundation itself.

4.4 Turnover as a Symptom

"Excessive" turnover frequently provides the first signal that something is wrong with a company's sales compensation plan. Although turnover is observable and would appear to present a clear message to management, it is not as obvious an indicator as you might think. In fact, sales managers who are experiencing serious defections need to examine the nature of the turnover closely:

▪ The level of turnover as compared with previous years or industry average.

▪ Who is leaving. Are they recruits or veterans? Are they sales leaders or poor performers, reps from all regions or from specific locales? And at what career stages are they leaving?

▪ The factors causing the turnover. Are defections pay related? If so, is the principal reason base salaries, incentive opportunities, or total cash compensation? Or is turnover due to sales organization and career path concerns; sales burnout, stress, or territory coverage; or inadequate sales management direction, concern, guidance, or communication?

If pay is responsible for the loss of sales reps, is it a problem or a blessing? Perhaps the compensation system is merely weeding out underachievers. Exhibits 4-3 and 4-4 illustrate a pattern of sales force turnover experienced by a typical high-tech company.

Exhibit 4-3 shows an analysis of turnover by service. Is the company losing recruits or veterans? Similar analysis might be done for other types of sales reps (e.g., direct versus distributor) and at different levels. Each bar represents a group of equal service employees. The height of the bar indicates the percentage of employees re-

Exhibit 4-3. Sales Turnover Analysis for Field Sales Positions.

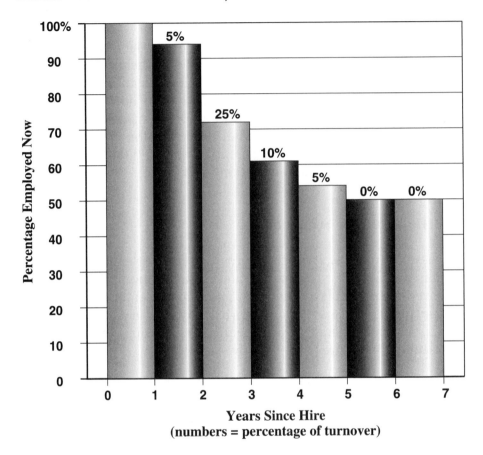

maining for that group of the total hired. The number above the bar shows the turnover from one year to the next. For example, the third bar shows that of the employees with two to three years of service, 70 percent have remained with the company, a decrease of 25 percent from the prior year's retention. The exhibit fairly clearly points to years 2 through 4 as the danger zone: This company retains most of its veterans (turnover is only zero percent to 5 percent a year) and its recruits (turnover is also zero percent to 5 percent) but not those in between.

Unfortunately, in most sales organizations, it is the two- to four-year group that is most productive (and most vulnerable to being raided). This analysis would suggest that management give additional attention to this group of sales reps. Although we now know more about where turnover is occurring, we don't yet know why.

Exhibit 4-4 analyzes compensation trends over time to help answer the question of why turnover is concentrated in the second

Exhibit 4-4. Pay Progression Analysis.

through fourth years. It shows compensation progression for sales-people with fewer than four years of service. Indexing pay (dividing actual pay by pay at hire) makes it apparent that pay increases decelerate around the second year, encouraging employees to consider opportunities outside the company. Why does pay progression slow down after two years? Many companies provide more frequent reviews during the first year or two of a rep's tenure, with the expectation that incentives will kick in after this point. Sometimes they don't.

The curve flattening in this particular company was caused by a salary increase moratorium. The reason that the curve flattens out in the last few years for both populations, of course, is the salary increase moratorium. Employees who have been with the organization for five years before the moratorium can view it with some perspective. Employees with shorter tenure can't.

What does this analysis suggest for the compensation program? There isn't a systemic impediment to pay progress; the moratorium was a one-time event. But it might not hurt to consider some tenure-based focus in incentive design or other rewards. For example, the incentive might not be applied to employees with less than a year of service (a "compensation" solution). Alternatively, the company might spend extra effort to find career growth opportunities within the organization (a "career path" solution).

Which is the right answer? It still is not clear, because the quali-

tative turnover analysis should be supplemented by structured interviews with sales reps and managers. But these charts do give a better
idea about what questions to ask in those discussions.

To understand turnover data:

1. Break the figures down into their component parts, analyze
them, and make them tell a logical, qualitative story.

2. Analyze where various groups of individuals have gone, to
detect any patterns or reasons for leaving. To competitors or to different industries? To positions requiring similar selling skills or ones
that represent a complete reorientation?

3. Follow the money. If it is a sales compensation problem, then
money should have something to do with it: in the sales compensation program itself, the assignment of accounts or territory, or goal
setting, all of which are inextricably linked to sales compensation
opportunity.

4. Compare these levels of turnover to levels experienced in
prior years for comparable positions and to what industry competition is facing. There are industry segments where 10 percent turnover is high and those where 25 percent is low, so understanding of
the context is critical to assessing turnover data.

4.5   Rethinking Recruiting

Turnover problems can cut across all levels of the sales staff or focus
narrowly on new recruits. Be prepared to analyze recruitment procedures as diligently as you explore general turnover issues. In particular, you should investigate the following issues:

- The frequency of recruiting failure.

- The positions that experience the most difficulties. Are they
entry level or midcareer? Are all geographic areas affected or only
certain locations?

- The background of recruits. Is the company recruiting candidates with sufficient selling skills, experience, and background?

- The sources where recruits are obtained (competitors or unre-
lated industries?).

- The reasons given by candidates who turn down offers of
employment. Is it compensation or something else, say, training
opportunities, career development, position characteristics, or "chem-

istry"? If compensation is the critical factor, is it a question of salary levels, incentive opportunity, or total cash compensation?

In studying these problems, you should do the following:

1. Analyze the employment records of different types of recruits. The company may not be recruiting sales staff from the right sources, at the right levels, or with the correct competencies.

2. Compare current and past recruiting experience with that of the competition (by position level and geography), keeping in mind that pricing movements affect supply and demand everywhere, including the labor market.

5

What to Do Now?

5.1 Overview of the Analytical Process

Companies work hard to adapt their sales and marketing strategies to the needs of the marketplace and to exploit their specific competitive advantages. Yet when it comes to the design of a compensation program, few organizations develop custom plans. In most cases, their plans are arrived at through one of three ways:

1. *Compensation quilting*—tinkering with an established plan without addressing critical compensation issues

2. *Compensation plagiarism*—substituting a competitor's program and mechanics, irrespective of the rival's differing marketing elements (product, price, promotion, and physical distribution)

3. *Compensation shortcutting*—sweeping difficult problems under the rug and hoping that the sales force will not notice the dust

Compensation design, however, follows the principle that the quality of the output is directly proportional to the quality of the input. Designing or redesigning a sales compensation plan is a complex process with the following steps:

1. Define the sales role.
2. Study the "people" competition.
3. Determine the competitive pay range.
4. Relate external data to internal practices and policies.
5. Select a target salary and incentive mix.
6. Design the incentive component.
7. Test, communicate, and implement the plan.

Although the steps are sequential, they interrelate and overlap. Organizations will find certain steps more relevant to their particular needs than others. Steps 1, 5, and 6 relate closely to the company's internal strategy, objectives, and culture; steps 2, 3, and 4 focus on the collection, analysis, and application of external data. Although step 7 often follows plan implementation, it is integral to the development process and to the plan's success.

Step 1: Define the Sales Role

What is the role of the salesperson in the marketing mix? What duties, responsibilities, and impact does the rep have? Answers to these questions are not always obvious. Consider interviewing a representative cross-section of salespeople and making a sampling of joint calls with them to obtain information for various sales levels and market and product segments. Analysis of existing sales data and background information will aid in the role definition process.

Step 2: Study the "People" Competition

When asked to name the competition for salespeople, how often have you simply rattled off a list of your business rivals? It's a good start, but too narrow a working definition. Enlarge the process to consider which companies' sales jobs, regardless of products sold, share similar responsibilities, skills, and buying impact. A market-based indicator of these qualities is a "Where Got, Where Gone" analysis: Determine where your salespeople (at various levels in the organization) have come from and where defectors have gone.

Step 3: Determine the Competitive Pay Range

In determining the competitive pay range, you should obtain data from the "Where Got, Where Gone" sample on the overall pay range offered. W-2 data provide an excellent source. Yet the overriding rule is to take what you can get in the way of information—for example, highs, lows, medians, and single data points; starting salaries, incentives, and total pay; and magazine quotes and hiring and turnover interviews (from published surveys).

With these data, array a pay distribution from high to low. Ultimately, you will be designing a sales incentive plan that will offer a range of earnings opportunities—more for higher performance and less for lower—that parallels the marketplace practice.

Step 4: Relate External Data to Internal Practices and Policies

There are two critical steps in this process. First, segment the distribution of competitive pay; in other words, break it into bands (dollar ranges) that fit the hierarchy of sales positions found in your organization. For example, a competitive range of $40,000 to $80,000 might translate into:

Rep level 1:	$40,000–$50,000
Rep level 2:	$47,000–$62,000
Rep level 3:	$55,000–$75,000
Major account executive:	$65,000–$80,000

Second, determine your company pay philosophy. Is your intention to pay at the average or median levels, the twenty-fifth percentile, the seventy-fifth percentile, or the top of the market? (Choices can vary depending on the position.) The segmented ranges above would need to reflect the position chosen. For example, if you wanted to attach a 15 percent above-market premium to the level 3 rep, the revised range would be $63,250 to $86,250.

Step 5: Select a Target Salary and Incentive Mix

You might first view this selection as ranging from all salary to all incentive. On reflection, however, the likely choices will narrow considerably. The guiding principles are, first, that salary must be high enough to attract a qualified pool of potential employees. This aspect is, to a large degree, market driven within bounds for the "Where Got, Where Gone" group. Also, as might be expected, the greater the required experience, technical skills, competencies, and education, the higher this component of pay typically is. The second principle is that incentives must be attractive enough to provide motivation and direction appropriate for the degree of impact the position has on sales results. The company must be able to track individual performance in terms of both accuracy and timeliness.

Still, there should be plenty of flexibility. Moreover, how the incentive is structured will have an effect on the amount of de facto risk (real incentive) in the program. An 80 percent salary–20 percent incentive mix, where the incentive cuts in at 80 percent of quota, creates more risk (has less "fixed pay") than does a 60 percent salary–40 percent incentive, where the payout accrues from the first dollar of sales.

Step 6: Design the Incentive Component

Nothing is more fun for a sales manager than the design of the incentive component, and nothing is more critical to the company and the sales force in terms of the message that the plan delivers and the actions that it directs and reinforces on the part of the sales force. The key points to remember are these:

1. Don't rush; think it through.
2. Don't oversimplify. The plan should reflect the sales tasks demanded.
3. Think of the ideal plan and save important pragmatic considerations for later in the process.

Basic design issues include the form of the incentive, its threshold for activation, its limits or restrictions, the salary and incentive mix, the incentive period, and the performance measures.

The sales rep's role and impact and the market's characteristics drive the form of the incentive. It can be a bonus (defined as the opportunity to earn a percentage of salary or a set dollar amount or range), a commission (a percentage of a business result), or a combination of both forms relating to different aspects of the sales job. The incentive portion itself can accrue at a constant rate or can accelerate or decelerate as performance increases over various goal or performance levels.

Determining an entry-level threshold—a performance level at which the incentive plan will cut in—is critical. This will affect the degree of true risk in the program, as well as the leverage (potential reward) that may be expected. This threshold level should be set low enough so that the great majority of representatives (85 percent or 90 percent) can earn some incentive. At the same time, a company's philosophy will often dictate a culturally acceptable minimum threshold level.

Equally important is the determination of the high-water mark the incentive plan is likely to generate. Even if there is no formal maximum or cap, the plan's mechanics, when combined with territory assignment and the goal-setting process, will certainly suggest the range of realizable earnings to the various players. Caps are the enemy of all sales forces, yet they make sense in certain windfall situations, most notably on a per account or product basis and often structured as a *perforated cap* allowing some of the windfall to flow through. Thus, psychologically, reps feel that no matter how well they have done, there is always a way to make an additional dollar.

The time period of the incentive is important. It should conform to the rhythm of the sales cycle and yet motivate the sales force. When a time period is too long to retain the focused interest of the sales force, you can introduce progress payments. Often annual, semiannual, or quarterly plans have quarterly or monthly progress payments.

Perhaps the most critical choice involves the selection and relative incentive weights of the plan components, that is, the productivity measures. Two common mistakes to avoid are erring toward oversimplification (not considering performance factors outside of pure overall volume) and blind allegiance to uniformity (every territory should be subject to the identical incentive plan). Creative strategic thinking and a measure of flexibility are the keys.

You must address a variety of other issues in a company-specific vein, such as:

- Split credits
- Windfalls
- Special plan treatments covering promotions, transfers, and special assignments
- House account treatment
- Definition of a sale
- Eligibility criteria
- Effects of terminations and resignations
- Implications of benefit programs

Sales contests must also be evaluated and staged to blend meaningfully into the overall incentive strategy.

In incentive design, you can and probably should start out with a blank sheet of paper. By being thoughtful and creating an economic game that links a sales rep's financial success, within proper limits, to the measurable, strategically sought sales results over which he or she has control, you can create a win-win scenario. The sales force will be able to recognize a plan that is fair and motivational and provides a sense of needed direction.

Step 7: Test, Communicate, and Implement the Plan

This last step, if improperly taken (or ignored), is a certain spoiler. You must evaluate how the plan will affect various individuals, as well as its likely costs and expected overall results. Unfortunately, there is no control experiment to show conclusively the results of a new plan. But sound, logical assumptions will help point the direction. This testing can be done informally (on a case-by-case, what-might-have-happened basis), subjected to overall assumptions and computer simulation, or accomplished through the use of a pilot project on the part of the sales force.

In introducing a plan, you must decide how to accomplish the transition: all at once, on a phased-in basis, or with the use of grand-fathering or other transitional safety net procedures. Properly communicating a new program deserves the highest priority. Sales reps must understand why its features have been designed, how it works, and how (realistically) they can win. The plan should be written clearly and payout calculation examples provided. Clarity allows you to pack more design into the plan and have the plan remain fully understandable. In addition to the text, meetings, slides, and videotape presentations can play a vital role. So can having a set of preanswered, likely questions to prepare managers for their reps' inquiries.

Administration must be handled properly. Make sure that payouts are made in a timely fashion and that the sales force can understand the report on which payouts are based. Also, have a specific person to whom sales reps should inquire (and receive prompt feedback from) on specific problems or plan interpretation and calculation issues.

A sales compensation plan cannot last forever. Each year, think through your sales-related strategy, see how it has changed, and reassess the validity of the compensation program. You are, after all, sending a message to your sales force. Your sales compensation program ranks among the primary reasons that they work for your company. It greatly affects what they think of the company and how they will direct their efforts.

5.2   Setting Up a Design Team

Generally the best way to proceed with a review of a sales compensation program is with a reasonably sized design team or task force. Although such a group should comprise individuals with differing areas of expertise, it must be able to act as an interactive body as decisions go forward. A typical configuration might include:

- Two to three headquarters sales marketing managers
- One to two human resources or compensation managers
- One data processing or management information systems representative
- One finance manager
- One to two external advisers (sales compensation consultant, sales manager, or management consultant)

The sales marketing contingent is responsible for ranking the sales strategy to be accomplished and for isolating which activities and results that are falling short. They should also rank the performances of field reps. As the process goes on, these individuals will need to have a strong voice in the proposed program. They are, after all, the ultimate managers of the field force.

The human resources and compensation group gather the competitive pay data (sometimes supplemented by the "Where Got, Where Gone" analysis provided through the district or region sales organization), pull together internal pay data, and interpret the results of the pay program in the light of the range of performance. In the design phase, human resources takes an active role in sound compensation design and ensures that the task force evolves programs that fall within the company's available parameters. At the same time, it is incumbent on this group to recognize that sales incentives are a unique blend of sales and compensation and most often require considerable fresh thought and intentional differentiation from more traditional compensation systems. The human resources function should also provide an overview of such associated issues as hiring, turnover, and career development and participate in transitional plan changeover and communications issues.

Data processing must be candid about what information required to track plan performance and to trigger plan payouts may or can be provided. It should not create obstacles and delays. By and large, if the information is important enough to track for the purpose of measuring sales compensation, then it certainly is important to track in order to measure the accomplishment of sales strategy.

It is highly important to know what the company can afford at various levels of performance and what its cultural biases regarding payouts are, to provide a reality test. Finance, however, must not play an obstructionist role.

The role of the external adviser (consultant) can include any of the above (depending on how the consultant is used) but can and usually does involve some additional responsibilities. The consultant offers three significant advantages: specialized expertise and fresh ideas, confidentiality (regarding information gathering), and nonpolitical partisanship (greater freedom of expression).

The consultant also has a distinct advantage in obtaining honest answers from the field sales force in the interview process. This is also true of customer interviews and, to a certain degree, for interviews with headquarters executives.

In sorting through the interviews and background analysis, a consultant offers a wide array of experience to help pinpoint problems and lead the task force in an inductive, creative process that culminates in an appropriate solution. Keep in mind, however, that the consultant will never know your business and its nuances as well as you do. Consultants must be harnessed. You must be heavily involved, contributing to and buying in on the solution. Ultimately it must be your plan, not the consultant's.

Consultants need hold no punches. Use them to lay the groundwork for the difficult sell and, if need be, to take the lead in selling the plan to senior management.

There is no single, absolute course to take in structuring the team, in the relative roles that are played, or in the role of the external resource. It's a matter of what works considering the depth of the problem, the openness, the commitment and expertise of the task force, and the company's underlying culture. Budgets and timing constraints may be important as well, but it should be underscored that a sales compensation program that functions well has enormous sales and profit leverage and improvement potential.

5.3 Analytical Steps for the Team

Let's assume that you are given the task of auditing or redesigning your sales compensation program within three months. The greatest source of data for conducting a sales force compensation analysis comes from interviews with the sales force and field sales managers. Nevertheless, a thorough analysis of sales-related data and written materials, which already exist and can be accessed rather easily, can help pinpoint trends, problems, and opportunities in preparation for these interviews:

1. The sales and marketing strategic plan, to identify important objectives.

2. The sales compensation plan, to indicate the economic selling message being delivered to the sales force. The message can then be compared by sales position, geography, market, and product line to the strategic imperative.

3. Internal data (oral or written) that speak to your competitive position by market, geography, and product line.

4. Customer feedback on your strengths and weaknesses in relation to your selling activities.

5. Competitive pay data (salaries, incentives, and total compensation).

6. Internal pay data (salaries, incentives, and total compensation).

7. Rankings of sales force personnel (segmented by position), indicating performance assessment by managers versus pay element ranking. You can perform countless analyses on these data to identify problem areas.

8. Hiring and turnover data.

Armed with this information, you may begin the interview and discussion stage. The interviews should include such headquarters executives as the sales and marketing vice presidents, the national sales manager, and the human resources vice president, who can provide much-needed direction in terms of the overall objectives of the company and division and of shortcomings in the sales compensation program. Senior executives will have their own impressions of the problems and opportunities not addressed under the existing program. Exhibit 5-1 sets out the topics to cover.

At this point, you may have processed a considerable amount of information and could probably prepare a written document on the sales compensation program's strengths and weaknesses. Don't rush to conclusions. It's still early, and you have yet to gain information from the field. Keep in mind that the sales reps' impressions of their relative ability to affect the sales process (in relation to other factors) and to have their impact accurately measured and assessed may vary considerably from those of executives at headquarters. Most important, their interpretation of the overall sales compensation program and the incentive plan in particular—the message it sends and the direction they take—is critical. The company must deal with the perceptions of the sales force, accurate or not.

Sales force interviews expand your understanding of the sales force's efforts and their perception of and reactions to the reward systems and related management processes. To accomplish this, the interviews must be candid, confidential, and nonthreatening.

You must therefore determine if task force members are capable of keeping the information confidential. If not, would a third party provide that assurance? Incidentally, although individual interviews generally provide better-quality information, group interviews (typically two to four people) can produce a "safety in numbers" openness when interviews are conducted internally.

Inform the sales force of the process about to be undertaken, explaining the role of, the preparation for, and the "rules" of the interview. (A suggested announcement memorandum appears in

Exhibit 5-1. Topics for Headquarters Interviews.

- Company strategy, goals, and objectives: near-term and three to five years out, overall and by division
    - —Sales, profits, return on assets
    - —Position of company in each business segment
- Factors affecting the company's ability to reach each business segment
    - —Pricing, quality, production factors, sales reps, advertising, external factors (weather, housing units, economy)
    - —Overall, across enough territories or division, degree to which these factors balance out
- Elements of management's pay philosophy, including
    - —Pay position versus peer groups
    - —Definition of peer groups
    - —Position on caps, mix of fixed and variable pay
- Organizational structure in relation to the attainment of objectives
- Quality of current sales management process and planning process territory loading
    - —Planning—top downward or bottom upward
    - —Planning—accuracy, short and long term
    - —Goal clarity
- Prevailing attitudes among sales force and field sales management
- Perception of current compensation programs
    - —Level and form
    - —Specific policies (e.g., expense and car policies)
- Compensation programs and ideas for change
- Problem areas in sales management or sales
- Suggested sales force interviewees (number per division, representative districts, sales force priorities)
- Career pathing
- Competitor survey companies, especially where sales influence is roughly similar

Exhibit 5-2.) To reinforce the openness of the process, invite noninterviewees, on a confidential basis, to submit comments on the subject.

Begin each interview by giving the participant an overview of the interview guide, which can be used as a checklist of topics to be covered. As the interview moves toward its conclusion, the guide can help you to avoid missing important discussion areas. Further-

(text continues on page 64)

Exhibit 5-2. Suggested Announcement Memo.

TO: Sales Force

FROM:

SUBJECT: Sales Force Compensation

We have retained the management consulting firm of _____ to work with our management to review the present sales compensation plans, to identify opportunities for strengthening the existing incentive approach, and to recommend any modifications that will make the compensation plans totally consistent with the company's marketing strategies and goals.

The study will be conducted by _____ and a company task force, comprising _____ and _____ .

The consulting firm and the task force must thoroughly understand the roles of the organization, products, markets, sales strategies, opportunities, and field sales force in achieving sales and profit goals. Therefore, we shall invite a representative cross section of sales executives, district sales managers, and sales representatives to discuss these issues with the consultants in a confidential interview expected to last about ninety minutes. No preparation will be required. The consultants are interested in hearing your contribution to the company's profitability and your reactions to programs and possible modifications.

These interviews will be conducted during [*months*] in [*cities*]. Our internal staff will make the arrangements.

The consultants would also be pleased to read any written comments that others in the sales force would choose to submit regarding sales compensation. These may be sent directly to:

_____

_____

_____

The company recognizes that your participation in this review is essential. I know that we can expect your full cooperation.

Exhibit 5-3. Field Interview Discussion Topics.

I. Interviewee's background
- Professional history
- Educational and experiential credentials
- Territory locations
- Reporting relationships
- Perceived future career path

II. Territory characteristics
- Major accounts
- Prospects
- Key products, applications, and opportunities

III. Time allocation
- Basis for priorities
- Call frequency standards
- Typical day, week, or month

IV. Account and market characteristics
- Interviewee's perception of categorization of decision makers
- Factors causing difficulty or ease of sale to account

  —Account characteristics
  —Product characteristics
  —Competitive characteristics
  —Other factors (identify)

- What is the minimum education or experience needed to manage each type of account or prospect?
- What characteristics make an account or prospect easy or difficult to sell?
- How and when do you know you have been successful with each product and market combination?
- How much of your time and effort is spent helping shape the needs of customers and prospects?
- What competitive pressures are present in each product and account combination?

V. Measures of success
- Indications (examples: volume growth, overquota, market share)
- Difference of indicators' validity by product and market segment
- Time frame for each indication
- "Contaminants" to each indicator

(*continues*)

Exhibit 5-3. (*continued*)

VI. The company "value" system: field perceptions

  ▪ Perceived "standards" of performance

    —Goals and quotas
    —How set?
    —How communicated?
    —How measured?
    —Fairness or unfairness

  ▪ The pay system

    —Salaries: How set? Administered?
    —Incentive compensation
    —The measures

      • Fair and appropriate; which ones?
      • Potentially unfair; depending on what?
      • Suggestions for improvement
      • Definitely avoid; which ones?
      • What time frame is fair for each?

    —Related compensation elements: sales contests, recognition program perquisites, cars, benefits, etc.; strengths, weaknesses

more, this technique encourages open-ended interviews and allows you to let the interview flow around the key topics in a way that makes the interviewee comfortable. A list of the topics to be covered in these interviews is provided in Exhibit 5-3.

6

Organizing for Effectiveness

In the good old days, sales force organization was pretty simple. Top management decided how far away it wanted its trucks to be sent and then deployed sales reps to cover all accounts within that area. The number of customers was relatively limited, and almost all were concentrated in urban areas within one or two geographic regions.

Management charged the sales reps: "Go forth and sell as much as you can to everyone in your territory who will buy. And mail in your orders at the end of each week." Quotas were, in effect, the sales figures for the prior year, perhaps with some adjustments. Sales reps were paid simply—either all commission or all salary. The boss's son or son-in-law often served as the sales manager. He hired people to fill one type of sales position after running an advertisement in the local paper and conducting thirty-minute interviews. He sent the rookies out with the pros for a week and then gave the recruits sample bags and their own territories.

A lot has changed over the years. Market segmentation and business strategy make it less likely that a sales rep can, or should, sell to "everyone" within a territory. Computers, telecommunications, and the Internet have changed forever how (and how often) field sales reps and customers communicate with "the factory." Efficient and cost-effective transportation, physical distribution and warehousing, and telemarketing systems have made it unusual for a large company to serve only one or two regions of the country.

Today sales forces have evolved to the point where management has a very difficult time answering complex organizational questions:

- Should we have one sales force selling all products, or several sales forces focused by product group?
- How many layers of management do we need in the field?
- What's the right ratio of control for our district manager: seven, eight, or twelve reps per manager?
- Should a customer be served by one rep or a team? If a team, what players should be on the team?
- Should we have a national or a key accounts organization?

- How much teamwork and coordination do we need for our accounts?
- What type of support should we provide at headquarters and at regional and district offices?
- Do we really need all those positions and people?
- How much should our field sales force cost? How much should it produce?

Today, we see sales forces organized and deployed in various ways:

1. Geography

2. Product

    - Product line or group
    - Custom or off the shelf
    - With specialists and generalists

3. Market

    - Industry or segment
    - Channel of distribution (original equipment manufacturer, direct, dealer)

4. Customer

    - Customer classification based on such factors as size, current or potential profits, or sales volume
    - Type of customer (user, dealer, retailer, wholesaler, institution, government)
    - Customer decision-making process (headquarters, purchasing, general management, committee, buying group); new versus old customers or accounts; other customer characteristics (culture, sex, race, religious affiliation)

5. Individual account teams
6. Other factors

    - Value-added opportunity (tech service, applications, R&D, just-in-time, custom, or off the shelf)
    - New versus old territories
    - Skill level required for the sales reps ("easy" or "difficult" territory)

Exhibit 6-1. Elements of the Sales Process Driving Organizational Decisions.

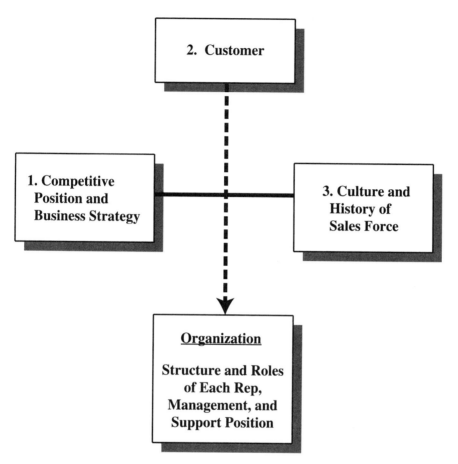

6.1 Developing the Best Sales Organization

There are three key elements of the sales process that dictate the best roles and positions for any sales organization: competitive position, customers, and corporate culture (see Exhibit 6-1).

Competitive Position and Business Strategy

Examine your overall business strategy from the perspective of your sales force. It is particularly important that you understand:

• Why your company has been successful in the past relative to your competition (product or service features, price, quality, innovation, delivery, service, technical capabilities, salespeople, and so on)

- Where your company is heading strategically (how you are investing to establish a position of advantage)

- Which objectives, when achieved, will tell you that you have arrived

- Which markets you will pursue

- What the best means are of approaching those markets (directly or via distribution, brokers, or reps, direct mail, and so on)

Most important, you must understand what role the sales force has played and will play in implementing your strategy.

Business strategy has gone through an evolution that has benefited the sales force and drawn more attention to how sales efforts are organized and managed. In the 1970s and early 1980s, top management focused on the best businesses to enter, not on how to make the most of the businesses that were already in the portfolio. (The exceptions were businesses selected for investment.) In retrospect, the focus on portfolio strategy provided little help for the sales force, unless it was fortunate enough to be in a star business, and was actually detrimental, given the excessive short-term concern about field expense-to-sales ratios in businesses deemed "cows" or, even worse, "dogs."

Current strategic thinking suggests that management concentrate on improving the businesses that the organization already operates. This directs us to three variables that greatly influence the structure and operations of the sales force: (1) *service* to the customer, (2) *profits* at the individual customer level, and (3) *time* to respond to and service customers.

The following trends, consistent with current strategic thinking, are evident in sales organizations across many industries:

- Sales organizations are becoming flatter and much more service oriented than they have been in the recent past. This is consistent with the overall emphasis in every industry on time-based competition, service, and attention to the customer.

- Each sales rep and account manager tends to have fewer but larger customers than in the past. In many industries, this is true because customers are reducing the number of their suppliers and increasing the importance of, and dependence on, the remaining "partners" that supply them, primarily on a just-in-time basis.

- Relationships with customers are becoming stronger and tend to involve top management of both supplier and customer, particularly in customer industries where the number of suppliers has been greatly reduced.

▪ Manufacturers are restructuring their sales forces, placing much more emphasis on the account manager position.

▪ The need for coordination among the various customer contacts and supporting positions has complicated the jobs of most sales reps and account managers and sales managers.

▪ The number of management levels in the field has been reduced, placing greater responsibility, authority, and accountability on the first- and second-level management positions. In many companies, this has actually increased the number of field managers, each of whom is responsible for fewer sales reps.

▪ Telemarketing units have assumed the responsibility for covering medium and small accounts and have proved to be quite useful in maximizing the effectiveness of costly (and valuable) field sales resources.

▪ Companies pursuing time-based strategies are decentralizing their sales forces and giving more decision-making authority to field managers to minimize response time to customers.

▪ More managers are being moved to the field, along with additional supporting resources.

▪ Field managers and some key salespeople are being given responsibility for bottom-line profits.

▪ Many consumer product sales forces are in transition as customers—grocery, retail, and discount chains—shift decision making from the store or local department level to headquarters.

▪ Many of the tasks and responsibilities traditionally fulfilled by direct field people are being subcontracted to third parties.

Customers

Not surprisingly, customers can provide the answers to most important business decisions. Therefore, fundamental to organizing any selling effort is a thorough analysis of how your customers think, how they do business, how they make buying and new product decisions, how customer buying centers vary across your product line (if they do), what customers are buying from your company (product, service, value-added by sales rep, tech service, dependability, and so on), and what it costs (and with what profits) to sell and service each account:

- How complex is the sale?
- What is required to win the order?
- What resources are needed to support the sales rep and serve the customer?
- Are your customers interested in partnership relationships with suppliers, or are sales of a more transactional nature?
- What is the potential of each account, and what, if anything, can be done to expand sales potential?
- Is there an attractive cost-benefit relationship associated with that expansion opportunity?

Keep in mind that these practices and characteristics differ by industry, segment, and, most important, customer.

Examine the field decision-making, coordination, and communications processes in the light of what is needed to implement the business strategy. If you are to establish and maintain a strategic edge on your competition, how quickly must pricing, new product development, and project priority decisions be made to respond to and service customers and prospects? How many layers of management are needed—or can be tolerated—between the customer and your final decision makers to make those decisions? What type of coordination is needed among various levels and positions to pursue, respond to, and service your accounts? What field and headquarters costs can be tolerated to meet those times and authority requirements called for in your strategy and by your customers?

Culture

Company culture—the company's value system and the way it gets things done—has a tremendous influence on field structure. Whether the culture is as good as it should be is irrelevant; it will still have an influence that must be accommodated. Independence and levels of authority; the relationships of marketing, manufacturing, and financial orientation of management; short-term versus long-term focus; risk orientation; innovation and creativity; sense of urgency; customer orientation; position of sales in the professional and management career tracks—all will influence the type of people drawn to the sales organization, how responsibilities are allocated among them, and how they are deployed.

You must determine, on the basis of these factors, how people in each position should spend their time during a day or a week. The best way to do this might be to conduct a detailed activity analysis of your sales force, comparing the current tasks, call frequency and times, and call routing patterns with those that are needed to serve customers and implement strategy. This analysis will indicate the proper staffing levels for each position. Where you find gaps in responsibilities or coordination, you will have to create, modify, or even eliminate positions.

The number and type of field management positions and the appropriate staffing levels of field managers are functions of several variables, many of which are cultural in nature—for example:

- Management's role in each sale and its relationship with customers
- Levels of authority
- Management's need or desire to be close to customers
- The span of control
- The sales reps' skill level, competency, or experience

6.2   Who Is the Entrepreneur?

Every sales force in every industry has at least one position that is the entrepreneur, or mover and shaker—by tradition, market or strategic need, or both. This position controls sales and the relationships with the decision makers in customers' organizations. The entrepreneur may be the account manager, the district manager, or even the president. (If the role of entrepreneur varies with the individual, an organization is not under control.)

The two questions you need to ask are:

1. In which position or positions are the entrepreneurs?
2. In which ones should they be?

The answers should be functions of the marketplace and the fundamental strategy of the company.

In markets where there are very few customers and every one is necessary for the company's success (e.g., a one-product company with a monopoly ingredient for brewers), the vice president of sales or even the president may be the best entrepreneur and in control of the sale, particularly for crucial pricing negotiations. In markets where there are pockets of major accounts, say, hospital buying groups which purchase on contract, the district, regional, or national account manager might be the best one to direct and control the sales relationship with each account, leaving the sales reps to service the individual accounts and ensure local compliance with the group contracts.

In a highly fragmented marketplace (e.g., hospitals, before buy-ing groups were significant) where there is a broad product line to sell, the sales rep is probably in the best position to control all as-pects of the sale as well as the overall relationship. If the account manager provides or controls the flow of technical and problem-solving skills to the customer, and that is the source of the value-added that the customer is buying, the account manager is probably the entrepreneur.

It is important to identify the entrepreneur because the organi-zation should be structured and managed to support and reward the entrepreneur in all efforts to serve the customer. If it is not, the organization is not functioning as efficiently as it should. Strategy and marketplace—that is, customers—dictate which position (or po-sitions) should be the entrepreneurs in the sales organization. The position that actually is the entrepreneur, however, is more than likely determined by a combination of tradition, culture, and the specific individuals in the sales organization.

This analysis of business strategy, customers, and culture will allow you to identify the tasks and responsibilities that are needed and the emphasis you should place within the sales organization. You will determine the appropriate role and impact of the various types of sales reps, field managers, and support people. Most impor-tant, you will understand what positions *should* be entrepreneurial, as well as their appropriate support systems.

In this discussion about organizational structure, we have not used a single organizational chart. This is deliberate. Organizational charts tend to oversimplify how organizations actually function. They focus too much on internal relationships and not enough on what the sales organization is trying to accomplish: serving custom-ers better than competitors do. We have tried to help you determine what types of positions and people you need to implement your sales strategy. You may draw boxes around the positions with lines connecting many of them, if you wish. But before you do, think through what's needed in a thorough, logical, and strategic way.

6.3   Deploying Resources Effectively

A common but inadequate measure of sales force efficiency is dol-lars of sales revenue per sales representative. By dividing total sales by the number of sales reps, many managers think they have deter-mined the contribution of their sales reps. By comparing this ratio with those of the competition and companies in similar businesses, they gauge their company's efficiency and reduce or expand their sales forces as a result. Because it ignores the complexity of the sales task and draws comparisons that fail to highlight important differences between sales forces, this ratio is too simplistic a way to measure the efficiency of a sales force and make staffing decisions.

To improve the use of sales resources, begin with a careful analysis of the sales requirements, based on an assessment of the market and consideration of alternatives. There are four specific steps in this process:

1. Segment the customer base by priority and by the requirements to be met.
2. Analyze each group's selling task.
3. Evaluate alternative ways to perform sales tasks.
4. Establish sales assignments.

A disciplined analysis of the market provides the foundation for this process. It will help you achieve a better understanding of sales needs, so that you can effectively match sales capacity to the needs of the marketplace.

Step 1: Segment the Customer Base

The first step is to segment the account base by type of customer, considering both the priority given the accounts and their requirements to be met. Rank accounts by size, profitability, and growth potential. What you must provide a customer group is determined by the customer product-user requirements and the way the client company makes purchase decisions. Product- and service-user requirements include such factors as level of service, product quality levels, variety of products, and delivery and response time. To understand the purchasing decisions, you must have a good grasp of who makes and who influences the selection of vendors, the importance the customer places on price versus quality, and purchasing cycles and needs for special terms. Customer segmentation is discussed in greater detail in the following section.

Step 2: Analyze the Selling Tasks

The next step is to specify the sales activities required to serve each type of account and the time that should be allocated to each activity. Determine the type and estimate the number and frequency of in-person calls for sales, reorders, relationship maintenance, and technical service; telephone contacts; correspondence; and other activities associated with each account.

The set of activities will differ for each customer group. For example, potential new accounts require prospecting and familiarization activities, established accounts need an emphasis on account maintenance and service, and highly competitive accounts call for intensive coverage and a strong selling effort.

Although the program for each customer group will be different, be sure that each group's sales program meets the following criteria:

1. The program reflects the mutual needs of customers and the company.
2. The set of activities effectively counters the competition.
3. The nature of the activities and the time spent reflect the priority given to each customer group.
4. The program provides the required level of account coverage at the lowest cost.

Step 3: Evaluate Alternative Ways to Perform Sales Tasks

Developing the best program is usually a process of trial and error. For each customer group, you must consider a number of approaches—for example:

- Different levels of attention to the top accounts
- Reducing the number of, or even eliminating, calls to the smaller accounts
- Using more telephone contact to reduce in-person calls
- Moving from direct calls to direct mail to replace prospecting calls

Developing a sales program is not an exact science, and not every contingency affecting a sales activity can be anticipated. Certainly, the program cannot be refined in the same way a time study calculates production line activities. However, if you carefully analyze and assess alternative approaches for each customer group, you will obtain useful results.

Step 4: Establish Sales Assignments

Once you have developed the sales program for each customer group, you can establish territories for the field sales reps. To determine the territory size that can be covered effectively by each sales rep, add the time needed to serve each customer and the associated travel time. A visual technique is to mark the accounts and prospects to be covered on a map, coding them by type and priority. The clusters of accounts may indicate natural territories.

The process of developing efficient territory assignments also involves some trial and error. When extensive travel time is required, such as when large geographic territories must be covered with many in-person calls, you can design alternative travel schedules and routes then calculate costs to achieve better territory structuring and sales rep placement. You may want to use some of the available computer programs to design the deployment of very large sales forces.

Field sales costs are the major cost element in sales and marketing. To make the most of your sales resources, match them with the requirements of the marketplace in a comprehensive analysis of the sales tasks the reps should perform, the time allocated to perform these tasks, and the ways they will differ among customer groups. Once you have determined these factors, you can design alternative ways to perform the sales tasks and to size and deploy the field sales force for the best effect.

6.4 Market and Customer Segmentation

Customer types, buying processes, and product applications vary dramatically. For example, although the same product might be sold to both universities and private companies, educational institutions usually have pricing needs that are much different from those of private companies. Marketers try to manage these differences by establishing *market segments,* or groupings of similar accounts for strategic marketing purposes. Marketers might then use particular advertising media to reach these groups.

Segmentation can be extremely valuable in the sales effort as well. It can provide important clues as to what to find out about account and selling strategies and information that is vital to sales organization and deployment. For example, customer characteristics that differ substantially and a product or service that demands a lot of adaptation from one situation to another argue for separate, or at least specialized, sales organizations. If the differences in customer characteristics are greater than or even close to the differences in product technology, the organizational lines are best drawn along market rather than product lines. Information available about the number and size of customers in each market segment can provide crucial insight into sales deployment (size of the sales organization).

Sales role characteristics must serve as the primary criteria in segmenting customers. For example, companies often establish market segments according to industry. This makes sense if the product sold, its application, and the buying process vary significantly from industry to industry. But even if the sales role is the same for similar industries, it may differ according to the sophistication of the account. So, for the purpose of managing the sales force, a different (or modified) segmentation from that used in the marketing process might be advisable.

Alternatively, customers are frequently classified by volume (or potential volume), with sales reps told to call more often on "A" accounts, less often on "B" accounts, and so on. This sort of classification scheme might help reps be more efficient, but it doesn't make the sales force any smarter. To match selling skills and customer needs effectively, customers should be classified according to their decision-making processes—for example, how will the buyer *use* the company's product, and what variables will the buyer consider in choosing vendors? Exhibit 6-2 summarizes some of the segmentation alternatives.

Selling specialized products, such as medical equipment, usually requires the ability to communicate technical information to sophisticated customers. The sales rep will, of necessity, develop a narrow product specialization. Therefore, a number of reps may have to call on a single customer, a situation that demands careful account management. If, on the other hand, distributors play a major role in decision making, they might provide a reason for segmentation. The sales organization can accommodate differences in the products purchased, the competition, or the service required. A less conventional criterion for segmentation might be the customer-vendor relationship itself.

The sales force may also be partially segmented. This is common when segmentation is based on account size. Partial segmentation can fit other situations, too, such as uneven geographic distribution of customers, which may warrant industry specialists in dense territories and generalists in sparse ones.

Specialization strengthens sales force effectiveness, but it is not without trade-offs. Specialization often increases travel time, which decreases the time available to spend with customers. In addition, travel is expensive, as is the more complex management of a segmented sales force. Is this greater cost worthwhile? If the probable

Exhibit 6-2. Sales Force Segmentation Alternatives.

Specialization Strategy	Situations Where Most Applicable
Product	• High degree of technical issues determine sales to sophisticated buyer. • Little commonality occurs along other dimensions (e.g., industry).
Large account	• Buying process changes significantly based on the size of the organization (e.g., national organizations). • Large, multisite accounts want a coordinated sales approach.
Industry	• Nature of product, product application, or buying decision differs significantly from industry to industry. • One or more industry segments have tightly knit relationships or unique business jargon.
Distribution channel	• Product must be sold not just to the end user but to others at various points in the distribution channel. • The nature of the sales role varies (e.g., selling electronic components to end users differs from encouraging a distributor to spend more time on the same products).
Customer-vendor	• Personality issues represent the most important relationship factors in buying decision. • Skills in different parts of the sales relationship (such as securing new accounts versus maintaining old ones) differ, and a graceful transition is possible.

benefits outweigh the cost and if similar benefits cannot be achieved by less expensive means, the answer is yes.

Examining a specialized approach is almost always worthwhile, because the process helps identify the best selling approaches for each market segment. Even if the economics do not justify a specialized organization, disseminating segment-specific information can help sales reps develop strategies that are more closely tied to account characteristics. The information can also help in training and troubleshooting problem accounts.

Companies with a market focus obtain the information they

Exhibit 6-3. Strategic vs. Product Information.

MedElect, a manufacturer of medical devices, introduced a new product, accompanied by a great deal of technical product literature (and trade advertising). The device sold poorly in most territories, although a few reps did well. Why didn't all do well? Here's what MedElect discovered:

- Although most of the company's other products were sold to individual practitioners, the new device, used primarily in hospitals, was bought by hospital purchasing committees. The reps that had experience selling to hospitals were more comfortable and more successful selling to them than were the reps without that experience.
- The new device had several possible applications. In the most obvious of these, it competed with a number of other products. Although it was arguably a "better mousetrap," the competitive products worked satisfactorily. So why would a hospital risk using something new, and increasing its inventory, when existing products sufficed? The successful reps focused on the applications where competitive products either did not exist or worked poorly—and where the new device filled a real need. The other reps, struggling with a new product in a less familiar environment, focused on the more obvious applications, which were easier to understand, because they didn't realize this decision made the sale more difficult.

---

need to formulate business strategies by examining customer rather than internal characteristics. Exhibit 6-3 illustrates the value of a customer rather than a product perspective on sales information. Once the company understood what was happening, it took two steps to present the new product better. The first was to specialize the sales force; in geographically concentrated markets, different reps covered the old and new products. The second step was to provide more information to the entire sales organization about those product applications where the company had an advantage. The company also advised reps on how best to explain product advantages in the marketplace. With these changes, product sales improved significantly.

7

The Linkage Between Sales Roles and Compensation

7.1 The Importance of Defining Selling Roles

As we have noted in earlier chapters, the design of sales compensation plans must be driven by an understanding of a company's overall business objectives, its marketing strategy, and the requirements of the various customer segments it serves. The intersection of these factors ultimately defines the key selling roles for a given sales job. One without the others is insufficient to tell you what you need to know about a job's key roles and tasks. The business objectives define the ultimate benchmark for the measurement of success or failure for the company. The marketing strategy governs the products and services, technologies, market segments, distribution channels, and distinctive capabilities your company must develop or emphasize; and the types of customers it must attract and retain to achieve its business objectives. Customers themselves, each with specific vendor requirements and selection criteria, govern the attributes a sales force must exhibit to be successful.

Where customers are stable and essentially committed to a vendor and such factors as regulation and economics restrict competitive entry into your marketplace, there may be no need for a true sales function. Organizations of this type need service personnel and perhaps a public relations function, but few of them need salespeople unless there is a requirement to focus on additional services or products for which there is no established demand.

In other words, there is no requirement for a sales function if there is no need for advocacy. The customer must have purchase options to consider, including the alternative of doing nothing, before a sales force is appropriate. In addition, the vendor organization must derive some practical value from using personal selling to deliver the marketing message, as opposed to using media, direct mail advertising, automated telemarketing, or the Internet. The use of

Exhibit 7-1. Traditional Sales Force Activities.

Customer Identification and Acquisition	Customer Development

▪ Market analysis and segmentation
▪ Cold calling and prospecting
▪ Lead generation and qualification
▪ Lead follow-up
▪ Proposal preparation
▪ Proposal presentation and
  negotiation
▪ Trade show participation
	▪ Demonstrations and tests
	▪ Add-on selling to broaden product
	  mix
	▪ Installation support
	▪ Training and consulting
	▪ Service and relationship management
	▪ Entertainment
	▪ Receivables management

salespeople is usually necessary when the organization has exhausted other means of cost-effectively attracting, retaining, and growing the business. When advocacy plays a key role, organizations typically turn to alternatives such as telemarketing or advertising when the cost of direct sales is prohibitive.

In organizations that need the sales function, the variety of actual selling tasks can be immense, even within a particular industry. However, most selling tasks can be categorized as either customer identification and acquisition or customer development activities. Exhibit 7-1 illustrates some of the traditional sales force activities in these two categories.

Even in organizations where significant market research, lead generation, and lead qualification comprise the sales process, there is usually some additional customer identification work left to be done by the sales force. So while a sales rep may not be required to perform initial customer identification tasks, the opportunity often exists to uncover other decision makers or individuals who influence the sales process, or to find new accounts that weren't targeted by prior research.

Indeed, a clear definition of a sales organization's key selling roles is critical to the design of an effective sales compensation plan. An understanding of these roles will largely determine whether a single or multiple incentive plans are required to support the company's marketing strategy and fit the unique characteristics of the different customer segments. Furthermore, role definitions shape the basic components of a sales compensation plan, including the most appropriate performance measures and their relative weighting or importance, and the amount of risk in the plan (that is, the mix of fixed compensation and incentive pay).

Exhibit 7-2. Sales Roles and Key Success Factors.

Sales Role	Common Titles	Success Factors
Prospector/closer: identifies and closes sales; develops a large base of new and existing customers	■ Sales representative ■ Account manager ■ Sales executive ■ Marketing representative	■ Revenue volume ■ Gross margin volume ■ Gross margin percentage ■ New account sales volume ■ Unit sales volume ■ Order size
Account manager: develops and maintains relationships; concentrates on a few large customers	■ Account executive ■ National account manager ■ Key account manager ■ Industry account manager	■ Revenue volume and growth ■ Market share ■ Account share ■ Account profitability ■ Product mix ■ Customer satisfaction and loyalty
Technical sales support: provides presale or ongoing postsale technical support	■ Field engineer ■ Sales engineer ■ Technical sales representative ■ Technical product specialist	■ Revenue volume for team of supported direct salespeople ■ Retention of business in assigned accounts ■ Product mix
Facilitator: coordinates product delivery and availability	■ Sales representative ■ Merchandising representative ■ Account manager	■ Distribution fill ■ Market share ■ Special products sales volume

7.2   Sales Role Definition and Key Success Factors

After examining the many roles a sales rep plays, you must define specific approaches to compensation that match the success factors of each role. These success factors often determine the performance measures that form the core of the sales incentive plan. Exhibit 7-2 illustrates roles a sales rep can play and the success factors that could provide the basis for all or part of the sales rep's incentive opportunity.

Before we look at methods for defining sales roles, we will discuss a topic that has significant implications for matching pay to a given sales role: the issue of sales force prominence.

7.3   Prominence

The mix of sales compensation (the percentage of target total cash compensation provided in fixed compensation relative to the percentage provided in variable incentive pay) is driven by one critical factor:

> The influence of the sales rep in the mix of all the marketing variables that collectively create the message heard by the buyer

Prominence is a measure of the degree of personal persuasion or influence a seller has on the buying decision. In other words, it is a measure of a sales rep's ability to cause the customer to act favorably to the sales rep's offer. It is not an absolute measure. It captures the relative influence of the sales rep compared to the influence of other factors, such as pricing, advertising, product quality, sales organizational structure, customer service levels, and the proximity of the sales force to the ultimate user or consumer. When prominence is high, the sales rep is heavily involved in differentiating the company's offering from those presented by competitors. When prominence is low, the sales rep is unable to exert much positive influence on the prospects for new business.

Four Key Indicators of Prominence

The amount of prospecting, the creativity of the sales process, the level of support provided to the sales rep, and the competitiveness of the product are the four key indicators of sales force prominence. In general, the more creative, entrepreneurial, and unsupported the sales process—and the more improbable, untested, and unknown the product or service offering—the more critical is persuasiveness or advocacy. This equates to a highly prominent sales job, one in which the sales rep is crucial in differentiating the company's sales message to the market. The nature of the sales process requires the sales rep to demonstrate spontaneous creative skill. Such skill is not easily replaced by another marketing tool.

Conversely, the more routine, established, and supported the sales process—and the more straightforward, proved, and visible the product or service—the more the sales process consists of managing a customer relationship. In this case, persuasiveness or advocacy on the part of the sales rep is less important. Consequently, the sales rep will have a low level of prominence relative to other factors in the marketing mix.

Examples of Prominence

High-, medium-, and low-prominence sales jobs are easy to recognize. A telemarketing sales rep making outbound calls or the classic door-to-door seller who seeks to sell an unadvertised and unknown product is prominent in the success of the business. This sales rep must frequently overcome the extreme reluctance of a prospective customer, and the job usually requires a substantial tolerance for negative responses. The sales rep's challenge is to make the customer receptive to the form and medium of the contact, the product or service category, and the specific brand.

High-prominence sales positions are usually found in businesses where few resources are available to manage or support a field sales effort, or where the only practical access to the buyer is through direct, personal selling. Many sales positions that involve professional selling to sophisticated commercial customers, where in-depth knowledge of how and why the customer buys is critical, are prominent in the overall mix of marketing elements. As a result, the mix of assured and variable compensation opportunity for these positions is usually skewed toward the variable component. Because the skills and industry experience required to be a successful participant in the professional sales arena can be significant, however, there is also a need for the pay package to reflect the market value of these resources through some base salary.

A department store sales counter clerk may be minimally important in the process that leads the customer to make a purchase. The prominence of this job tends to increase to the extent that the product lends itself to consultation and the clerk is expected to advise the customer. Yet even at the extreme, where the counter clerk's role is to move the customer up the line to higher-profit selections and to answer an array of questions and even demonstrate the product, this sales job can achieve only moderate prominence relative to sales jobs in other industries. In retail, the store and its location, merchandising philosophy, advertising commitments, and pricing practices usually play a larger role in the customer's decision to walk into the store, approach a specific counter, show interest, stay long enough to make a purchase, and buy the items that offer the best return to the store.

How Prominence Varies

The prominence of a sales job in the marketing mix should be understood as a dynamic concept. Prominence varies as the point of customer contact, the product mix, the sales message, the sales role, and the type of customer vary. Because there is usually some change in all or some of these factors in a given business, the prominence of a given sales job will usually change over time as well.

Because prominence is essentially a function of account control by the sales rep, anything that tends to alter the level of control also alters prominence. A common example will help to illustrate this point. Once the buyer has decided to purchase selected components from a specific supplier, the supplier must deliver what has been promised and perhaps attempt to broaden the business relationship to include other components. As contract terms are being finalized, the sales rep is usually very prominent in closing the sale.

After the contract is signed, the nature of the sales role usually changes. Part, if not all, of the work on the account now involves fulfilling the contract and servicing the needs and requests of the buyer. At this point, the prominence of the sales rep declines as the importance of postsale support increases, with other nonsales functions of the supplier becoming involved in determining the level and quality of the business with the customer. Sales force control over the relationship—its prominence—has usually been reduced.

If the supplier relies on the same field sales position to close deals *and* provide postsale support, the prominence of the sales job may change even further as more of the sales rep's attention is focused on account maintenance rather than new business development. Problems with declining sales force motivation and increasing costs of sales often emerge as the compensation program, which may have been designed to support aggressive selling, no longer reflects the content and prominence of the sales job. As a result, the program is too lucrative for a role that is largely maintenance oriented.

7.4   Sales Compensation Plan Design

Prominence

Prominence is the key concept in the design of effective sales force compensation programs, as well as organizational roles and structures. It is also a complex concept that is neither readily identified nor easily measured. Because different sales roles will be more or less prominent in the marketing mix of a specific business and the same roles may have a different prominence in different business environments, skilled observers occasionally disagree about a specific job's prominence.

Far from sufficient for telling us how to structure a compensation plan for a given sales position, prominence is nevertheless a helpful tool. In the main, two incentive design factors are driven by the level of prominence: (1) the mix of fixed and variable compensation and (2) the amount of potential incentive earnings opportunity a position is given.

Taken alone, higher prominence suggests a closer linkage between sales results and pay because higher prominence means more control over, and direct responsibility for, those sales results. At the extreme end of the scale, this logic suggests that the income of very high prominence sales jobs should be *only* variable (no fixed base salary or assured income).

At this extreme, we would be tempted to conclude that the pay of a high-prominence job, such as selling integrated telecommunications systems to expert buyers who routinely negotiate acceptable terms and prices, should be fully variable, probably in the form of a straight commission. Notably, however, this is almost never true. There are at least three reasons for adopting another pay design:

1. If sales cycles are long, a straight commission plan can result in extended periods without any income.
2. New or unavailable technologies can disrupt the sales rep's ability to offer a competitive product or system.
3. The sales rep's skill and experience will probably command a minimum level of pay in the marketplace.

Thus, high-prominence sales positions may receive substantial levels of assured income, in the form of either base salary or a nonrecoverable draw. However, it is also possible for high-prominence sales positions to receive no assured income. This commonly occurs when few acquired skills and little experience are required and the sales rep can close sales frequently and quickly.

In general, the dollar amount of variable pay *opportunity* will usually increase with increasing prominence. This means that high-prominence positions commonly require significant incentive opportunity, and low-prominence positions commonly have little, if any, opportunity. The total level of compensation will be determined by market practices and the need for base salary. The converse is not necessarily true; the absence of significant incentive opportunity does not prove that a position has low prominence in the marketing mix.

National account managers (NAMs), for example, are frequently very visible and influential in the execution of the sales strategy and are often more important to the success of the business than many other factors. Yet most NAMs are given only moderate amounts of incentive income relative to assured income and have low incentive opportunities, partly because it is inappropriate to tie substantial variable pay for such a national sales role to conventional measures of performance, such as revenue and profit. Indeed many NAMs are engaged in a complex and lengthy sales process in which results must be measured less frequently, thus making it difficult to rely too heavily on variable incentive pay relative to base salary.

Barriers to Entry and Barriers to Exit

The second most important factor that should influence the design of a sales compensation program is the presence of barriers to entry into the job. A barrier to entry is a qualification the candidate must meet to be considered for the job. The greater the number, specificity, and value of these qualifications, the greater the barriers to entry.

In general, as barriers to entry increase, the available labor pool decreases, and the new employee's minimum economic value increases, if only because the employer's requirements bid up the value of the labor supply. In addition, the skills and experience required of high-barrier sales reps probably command some kind of guaranteed income, because these individuals often have access to alternative employers and labor markets. The implication of both factors is that many sales positions require some level of fixed compensation even though it may not be warranted on the basis of the position's prominence.

Barriers to exit also reflect the sales rep's valued skills and experience. These are barriers erected to retain qualified and seasoned employees who might be tempted to accept a competing offer, and they are designed to reduce the appeal of such offers by providing some combination of competitive total and assured cash compensation, recognizing performance with noncash awards, and promoting star performers to higher or more prestigious positions. Erecting barriers to exit is particularly important for businesses that invest heavily in training and developing their salespeople. Where key skills are often lacking, many smaller and less organized companies would welcome a competitor's well-trained sales rep.

The Relationship Between Barriers to Entry and Prominence

It's essential to understand four basic combinations of barrier and prominence relationships when reviewing or crafting a sales com-

Exhibit 7-3. Common Characteristics of Basic Barrier/Prominence Relationships.

Barriers to Entry

		High	*Low*
Prominence	*High*	• Expert or experienced rep • Product, company, application must be sold	• Minimally trained rep • Heavy prospecting • Multiple suppliers
	Low	• Technically skilled rep • Complex product, need seen, few suppliers	• Minimally trained rep • Familiar products • Established customers

pensation plan: high barrier/high prominence, high barrier/low prominence, low barrier/high prominence, and low barrier/low prominence. Each of these relationships represents a product-market-rep scenario that should prove instructive throughout the review or design process. Exhibit 7-3 illustrates the common characteristics of these relationships.

A high-barrier/high-prominence sales position clearly requires demonstrated sales skill and perhaps some scarce technical knowledge in situations where the business relies heavily on the success of the sales rep in achieving its goals. The most extreme case of high prominence occurs when marketing is a critical activity for the business and the sales force assumes a leading role in that activity. In that situation, the product must be sold in terms of meeting and even creating a need. Where the sales force is critical, the marketing message is usually too complex, or the demographics of advertising channels too broad, to permit reliance on less direct methods.

A low-barrier/low-prominence sales position represents the opposite end of this spectrum. Most low/low positions require no previous training or related experience. The risks incurred by the business in putting an inexperienced recruit in low/low jobs are usually minimal because the customer base is stable and the products are familiar and standard, requiring limited explanation or applications work by the sales rep.

Implications for Plan Design

The spectrum of low- to high-prominence sales positions ranges between positions that only facilitate orders to positions that create

Exhibit 7-4. Implications of Barriers and Prominence for Total Compensation.

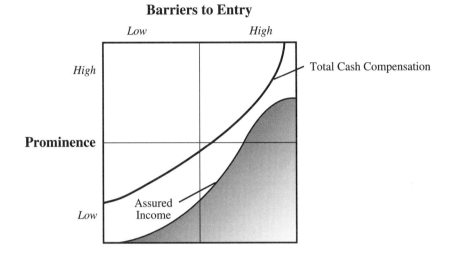

markets. Similarly, the spectrum of low- to high-barrier sales positions ranges between positions that do not require any relevant training or experience to positions that demand highly educated, expertly trained, and industry-experienced salespeople.

In general, as barriers to entry or exit increase, the level of fixed income, in the form of a base salary or nonrecoverable draw, also increases. Similarly, as prominence increases, the amount of variable compensation tends to increase. The actual mix of fixed and variable compensation that is appropriate for a position is largely determined by an analysis of the interplay between these two design factors, barriers and prominence, as they act to raise or lower total compensation and the level of income risk to the sales rep.

Exhibit 7-4 portrays this interplay and emphasizes the importance of judgment in arriving at the correct mix of fixed and variable compensation for any position. As barriers increase, we want to raise the base salary (or nonrecoverable draw), but as we do this, we reduce the percentage of pay that is variable and raise the total level of pay. If we are constrained by market practice or internal budgets to limit total pay, but still want to raise the base to reflect the role of barriers to entry, we are committed to reducing the *leverage* of the pay plan—the percentage of pay that is variable. This tends to be troublesome if the position in question is also highly prominent. It's easy to find other examples that illustrate the dynamic and complex behavior of these two factors.

The depiction of the basic variables in Exhibit 7-4 (prominence, barriers to entry, and total cash compensation) should be viewed as a rendering rather than an exact depiction of the most important relationships in sales compensation. The point of this exhibit is to show that assured income and total compensation rise as barriers and prominence rise, but not linearly and not at the same rate. Actual rates of change vary with the real circumstances of an actual business situation.

7.5 Defining Roles

One method for identifying the key roles for a given sales job seeks to profile the key characteristics of a sales rep's role within the context of the selling environment. A number of characteristics or factors can be examined comparatively across a variety of different selling jobs to distinguish the true nature of one sales job from another.

Following is a sample list of sales role characteristics that form the basis for comparing sales roles among different selling jobs. Carefully profiling a sales job along these dimensions will help clarify critical incentive design issues such as the number of distinct incentive plans required, the appropriate levels of pay mix and incentive opportunity, and the performance measures that best match the key selling roles.

Primary Charter

The *primary charter* of a sales job is a statement of the sales rep's core role, which is a direct reflection of a company's overall business objectives and marketing strategy. The job's primary charter will point directly to the optimal metrics to be used to gauge the performance of the seller—for example:

- Achieve target revenue volume levels with existing accounts in the assigned territory.
- Penetrate the assigned vertical market by identifying, qualifying, and closing prospective target accounts.
- Increase existing account penetration through the sale of the breadth of the company's product or service offering.
- Achieve target revenue volume in a particular product line by securing design wins with existing and prospective accounts.

Territory Characteristics

This speaks to issues of sales deployment, sales specialization, and the general size of the account or territory base:

- The type of deployment model employed (e.g., geographic territory versus assigned, named accounts)
- The level of sales force specialization (e.g., vertical market specialization versus horizontal market specialization versus product specialization)
- The size of the territory or account base assignment, including number of accounts, size of geography, and quota size

Territory characteristics have an impact on the definition of the selected performance measures, for example, whether revenue volume should be measured as all revenue dollars from a geographic territory as opposed to the revenue from a vertical market segment only.

Account Characteristics

These characteristics help to distinguish the nature of the assigned account base, along the following criteria:

- Minimum and maximum volume thresholds to qualify as a target account
- Account buying practices, including where the key decisions are made (e.g., central office versus local office)
- Single versus multiple buying locations

Key Decision Makers

Determination of the key decision makers and influencers to whom the sales rep must sell will provide an indication of the complexity of the sales process and the corresponding level of skill and experience required to succeed.

Key Buying Influences

This is an indication of the criteria against which a customer judges competing vendor offerings. Examples of key buying influences are product quality, level of service, sales rep relationship, brand awareness, and pricing and financial terms. The buying influences are an indication of the sales rep's prominence in the overall marketing mix, which determines how much pay to put at risk in variable compensation.

Length of Sales Cycle

The length of the sales cycle is a measure of the amount of time typically required from initial contact to the close of a sale. The length of the cycle has direct implications for the frequency with which incentives can be paid and the amount of pay to be placed at risk.

Sales Process Interdependencies

This is a measure of the degree to which the sales rep must effectively team with another selling or customer contact resource to execute the sales process. Interdependence in the sales process exists when various selling resources must interact to close a sale. For example, a technical sales engineer who demonstrates the technical specifications of a complex product might interact with the direct sales rep, who effectively negotiates and closes the sale. Such interdependencies may indicate the need to consider sales support jobs for sales compensation eligibility. Sales process interdependencies will also tie directly to the need for individual- versus team-based incentives.

Pricing Authority

This is an indication of the extent to which a sales rep influences the margins of the business. A high degree of pricing authority may indicate that an incentive plan measure of gross margin or profitability is appropriate. However, despite the fact that improving margins may be key to a company's marketing strategy, if the sales rep has no pricing authority, it will be difficult to justify incorporating such a measure into the incentive plan.

7.6   Illustrative Role: Direct or Geographic Sales Rep vs. Indirect Channel Manager

To illustrate how role definition determines key incentive plan design, we will compare two selling roles: a geographic sales representative who sells directly to the end user, and a channel manager who sells through an indirect channel of distribution. Exhibit 7-5 illustrates the various aspects of these two selling roles along the profile dimensions detailed in the previous section.

In comparing the two roles illustrated in Exhibit 7-5, there are

Exhibit 7-5. Comparison of Two Different Sales Roles.

Role Profile Dimension	Geographic Sales Rep	Channel Manager
Primary charter	▪ Identify and close new prospective accounts within assigned territory ▪ Maintain and penetrate existing accounts by selling additional products and services	▪ Support assigned wholesale distributors by ensuring adequate inventory levels of the entire product line ▪ Provide support by training distributor sales staff on product features and benefits ▪ Ensure compliance with distributor agreement and identify potential new channel partners
Territory characteristics	▪ Geographic territory by zip code assignment ▪ 65 existing accounts; 32 identified target prospects ▪ Annual sales quota: $2.5 million	▪ Seven named wholesale distributors headquartered in western region ▪ Annual quota: $12.0 million (measured as "sales-in" to the distributor)
Account characteristics	▪ Sales credit granted for accounts with average monthly sales greater than $1,000 and less than $5,000 ▪ Local buying decisions are prevalent ▪ Accounts average from one to three buying locations	▪ Central buying decisions for "sales into" multiple warehouses; influence "sales out" to local consumers ▪ One to four warehouses per distributor—average of 2.3
Key decision makers and influencers	▪ General manager ▪ President/business owner ▪ Purchasing manager	▪ Vice president, purchasing ▪ Chief financial officer ▪ Warehouse manager ▪ Vice president, sales ▪ Regional sales manager ▪ Distributor sales rep
Buying influences	▪ Price ▪ Product quality ▪ After-sale service ▪ Relationship	▪ Breadth of offering ▪ Inventory financing terms ▪ Price ▪ Sales-out support (training and joint sales calls)

Length of sales cycle	• One to six months	• Six to 18 months for a new distributor • Monthly reorders with existing distributors
Interdependencies	• Product engineer • Installation support specialist	• Channel recruiting manager • Legal (new and renewal contracts)
Pricing authority	• Wide pricing latitude within a broad range; sales manager approval required for pricing outside stated range	• None; all pricing decisions made centrally

certain clues that indicate the relative level of prominence between the two jobs. For example, the fact that the geographic sales rep sells directly to the end user, must prospect for new business, and has a high degree of pricing authority suggests a relatively high degree of prominence. As such, the geographic sales rep would likely have a fair amount of the target total cash compensation at risk in variable pay.

The channel manager, on the other hand, sells through an indirect channel and only occasionally influences the end user through joint distributor sales calls. The channel manager also focuses on maintaining relationships with existing channel partners and has no pricing authority. However, the lower level of prominence for the channel manager does not suggest that the target total cash compensation level for the position is also lower. On the contrary, the skills required to manage indirect channel partners of this size—including ensuring distributor contract compliance, monitoring inventory levels, and selling to multiple levels of decision maker—may suggest a greater level of skill and experience. This greater level of skill would likely translate into a higher target pay level with relatively less pay at risk.

8

Selecting Performance Measures

Selecting performance measures is one of the most critical, and often one of the most time-consuming, tasks in the incentive design process. They become the most important link in aligning sales compensation with the role of the job *and* with the organization's broader sales and business strategy.

This chapter provides an overview of typical performance measures. It identifies a variety of measures—both standard and new or emerging measures—discusses their applicability in different situations, and reviews their pros and cons. Before launching into this review, it is worthwhile to discuss the process and criteria for assessing the appropriateness of different performance measures.

8.1 Assessing Alternative Performance Measures

The task of choosing appropriate performance measures can seem overwhelming, particularly as more and better sources of data become available and as selling roles and processes become more complex. To assess the appropriateness of any potential metric, there are three important questions to ask:

1. Is the measure aligned with the overall business strategy and objectives?
2. Is it a factor that the salesperson can control, affect, or influence?
3. Is the measure observable and trackable? If not,

    - Can we develop systems to measure it? How long will this take?
    - Can we use an alternative measure?

1. *Is the measure aligned with the overall business strategy and objectives?* This is the starting point for any sales incentive compensation

plan design. The choice of performance measures is the most critical link between salesperson behavior and the business strategy. For instance, if the strategy is to stay ahead of the competition by continually developing and releasing new products, it follows that the sales reps should be given incentives to promote sales of new products (which tend to be a more difficult and challenging sale than existing products, particularly when the reps must create a market for these new products). Therefore, separate measures that focus on both existing and new product sales may be appropriate. If sales of both new and existing products are not differentiated in the performance measurement system, reps will be motivated to achieve their sales numbers by focusing on existing products since they are an easier sale. The result is a fundamental misalignment between the business strategy and sales rep performance.

2. *Is the measure a factor that the salesperson can control, affect, or influence?* Just because a measure is aligned with the overall business strategy does not mean that it is also aligned with the role of the salesperson. Any one sales job has a specific role to play to help further the business in the attainment of its strategic objectives. Yet that role will not necessarily encompass all aspects of the overall business strategy. For instance, the business as a whole may have an objective of increasing sales revenue by 25 percent. This implies that the sales reps should be measured on the same basis: sales revenue growth. Yet different sales jobs will have different roles to play in driving the overall growth metric.

For instance, some sales organizations use the simple organizational construct of having separate "hunter" and "farmer" sales jobs—hunters being reps responsible for acquiring new customers and farmers being those who manage existing customers. Hunters clearly have a primary role to play in driving sales growth. Farmers can also play a role in sales growth to the extent that they have not yet fully penetrated their existing customers. Yet some farmers may manage a book of business that is fully penetrated. In this case, their role is to maintain that business and minimize any losses. By definition, it is impossible for them to increase their business any further (assuming there are not new products being released or new markets being created within their customers). Therefore, it would be inappropriate to establish a growth-based performance measure for these salespeople since such a measure is clearly not aligned with their role.

3. *Is the measure observable and trackable?* In selecting performance measures, there is a simple and seemingly obvious (yet often

forgotten) rule that must be remembered: It is impossible to pay for something that cannot be measured. Many well-intentioned incentive plans (and often otherwise well-designed ones) have failed miserably because the organization could not measure performance in an accurate and timely manner. This is not to say that the measure should be disqualified automatically. Rather, if management agrees that the measure in question truly is the most appropriate and that it offers clear benefits over alternatives, then further investigation is in order.

At issue is how long it will take to develop the appropriate systems to ensure accuracy and timeliness. If tracking mechanisms will not be available in time for the new incentive plan year, then an alternative measure must be chosen. This option may be used until the desired measure is trackable or the second-best alternative may be used as a replacement altogether for the desired measure, particularly if the costs and time required to monitor the desired metric are deemed to be excessive.

8.2   Common Measures of Performance

Sales Volume

Volume or production is the most basic of the measures outlined here. Most often volume is measured in terms of the number of units sold or an aggregation of individual units, such as cases, pallets, or containers. It may also be measured in terms of weight, area, or cubic volume, particularly for commodity or natural resource products.

A key advantage of volume as a measure is its simplicity. A volume measure is generally very easy to understand. It also can be ideal in highly transactional-based sales environments, where a primary role of the sales rep is to maximize short-term sales results (as opposed to other sales roles that may have a greater focus on building long-term customer relationships). Hence, volume is a common measure for commission incentive programs, though it can be appropriate for bonuses too. Another potential advantage of volume is that it eliminates the impact of price distortions on rep performance. This is mainly relevant where reps have little to no control over pricing (e.g., commodity sales where price is set to match the current market price) and price can fluctuate wildly in short time spans.

The very simplicity of the volume measure, however, can also be a disadvantage. The most obvious disadvantage is that a volume measure is not directly linked to business results such as revenues and profits. If reps are selling a variety of products, it may be necessary to set separate product volume goals in order to ensure the proper link is established between sales rep performance and business results. For instance, if reps have five products to sell, but one (product A) is an easier sale than the others, reps will tend to gravitate toward selling more of product A. If product A is also a relatively lower-value and lower-profit product, the reps may easily meet their volume goal while the company misses its revenue and profit goals. Although this may be corrected by introducing individual product goals or weights, this also introduces additional complexity. If only a handful of products are involved, such that no more than three to five separate product or product category performance measures are required, then this may not be a problem. But when the number of products and part numbers sold moves into the hundreds or even thousands, a volume measure becomes relatively meaningless. The main exception is if the different products are packaged similarly and sold at similar prices. For instance, a route sales rep selling ten different beverage brands or lines in a variety of packaging (12 ounce cans, 1 liter bottles, 2 liter bottles, and others) can still be measured by one volume measure for all of these hundreds of products (cases, liters, or gallons could easily be used). But where the products are hundreds of different brake parts and components, volume is not the optimal performance measure because it does not meaningfully communicate the true sales results.

Revenues

Revenue is probably the most commonly used measure of sales performance. It creates a stronger, more direct link with business results than volume. In addition, it is a useful measure for dissimilar products and is more convenient for measuring aggregate sales results of dissimilar products. For instance, if a rep is selling five differentiated products, it may be meaningless to know that he sold 10,000 units in total, particularly if these five products have vastly different levels of pricing and profit contribution. To know that these 10,000 units produced $1 million in revenues is far more informative.

One of the biggest disadvantages of revenue as a measure is the impact that price changes will have. If price changes (whether up or down) cannot be predicted at the start of the plan year, this means sales rep goals do not reflect the impact of these price changes. If prices increase twice by an average of 10 percent each time during the course of the year, the company must recalibrate sales rep quotas to reflect these price changes. Otherwise reps' sales results will be artificially inflated for sales following the price increase, such that they may meet their quotas but the company will fall short of its goals. This recalibration of quotas can be a time-consuming process, and if reps' expectations have not been managed well in advance, it can inadvertently become a demotivator for the sales force.

In many cases, prices can be established in advance for the year, and price changes that will occur during the year can be estimated in advance and built into reps' quotas. Where this is not the case, the process and rationale for recalibrating quotas should be clearly explained to reps at the start of the plan year so they are not caught by surprise. If prices are subject to large, frequent, and unpredictable swings, an alternative measure, such as volume or market share, may be more desirable.

Market Share

Whereas the other measures discussed thus far focus entirely internally, market share focuses on a sales rep's performance in relation to the marketplace. Market share can be an especially useful measure of sales results in rapidly growing markets, where a company's success is best measured by its penetration of that market. It also has applicability in declining markets where, although a company's expected revenues or volume (or both) may be shrinking, its market share needs to be maintained or even expanded. Market share can be useful measure in this case, since it can be very demotivational to tell sales reps that their goal is to shrink revenues by 25 percent. To say their goal is to maintain a market share of 30 percent, although it may result in a shrinkage of revenues, sends a far more positive and motivational message.

The greatest problem with a market share measure is the availability of good, accurate data. Outside of industries such as consumer products and pharmaceuticals (where third-party data vendors collect and report sales data on a highly delineated basis), it is costly and difficult to get good market share data, particularly on the level of the individual sales rep. Thus, market share is not even an option for many sales forces.

When market share is an option, it remains a very product-focused measure. For reps concentrating on a narrow range of products with a largely homogeneous group of competitors, this works fine. But unlike revenues, market share cannot serve as a common denominator for measuring aggregate performance across a wide variety of dissimilar products. As a result, if a large number of different products are involved, measuring market share would require a separate metric for each. In addition, if the market is highly fragmented across a large number of competitors, market share (at the rep level especially) may not be particularly meaningful. In many markets, the top competitor may hold no more than 5 to 10 percent of the total market. Increasing market share from 1 to 2 percent may be a far less meaningful (and less motivational) goal than increasing revenues from $1 million to $1.5 million per rep.

Profits

In recent years, many sales organizations have taken moves to tie their sales reps' compensation, in whole or in part, to profitability. This has largely stemmed from the increasing pressure on senior management to increase returns to shareholders and the trickling down of a more profit-centered focus throughout the organization.

In many sales organizations, there has traditionally been little to no motivation for reps to focus on growing sales profitably. Rather, given the preponderance of traditional measures like volume and revenues, they have tended to focus on increasing sales at any cost. True, reps often have specified expense budgets within which to operate, but the rep who sells $1 million worth of product at a 10 percent profit margin is often rewarded the same as the rep who sells the same amount at a 20 percent margin.

Where a measure of profits has been introduced to sales rep compensation, it has often been at a high level of measurement—at the company, division, or perhaps regional level. The intent is to tie a portion of rep pay to overall profitability. While in theory this may seem to align rep and management pay better, in practice it often is not fully effective. Such high-level measures are too far away for the rep to feel that individual actions can truly have any impact on profits at the end of the day. As a result, reps will tend to focus on the other factors (such as volume, revenue, or market share) that are measured on a territory or individual level and hope for the best with profits. And, as noted, this dysfunctional behavior is frequently rewarded by incentive plans of marginal quality.

Many forward-looking companies have taken a further step and developed territory or account profit and loss statements (P&Ls). There are two basic approaches that can be taken: measuring the net profit or the gross profit. The net profit approach basically allocates all costs in the company's or division's P&L down to the individual territory (or account) level. The result is a series of territory P&Ls

that, when summed together for each territory, will add up to the total P&L for the company or division (which may measure a variety of things, depending on the level of profits the company has chosen to focus on). Reps often argue that the net profit approach is not fair because their performance is subject to many factors outside their control, such as raw material costs, R&D expenditures, and production efficiency.

The alternative is to develop a gross profit P&L, which can take a variety of forms. The key distinguishing characteristic between the net profit and gross profit approaches is that the gross profit approach subtracts fewer line items from revenues to arrive at a measure of profitability. Thus, it may deduct only selling costs and the cost of goods sold from the revenue line item to arrive at gross profits for the territory. Note that revenues now become just one of several components in the performance measure. Hence, reps can achieve their gross profit objective through a combination of results:

1. Increasing sales revenue (to drive the top-line revenue item)
2. Reducing sales expenses (to reduce one of the cost line items)
3. Selling a different mix of products (focusing on those products with a higher profit contribution)

Linking sales reps to a P&L measure requires a careful balance of interests. On the one hand, there is a desire (and often a financial need) to link reps' incentives to the organization's overall profitability. But at the same time, the motivational impact must be considered. If rep incentive earnings are significantly reduced (or eliminated) because of poor profitability, driven largely by factors outside their control, this will likely have a negative impact on future performance and make it difficult to retain top performers. In short, more so than the other measures discussed so far, P&L measures of profitability can be greatly affected by factors on which reps have little control. If reps believe their compensation is largely determined (or that it has the *possibility* of being largely determined) by factors outside their control, then that compensation program will tend to be viewed as unfair, arbitrary, and demotivational. In other words, it will fail to drive behavior and performance.

Because of the inherent challenges in measuring profits on a territory or account P&L basis, many companies develop proxies for profitability in the incentive program. These proxies focus specifically on the one or two factors through which reps can have the greatest impact on profits. For instance, if reps are freely able to negotiate pricing but management believes discounting is rampant, a specific measure linked to price realization could be introduced. In this case, the goal may be to realize a 5 percent price increase over the next year, or it may be simply to hold prices steady (and not discount any further). Another proxy for profits is the use of a product mix factor, whereby reps are rewarded more for selling a targeted mix of products or for selling more profitable products. Both approaches are easier to measure and implement than territory or account P&Ls, and they tend to be more motivational because there are fewer factors in these measures that are outside reps' control.

Some companies use an expense control factor as a means of linking reps to profitability. The basic premise behind this measure is that reps who do a better job of controlling their travel and entertainment get rewarded more. This measure can backfire if it motivates reps to focus so much on controlling expenses that they miss or forgo key sales opportunities. This flaw can be corrected by designing the measure such that it does not provide additional rewards for exceeding targeted performance. For example, if the goal is not to exceed an expense budget of $30,000 or 3 percent of revenues, to the extent a rep spends less, there is no additional reward. However, this creates another issue: with no upside opportunity, the measure is no longer an incentive but rather merely a control mechanism. It is all stick and no carrot, so it can only harm rather than help reps. If they exceed their expense budgets, they get penalized, but if they meet them or come under, they get no additional reward. Therefore, this type of measure is generally less desirable than other measures of profitability. If it is deemed to be an important measure to include (again, based on the business strategy and the role of the sales reps), it needs to be calibrated and managed very carefully. (Exhibit 8-1 summarizes these measures.)

8.3 New Measures of Performance

Customer Satisfaction

As companies have shifted toward a more customer-focused philosophy and selling approaches, there has been a tremendous growth of interest around linking sales rep pay to customer satisfaction. The premise is simple: to have a customer-focused sales effort, the interests of the company and its reps must be linked to (or at least aligned with) those of the customer. Since compensation is often seen as the primary motivator of salesperson performance, this has fostered an interest in developing customer satisfaction measures for

Exhibit 8-1. Summary of Advantages and Disadvantages of Common Performance Measures.

Performance Measure	Advantages	Disadvantages
Volume	• Simple and easy to understand • Eliminates potential price distortions on sales results • Works well in transaction-focused commission programs	• Not directly linked to business results (e.g., revenues and profits) • Impractical for a large number of dissimilar products
Revenue	• Stronger link with business results • Creates a common measure for dissimilar products	• Can be distorted by unpredictable price changes • Not directly linked to business profitability (but can be modified to reflect profitability)
Market share	• Provides an external focus (whereas the other measures are purely internally focused) • More meaningful measure for: —New, high-growth markets (where total demand is hard to predict) —Stagnant or shrinking markets (where zero or negative growth goals can be demotivating)	• Reliable market share data are often not available in many industries • Very product focused; impractical for a large number of dissimilar products • May not be a meaningful measure in fragmented markets with a large number of competitors
Profits	• Strong link with bottom-line results of the overall business • Usually is more aligned with the overall business strategy • A number of alternative measures can be used as proxies for profitability (these measures are often easier to measure at the rep level and are often more directly linked with the role of the sales rep)	• A profit measure is often not well aligned with the sales rep role (many reps have little to no ability to drive profitability) • Profit measures are often too far removed from the rep to be meaningful (at the company or division level)

sales incentive programs—specifically, the customer's satisfaction viewed as the result of the salesperson's effort.

Measuring customer satisfaction creates several unique challenges in comparison to the metrics discussed so far. First, and most important, traditional measures focus on either sales or market penetration results that are quantifiable, objective measures. In contrast, customer satisfaction is a much less tangible concept. The way in which it gets defined, measured, and interpreted is subject to much more subjectivity than are the traditional measures.

Ideally, if customer satisfaction is used in incentive design, it should be based on quantifiable survey data with a statistically acceptable degree of scientific rigor. Yet even in this best-case scenario, customer satisfaction is still at heart based on the quantification of opinions of individuals, which of course have some degree of built-in subjectivity.

The ability to measure customer satisfaction is often the greatest obstacle to using it as a performance measure. Many companies have no existing or regular customer research program. If they do, it often needs to be modified to provide the appropriate compensation measures that reflect the rep's true contributions.

Ideally, a customer research methodology should be in place and tested for at least one to two years before it is linked to compensation. Otherwise management runs the risk of implementing a measure (and setting goals against it) that may perform much differently over time than expected. If not done carefully, the end result may be a measure that not only fails to align reps' interests with customer interests but that also demotivates and frustrates them. In general, most companies have found it desirable to spend a few years getting comfortable with their customer research methodology, using the results as input for general business management purposes such as staffing, territory alignment, and product offerings and product development before taking the final leap of linking it with sales compensation.

There are alternatives to a survey-based approach. One is for managers to conduct some of their own information gathering at year end, interviewing selected customers regarding rep performance. Although it does not provide data that are as quantifiable or as statistically rigorous as a survey approach, it is a far less costly approach and can be completed relatively quickly. This method is often a good interim approach, to be used while a more rigorous survey method is developed and tested.

Some companies have begun rewarding for customer satisfaction outside the formal compensation program. For instance, some offer spot awards of perhaps $100 to $500 for every unsolicited letter of praise that a rep receives from a customer. Others provide the reward for any customer letter, whether offering praise or voicing concerns, and whether focusing on rep issues or broader company issues, under the premise that any customer input is of value to the company.

Other, more quantifiable measures can be used as proxies for customer satisfaction. For instance, customer retention and customer penetration can be used as gauges of satisfaction. Perhaps more important, they begin to get at the intended results of customer satisfaction: customer loyalty and the bottom-line impact on the business. (The distinction between satisfaction and loyalty is an important one. Satisfied customers are not necessarily the same as loyal customers, and it is loyal customers who ultimately are of the greatest value to the organization. A loyal customer is, by definition, someone who maintains and increases business with the company.) Hence, measuring customer retention and penetration can quantify some of the key results of customer loyalty.

Besides customer retention and penetration, it can also be argued that the results of customer satisfaction and loyalty can be measured in terms of total sales results (whether defined as volume, revenue, market share, or profits). In other words, this assumes that reps who achieve the higher levels of sales also tend to have more satisfied customers, hence the higher sales results. This may often be true, but there is some danger in relying exclusively on sales results measures as proxies for customer satisfaction. For many companies, it is hard sales results that are of greatest value to management and the company's shareholders; customer satisfaction and loyalty are of value to the company only to the extent that they ultimately drive overall business performance. Yet short-term sales results are reactive measures of customer satisfaction and loyalty; they indicate only what happened *after* customers became either satisfied or dissatisfied. On the other hand, customer satisfaction is a more proactive measure. Given the right customer research program, a company can use customer satisfaction data to help reps modify their behavior, thus taking corrective action before a customer becomes so dissatisfied that she takes her business elsewhere. A well-constructed customer research program can also help direct reps to ensure that satisfied customers remain loyal ones.

Value-Based Measurement

Value-based measures of performance have been employed with increasing frequency in the 1990s, primarily at the executive level of an organization. However, there is growing interest in expanding this approach throughout all organizational levels and functions. How does a value-based management (VBM) approach get translated to the sales organization and, ultimately, how can it affect the compensation program?

By the simplest definition, VBM is a strategic management process for building and maximizing shareholder value. VBM measurements tell companies whether they are creating or destroying this value over the long term. Yet VBM is more than simply another alternative performance measure, such as revenues and volume. It is a framework through which an organization can help clarify and establish its strategic priorities and translate these strategic priorities into actionable tasks for the entire organization.

A VBM approach helps ensure the appropriate alignment among sales force performance measures, compensation, and the overall strategic intent of the business. At the end of the process, many or all of the performance measures identified for the sales organization may look just like the traditional measures. A VBM approach can help clarify, for example, the rationale behind why revenues are more important than market share, or vice versa. In addition, a VBM approach can provide rich additional information about what it is that reps (and others) must do to drive revenues, market share, profits, or whatever else the appropriate measures are. In this sense, VBM can help not only in identifying performance measures for the compensation program (which tends to focus on results achieved), but it can also identify measures and criteria for the performance management program (which tends to focus on *how* those results can be achieved).

For example, revenues may be identified as a key performance measure for sales reps. A VBM approach will break revenues into their component parts (e.g., which specific products are likely to increase shareholder value in the long run). From this, one can determine to what extent the sales reps influence each of those component parts, ultimately providing greater direction to them.

8.4 Other Sales Objectives

Most of the performance measures described so far are quantitative—the one exception being certain types of customer satisfaction measurement data (such as manager interviews with customers). Traditionally, incentive compensation performance measures have focused largely or exclusively on quantitative sales results. Yet as selling processes become more complex, it has often become increasingly difficult to measure an individual sales rep's contribution to quantitative sales results.

As a result, companies have turned to a variety of alternatives. Broadly, these alternatives can be categorized as performance objectives (often called MBOs). Such objectives will in many cases be integrated side by side with quantitative measures of sales result. For instance, a rep may have a 75 percent weight based on revenues and 25 percent based on MBOs. MBOs may include such things as:

- Qualitative measures (also referred to as subjective or discretionary)
- Activities (e.g., number of calls per week; number of in-store displays installed)
- Personal development goals (e.g., completing a financial analysis course, completing specific sales training courses)
- Other quantitative or quantifiable results not directly measured in the rest of the incentive plan (e.g., sales to one particular strategic account; number of new accounts; number of new contracts signed)

Of the four categories outlined above, the first three, although quite common, are generally *not* desirable measures to include in a sales incentive compensation program, for the following reasons.

Qualitative measures tend to be demotivational because by their very nature, they are difficult to define and clarify in advance, difficult for a rep to track performance against, and subject to different interpretations of performance against the objective. This is not to say that subjective assessments of performance are always inappropriate. Rather, they are best left within the context of performance management and used as an input to identify development needs, rather than as a determinant of sales compensation.

Activities, although clearly quantifiable, tend to focus a sales rep on quantity rather than quality. The danger is that reps will achieve the activity goals, but not in a way that actually contributes to sales results (however they may be measured). Hence, reps may not be aligned in an optimal manner with business objectives and results.

Personal development goals have an important place to play in managing a rep's performance and building long-term career success, but these goals belong to the overall performance management program, not the sales incentive compensation program. To maximize its effectiveness in driving performance, the sales incentive compensation program should focus on the achievement of sales results. Other elements of compensation (such as base salary and base salary merit raises), in combination with other management tools (such as the performance management program), are more effectively used to focus on the development of knowledge and skill sets that will better equip the salesperson to attain selling success.

When used appropriately, MBOs can create additional flexibility in the incentive plan, providing a means of customizing the measures and goals for each individual rep according to what is most appropriate for the assigned territory. They can be effective tools to focus the salesperson on specific tasks that will lead to overall success and contribute to achieving the bottom-line quantitative sales result goal.

To work effectively, MBOs must be managed very carefully. One of the critical success factors in an MBO program is ensuring consistency in the rationale and criteria for establishing individual MBOs. This requires comprehensive training for the managers who will be setting individual MBOs. Those programs that have been most effective provide managers with a template of categories to choose from, with suggested examples of appropriate and inappropriate measures and goals. Different managers can then use the same criteria to establish MBOs, which is crucial in determining whether reps see the MBO program as motivating and unbiased, or arbitrary and unfair.

8.5 Team vs. Individual Measures

As selling has increasingly become a joint effort, companies must rethink how they measure and reward sales rep performance as traditional measures have increasingly become less appropriate in many cases. Of course, team-based performance measures are not right for every sales force. Indeed, there still exist (and will continue to exist) many sales jobs that are essentially handled by individuals. In this case, it would be a mistake to force team measures that are clearly not aligned with the sales role.

But team sales approaches are important, and team performance measures need to be considered. In developing such measures, careful consideration must be given to creating a balance between team and individual metrics. Many companies have inadvertently created extremely demotivating sales compensation programs by changing from 100 percent individual measures to 100 percent team measures, simply because they believe they now have sales teams. Despite the use of a sales team, it is vital to balance these two forms of measurement. Salespeople tend to be demotivated by performance measures based 100 percent on team results, viewing such programs as socialistic. At the end of the day, the team is only as good as the collection of individual efforts on that team. It requires *both* team and individual behaviors, and therefore requires measures at both levels of performance.

There are a variety of different types of sales teams, both formal and informal. The structure and nature of the team should drive the type of team measures integrated into the sales compensation program. Here are some examples of typical sales teams:

Geographic-Based Teams

- A group of reps in the same geography (i.e., a district or a region) calling on the same customers.
- Reps may typically be product specialists.
- Typically dedicated full time to the team.

Account-Based Teams

- A group of reps who together call on or service one account, typically a large account with multiple locations nationwide or regionally.
- Typically includes reps from a variety of geographies.

Members Dedicated Full- or Part-Time to the Team

- Part-time team members may serve on similar account teams for other accounts and/or may manage their own individual (smaller) accounts.

Cross-Functional Sales Teams

- Involving individuals from a variety of corporate functions outside sales, such as marketing, distribution and logistics, manufacturing, engineering, R&D, or finance.
- Team members may be dedicated full time or part time.
- Teams may be constructed around such things as a common product, account, industry or segment, or geography.

In addition to the type of team, its size will determine the balance between individual and group measures. If the team consists of two reps with overlapping coverage in one area, the measures could largely be team based. If the team is twenty reps in a large geographic area, some individual measurement should be retained.

Exhibit 8-2. Example of Team Responsibilities and Performance Measurement.

National Account Team Rep
- Majority of time spent as customer focal point for eight assigned local accounts (individual accounts)
- Also assigned to two national account teams to support the national accounts on a local facility basis

Incentive Weights	Performance Measures
50 percent	Individual accounts • Aggregate sales revenues versus goal for all eight accounts
30 percent	Local facilities of national accounts • Two accounts, ten facilities total • Aggregate sales revenue versus goal for all ten facilities
20 percent	Total national results • Two accounts • Aggregate sales revenue versus goal for all sales to these accounts nationwide

Team measurement does not necessarily mean that all team members must have the same exact measures, even for the team component. Exhibit 8-2 illustrates an example of a rep who has a combination of local accounts, where she is the only assigned sales rep, and a number of local customers who are part of a larger national account organization. Hence, she works as a part-time member of two national account teams. Most of her focus as a member of these teams is on developing and maintaining relationships with the local facilities in her territory.

She is regularly asked by the national account managers of these two accounts to perform certain service activities and other tasks that may contribute to sales results in areas outside her territory. She is also occasionally asked to help reps in other territories cover the local offices of these accounts. Hence, measuring purely local sales results does not recognize and reward her for the time she spends working on broader account initiatives, some of which may not directly contribute to sales in her territory. Therefore, a portion of her compensation is also linked to the total account performance on a national basis.

Exhibit 8-3 illustrates another example. In this case, there are three product specialists with perfectly overlapping territories. All

Exhibit 8-3. Example of Team Responsibilities and Performance Measurement.

Product Specialist Team Rep
- Works full time on ten assigned accounts
- Focuses on one specific product line (out of three)
- Two other reps call on the same ten accounts, specializing in one of the two other product lines

Incentive Weights	Performance Measures
75 percent	Individual product sales • Total revenues versus goal for assigned products sold to assigned accounts
25 percent	Team sales • Total revenues versus goal for all products sold to assigned accounts

three cover the same accounts in the same geography; however, each rep is responsible for a different product line. These reps are expected to maximize sales results for their assigned product line, but they can do so only if they work together in managing their customer relationships. Hence, their performance measures all have a strong focus on individual sales results (75 percent), but a significant portion (25 percent) of their total incentive payout is determined by total sales results for all three team members.

Both examples illustrate the fact that team measures do not mean that everyone is measured on the same results. Although the reps in both examples had one measure shared entirely with other team members, both also had unique individual measures of performance as well.

Designing incentive plans for team-based sales personnel is discussed more fully in Chapter 19.

8.6 Defining Performance Measures

Selecting performance measures involves far more than simply sketching out how the incentive plan might work. To create a well-functioning plan, a number of key questions must be answered:

1. What products are to be included? Are reps to be measured and paid for each product individually or for sales of all products in aggregate?

2. What results are included in the measures: growth, maintenance, or both?

3. What is the level of measurement: an individual, territory, or account portfolio or a team (geographic, account, cross-functional, or product-based)?

4. What is the frequency of measurement and payouts: monthly, quarterly, semiannually, or annually?

5. What is our ability to measure it? What are the accuracy and quality of the data and the timing?

6. Are gross or net sales to be used? If net sales, net of what (returns, discounts, chargebacks, etc.)?

7. When is the sale recorded or credited to the salesperson: booking, shipment, installation, invoicing, or payment?

Clear definition improves the communication of both the plan mechanics and management's sales performance focus.

9

Making Pay Comparisons

9.1 Base Salary Philosophy and Administration

When evaluating the appropriate level of base salary, first consider the salesperson's role and level of influence in the sales process. Typically, managers take an overall view of total compensation first and then determine the relative role of base pay and incentive pay.

Base salary and other income play two primary roles:

1. To compensate an individual for the minimum "going value" of the experiences and skills required by the job and to retain top sales talent.
2. To provide a cash flow floor for the rep when there is a risk that routine personal needs cannot be met with incentive income.

How this fixed compensation is delivered is critical: in the form of a base salary, a draw against future incentive income, or a guaranteed level of incentive income earned on an established "book of business." The choice will have a profound impact on the overall design of any compensation plan.

Many managers believe that base salary is delivered for a minimum level of expected sales performance. If it is, a base salary may purchase some degree of rep commitment to the job. An employer, on the other hand, may expect significantly more than this for the investment. Some sales managers speak of basic sales activities (as distinguished from end results) as being "paid for by the base." Other managers see base salary as representing the rep's long-term success in fulfilling the enduring accountabilities of the job.

In theory, higher base salaries are effective in gaining sales rep commitment and management control over rep activities. In reality, higher base salaries may purchase only passive commitment (not looking for another job) rather than active commitment (performing the current job with skill and energy). This proves especially true in industries where sales reps are accustomed to high incentive opportunity and their high base is offered at the expense of such opportunity. This is a common challenge for sales and human resources managers as they sort through the complex interplay of two key factors: competitive labor costs and the latest market trends for those costs and the budget and criteria for merit increases to base salary.

The role of base salary is to deliver the compensation needed to attract and retain the skills and experience required by the sales job. It does this in a decisive way: the base is virtually guaranteed as long as the rep is an employee in good standing in the job. This role can be enhanced by linking any increases in base salary to the achievement of identified objectives. Unfortunately, the traditional performance appraisal process is a particularly difficult tool for sales managers to master in their effort to separate the performance that justifies base salary adjustments from the performance that triggers incentive payments.

Drivers of Salary Levels

Characteristics of both the external marketplace and the individual salesperson drive the base salary rate. In industries experiencing a shortage of seasoned sales talent, the price of that talent is usually bid up until price and supply reach some equilibrium. Higher market rates attract sales reps from other segments of the same industry and even other industries and also encourage salespeople in the host industry (particularly those with alternatives) to consider a change. In a rising compensation market, this can be the quickest way to raise personal income. It also represents a competitive climate in which pay plan provisions are critical to attracting and retaining talent.

On the other hand, internal factors that drive a rep's base salary are more easily characterized. They are:

- Inherent skills and personal competencies of the individual
- Performance over time
- Tenure in the job
- Tenure with the company
- Specific pay practices of the company
- Promotions to higher positions

Base salary can also reflect the pattern and frequency of changes in employer, especially if these changes are in response to changes in the industry.

Sales rep attributes should only partly determine a company's hierarchy of base salaries. Customer characteristics should also play a role. If all sales reps serve the same types of customers, it often makes sense to provide a higher base to reps with greater experience, success, and tenure simply to avoid losing more experienced salespeople. In this case, base salary acts as a retention mechanism.

In summary, the hierarchy of base salaries should reflect the following key considerations:

- Labor market practices
- Individual characteristics (e.g., experience, tenure, and current performance as measured against qualitative and longer-term goals established for the position held)
- Organizational characteristics (e.g., the need to lay out a career path for salespeople that permits increases in base to match increases in job content)
- Customer characteristics (e.g., complexity of purchase decision, buying cycle, size, local versus national scope of customer operations, and number of decision makers)

Administration of Base Salary

There are five general approaches to administering base salaries for salespeople, each appropriate in a given context:

1. Single rate
2. Experience or tenure
3. Stack ranking
4. Merit
5. Discretionary

With the exception of the single-rate approach, these methodologies do not strictly conform to their theoretical descriptions. For example, most longevity programs simply give more weight to tenure or experience than to the results of a performance appraisal. Similarly, most programs based on an evaluation of the rep give more weight to the appraisal process than to tenure or experience. The principal characteristics of each of these approaches are summarized in Exhibit 9-1.

Single-Rate Approach

In those relatively rare situations in which the sales force is unionized, labor negotiators often argue for the single-rate approach.

Exhibit 9-1. Common Salary Administration Approaches.

Approach	Characteristics
Single rate	• Union sales force • Maintains internal equity • Newly formed sales organizations • High-prominence sales jobs
Experience or tenure approach	• More base pay for tenure • Maturity ladder system • Multiple sales levels
Stack-ranking approach	• Rewards top performance • Budget set aside for base salary increases
Merit approach	• Formal appraisal process • Links merit budget to performance evaluation • Can be linked to competency development
Discretionary approach	• Based on "discretion," not a formula • Most flexible approach • Simple to administer • Delegates decisions to sales management

Unions generally try to ensure a contractual rate (free from management's discretion) at which all members will work, and to suspend or modify any compensation arrangements on which the sales force may have relied.

The single-rate approach can also prove useful in maintaining a sense of internal pay equity among salespeople when the incentive earning opportunities are significant and the control of the sales force over personal performance and income is great. In these situations, sales reps may interpret significant differences in base salary as arbitrary and unfair, because the opportunity to have more income through personal sales performance is clear and available to everyone.

Furthermore, in new sales organizations formal performance appraisal processes seldom exist. It may simply be necessary to use either a single-rate or an experience or tenure approach to setting base salaries. Often a rep joins the organization at a lower starting rate and, after successfully completing an orientation period of selling, quickly moves up to the control-rate, base salary level. Management should remember, however that single-rate approaches are best suited to high-prominence sales jobs with a clear and immediate opportunity to earn incentive income based on individual achievement.

Experience or Tenure Approach

The experience (maturity ladder) or tenure (longevity) approach delivers more base for more experience or tenure. In its simplest form, a maturity ladder system raises the base as years of relevant sales experience increase, *no matter where that experience was acquired.* Similarly, a longevity approach increases base as years of internal experience increase. The relationship between years of experience or tenure and base salary can be well defined or loose. Most companies prefer to avoid a strict relationship, whereby a qualifying number of years automatically ensures each rep a higher base.

On the face of it, neither experience nor tenure seems acceptable as a stand-alone practice because neither is directly related to performance. Yet each is usually related indirectly to performance, because increasing experience or tenure is normally difficult to acquire when one is not performing. The ultimate appraisal system is always at work, that is, the one that reaffirms periodically that the rep continues to meet the minimum standards for the job.

Stack-Ranking Approach

The stack-ranking approach to base salary administration, which is fairly uncommon today, has two basic elements:

1. A high-to-low rank ordering of each rep's annual performance in a given job
2. A budget set-aside for base salary increases for eligible employees in that job category

Once the budget has been established and each employee's annual performance has been graded, the highest-ranking individual receives the largest increase (in either percentage terms or dollars, depending on the system in use), followed by the second-ranking individual, and so on. In essence, this method tells the sales force that the reps with the highest grades receive the greatest rewards.

The only constraint on the size of the increase in a pure stack-ranking system is the overall increase budget. (Some modified stack-ranking programs also stipulate a maximum and a minimum increase in an effort to maintain some level of internal equity.) As compared with the experience or tenure approach, stack ranking focuses on what the sales rep has accomplished rather than on how long the rep has been working at it.

Stack ranking differs from the merit approach in its informal way of arriving at the actual size of the rep's increase. In a merit program, fairly strict rules determine a rep's percentage increase based on his or her appraisal rating, position in the salary range, and sometimes tenure.

Merit Approach

Human resources managers overwhelmingly prefer the merit approach to base salary administration for sales personnel. Enthusiasm for this method is not as pervasive among sales managers. The merit approach combines at least the first two of the following administrative elements:

1. A formal performance appraisal form and process
2. A budget for merit increases to base salaries
3. Salary change guidelines that link salary increases to the incumbent's current position in the salary range

A plain vanilla merit program establishes a budget for base salary increases that can be spent by the company as a whole, the exempt population as a whole, a functional area as a whole, or a department. It also creates a link between the budget and the performance evaluation received by a rep. To standardize this linkage, the evaluations are usually expressed by an overall numerical score, such as 3.00 out of a possible 5.00. A specific score translates into a specific percentage increase to the rep's base salary, or an increase range within which the manager may choose a specific percentage.

A more elaborate merit program links the merit budget, the performance evaluation, and the rep's current position in the base salary range to the increase percentage that is awarded. Under this approach, those with the highest evaluation and the lowest salary would receive the largest percentage increase because, relative to their performance, they are the most deserving. The most basic performance appraisal form or process for salespeople requires the manager to evaluate the rep's performance throughout the year against stated objectives, standards, key job responsibilities, and required competencies. Objectives can include traditional production quotas (such as revenue or gross profit goals), as well as special objectives for selected accounts, products, and marketing programs.

Standards usually include considerations of professional conduct, minimums for call frequency and production, and demonstrations of initiative, creativity, and teamwork where appropriate. Key job responsibilities outline the basic steps and end results expected of any satisfactory performer in the job. Competencies (described in detail in Chapter 22) might include business acumen, interpersonal capabilities, or teamwork orientation.

The most common concerns that sales managers express about the use of the merit approach fall into five categories:

1. Too structured, not enough discretion.

2. Not enough differentiation between the performers and the nonperformers. Under the merit program approach, everyone receiving an increase must get a raise of 2 percent to 6 percent. A less formal system allows greater differences.

3. Too time-consuming. The paperwork and face-to-face performance reviews are draining and yield questionable improvements.

4. The tendency to double-dip, that is, to count twice the performance to quota attained—once in the incentive plan and once in the base salary program—giving a rep a large increase in base when his incentive earnings for the year are also very good. This results in an increased fixed cost (a higher base), which is especially painful when yesterday's high flier is today's glider. Such a problem would be less likely with a single-rate approach or even a maturity ladder or longevity approach.

5. The sales force gets less than its fair share of budgeted base salary dollars (because other company functions complain that sales is already treated too well given its cash incentives and recognition awards). A single-rate or longevity approach might not produce the same reaction.

All of these concerns are legitimate because a merit program can be improperly designed or administered in each of these ways. A merit program also provides an easy target because it purports to link pay equitably to performance. Single-rate, longevity, and discretionary approaches to salary administration do not make this pledge. Pure varieties of the single-rate and longevity approaches use uniform rules for assigning base salaries, but that isn't the same thing as following equitable policy. A uniformly applied rule can be uniformly unfair.

Discretionary Approach

The discretionary approach refers to the practice of using discretion rather than a formula or a published guideline to determine the size of the base salary. This approach is less a stand-alone method than it is a technique to modify the three approaches previously discussed.

The power and appeal of discretionary practices are balanced by some potential drawbacks. These practices can be seen as arbitrary and are easily corrupted by bias and carelessness in arriving at a conclusion for each employee. To minimize the inherent weaknesses of a discretionary approach, a company can require one or more stages of management review before finalizing each rep's new base salary rate.

9.2   Incentive Pay Philosophy and Administration

A Telling Case Example

A medium-size industrial company that was struggling with the design of an incentive plan hired a new vice president of sales. After only two weeks on the job, the vice president offered her proposal for a new plan that had worked well at her two previous employers: a salary plus commission arrangement based solely on volume. The vice president argued that the plan would succeed and would require only limited fine-tuning. And, in fact, the plan appeared to work for about six months—before it went sour.

Under the new incentive plan, sales reps began to focus solely on high-volume accounts and to ignore lower-volume but highly profitable accounts. After a year, the company had experienced moderate sales growth, significantly lower profits, and record-high payouts to the sales force. The company changed the plan abruptly the next year to include a variable commission rate based on gross margin. Because this resulted in reduced commission payouts, the sales reps viewed it as unfair. They believed that the company was "changing the rules" because it didn't want them to earn large commissions. Many of the company's top performers left the organization over the next twelve months. Volume slipped, margins remained about the same, and the vice president of sales departed to "pursue other business interests."

This story demonstrates the potential pitfalls of installing a new incentive plan without a sufficient understanding of all the relevant factors and plan determinants. Simply copying another company's incentive plan can lead to disaster. An incentive plan will succeed only if it reflects the organizational dynamics of the particular company.

Designing an incentive plan is a relatively straightforward process once you have clearly defined the plan's objectives and performance measures, competitive practices, customer characteristics, barriers to entry to the sales position, and prominence of the sales force in the selling process. Exhibit 9-2 shows this process.

To determine the appropriate proportion of variable incentive pay to total cash compensation, you must consider barriers to entry and prominence. (Exhibit 9-3 shows the relationship of both in the marketing mix.)

Barriers to Entry

Barriers to entry are one determinant of the amount of low-risk compensation (e.g., base pay or virtually guaranteed incentive payout) needed to obtain a certain set of skills in the competitive marketplace. If the barriers to entry are high, you can expect the talent pool to be small. In this case, significant base salary is probably appropriate because the value of scarce talent will be bid up in the marketplace. The higher the barrier to entry, the higher the levels of base pay.

If the barriers to entry are low, management must provide little (if any) base salary. Any income that is required to meet the rep's cash flow needs can be provided by a *draw,* a minimum income level below which the rep's income cannot fall but against which all incentive earnings are netted before any additional income is payable to the rep.

Prominence

Incentive compensation will vary as every factor that affects sales opportunity, sales success, and sales event tracking varies. To the degree that the sales rep can control the frequency, extent, and timing of these factors—and where it is possible for the rep to establish a territory quickly that produces a sustaining level of sales on a regular basis—incentive compensation should reflect the rep's influence.

The influence or prominence of the sales rep in the organization's overall marketing mix plays a significant role in determining the proper combination of fixed and variable compensation. Gener-

Exhibit 9-2. Incentive Plan Design Process.

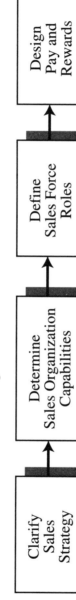

Clarify Sales Strategy → Determine Sales Organization Capabilities → Define Sales Force Roles → Design Pay and Rewards

Exhibit 9-3. Relationship Between Barriers to Entry and Prominence in Marketing Mix.

	Low Prominence in Marketing Mix	**High** Prominence in Marketing Mix
Barriers to Entry — High	**High Barrier/Low Prominence** A technically trained representative is responsible for selling a highly complex product or service; the need for the product is readily recognized, and there are few suppliers (perhaps only one).	**High Barrier/High Prominence** The sales representative must have extensive experience and technical expertise (or both); the product, process, or service must be sold in terms of both its need and the given company as the supplier. Creative, unique applications of the product or the process must be developed and integrated with the customer's production process in a manner that increases profitability.
Barriers to Entry — Low	**Low Barrier/Low Prominence** The sales representative has a maintenance position requiring minimal training or product expertise and circulates among a largely established customer base familiar with company products and applications.	**Low Barrier/High Prominence** The sales representative is required to find or qualify prospects and successfully persuade them of their need for a particular product, process, or service even though a tangible need for the company product cannot be documented objectively.

Barriers to Entry

Prominence in Marketing Mix

ally high-prominence selling jobs have significantly leveraged compensation packages with a large amount of pay at risk.

For example, a few well-known companies dominate the personal computer industry. These companies enjoy significant brand-name recognition, large advertising budgets, and well-developed channels of distribution. At the other end of the spectrum are companies struggling to survive with low recognition, small advertising budgets, and poorly developed distribution channels. The prominence of each company's sales force varies dramatically, as does the amount of incentive opportunity.

Clearly defining the selling role is a good starting point for determining the mix of pay. The following specific criteria will help in the definition process:

1. Level of influence in new sales
2. Amount of customer service required
3. Level of teamwork required in sales process
4. Responsibility to determine pricing

When Should Performance Be Recognized?

When designing any new incentive plan, you must consider two basic questions about timing:

1. When should performance be recognized?
2. How often should incentives be paid?

The correct approach depends on company-specific variables and the nature of the selling situation. There are no right or wrong answers, only general guidelines.

An order may be credited to the salesperson at one or several steps in the sales process:

1. Milestones prior to the order
2. Order booking
3. Shipping
4. Billing or invoicing
5. Installation or delivery
6. Payment or collection

Most companies recognize results when an order is billed or delivered. Some companies credit a sales rep for a sale at the time an order is booked, others at collection. Some give partial credit at one event and the balance of the credit at another event.

To maximize the motivational impact of an incentive program, it makes sense to recognize a sale at the time an order is booked. This ensures a rapid response to a desired behavior, and the rep is not penalized for events beyond his control, such as production delays or delivery problems. Without question, however, concerns about sales reps' submitting marginal orders are valid.

Management can address the company's cash flow issue by delaying the time at which an order is recognized for incentive purposes. For example, crediting sales reps when orders are invoiced is a reasonable way to cut the time between payment and collection. If there is a significant amount of time between entering the order and invoicing it, say, more than six months, some of the motivational impact of the incentive plan will be lost.

Waiting until an invoice is paid resolves the marginal order concern and encourages a rep to follow up on delinquent accounts. But the longer the period is between behavior and recognition, the more likely the motivational impact of the plan will diminish.

Many companies, such as those in the technology industries, give partial credit at two or more discrete events to address the issues raised and to preserve the motivational impact of the plan. A common approach in a situation where there is a long period between order placement and shipping is to credit a large portion of the incentive when the order is booked and the balance when payment is received from the customer.

How Often Should Incentives Be Paid?

In general, incentive payments should be made often enough to motivate a sales rep but far enough apart to conform to a company's sales cycle and ensure that individual goals can be accomplished in the time allowed. The frequency of incentive payments should also reflect the compensation mix. (These objectives often conflict, and an appropriate balance needs to be struck if a plan is going to be effective.) Finally, the greater the portion of incentive to total cash, the more frequently incentive payments should be made.

Sales reps in high-prominence selling jobs frequently receive more than half of their annual cash income in incentive payments. For these high-leverage jobs, incentives are paid at least monthly and sometimes every two weeks. This is especially true for low barrier-to-entry jobs, which typically pay low base salaries. In these cases, the rep often cannot maintain a modest standard of living with base salary alone.

What if a company has a particularly long selling cycle, where it often takes months and sometimes years before a sale is consummated? Should a company be expected to make incentive payments before the sales force has made the sale? Surprisingly, many companies answer yes.

Some incentive plans are designed to recognize the accomplishment of milestones toward a sale, such as getting a product specified. These plans reward the rep for doing the right things to make a sale likely, as well as for closing the sale. Quarterly payouts are made based on how well the rep has done in relation to the milestones or account objectives, and commissions on sales are paid when the company recognizes the sale (for example, at invoicing or payment).

Exhibit 9-4 summarizes the various factors that influence base salary and incentive levels, frequency of payment, and pay mix. For each of the general levels of risk, we have shown the business context in which it might be found.

9.3 Analyzing Pay and Performance Relationships

A good rule of thumb for analyzing sales rep performance is that the top performers should be the highest-paid reps. This concept is illustrated in Exhibit 9-5, which indicates that sales reps contributing the most profitable business were the highest earners. For many companies, the opposite is true, and they struggle with the symptoms of an ineffective plan: inadequate sales results, low employee morale, and high sales rep turnover.

Using historical information is a good tool for developing a thorough understanding of the effectiveness of the current plan, and, it provides insight as to individual reps' pay and performance. Exhibits 9-6 and 9-7 illustrate two types of this analysis.

In performing pay and performance analysis, look for two specific findings:

1. Does anyone fall well above or below the rest of the sales organization?
2. What is the distribution of performance of the entire sales organization?

In each analysis, you should begin to answer these questions:

- Is pay differentiation sufficient to reflect varying levels of performance and contribution?

(text continues on page 129)

Exhibit 9-4. Range and Characteristics of Base Salary and Incentive Combinations.

Incentive	Base Salary	Typical Emphasis on Compensation Security	Typical Job Prominence	Typical Barrier to Entry	Payment Frequency	Typical Business Context
75 percent	25 percent	Little or none	Very high	Very low	Biweekly	▪ Start-up company ▪ Door-to-door sales ▪ Strong selling orientation encouraged ▪ Commission orientation ▪ Little management control
50 percent	50 percent	Modest	High	Low to moderate	Monthly	▪ Sales force relied on heavily for generating sales ▪ Modest management control ▪ Service sales (e.g., insurance company, computer services)
25 percent	75 percent	Significant	Significant	Varies (typically modest to high)	Quarterly	▪ Mature company ▪ Sales force equal in importance with other elements in marketing mix ▪ Significant management control ▪ Industrial sales (e.g., chemicals, instruments)
10 percent	90 percent	Heavy	Low	Varies (typically low)	Annual	▪ Sales force has limited influence in marketing mix ▪ Sales trainee position ▪ Tight management control ▪ Paying for talent orientation ▪ Team-oriented sales processes

Exhibit 9-5. Last Year's Pay vs. Profit Contribution (actual personal earnings and "fitted").

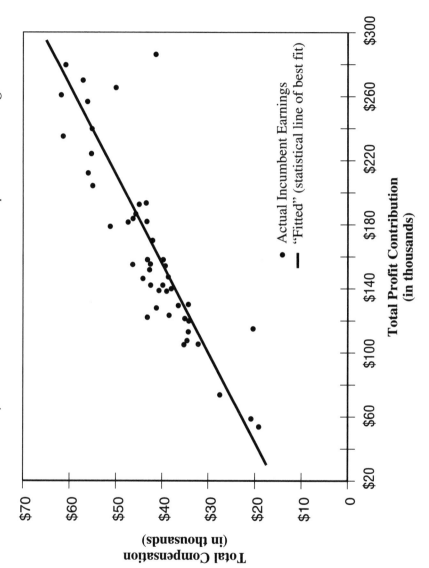

Exhibit 9-6. Distribution of Sales Personnel by Total Earnings.

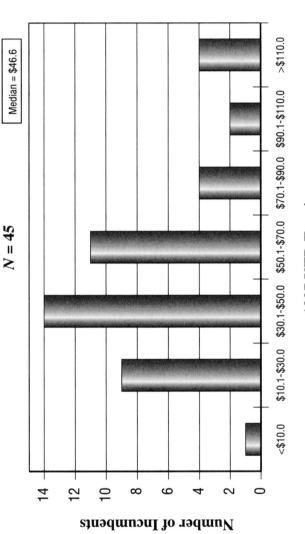

**Sales Representatives,
Total Earnings, 1997 October YTD**

N = 45

Median = $46.6

Number of Incumbents

1997 YTD Earnings
(thousands of dollars)

Exhibit 9-7. Correlation Between Seniority and Incentive Earnings.

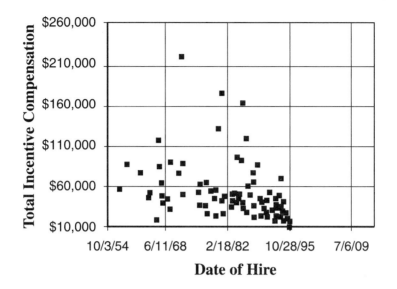

- Which elements of pay (e.g., performance measures) are causing problems?
- Are any other factors contributing to the problem (e.g., goal setting, sales management)?

9.4 Market Pay Comparisons

Defining Market Comparators

Of the various markets in which a corporation can be a player, labor resources is one of the most important. Skilled sales talent represents a rare and valuable commodity. To be a player, you must identify your company's position in the market and then develop your pay strategy. This strategy will be the basis for total compensation philosophy and should be aligned with current labor market practices.

How your total compensation compares to the market often is a driving force in attracting and retaining top sales talent. It is not always true that a company's position is the same from market to market, nor is its list of direct competitors necessarily identical.

As you consider the appropriate comparator group (the group of companies with which you compete for sales resources), also consider these key questions:

1. In what market segments are you competing?
2. Is the company's strategy changing?
3. What critical success factors are necessary for your sales force?
4. What industry or industries best reflect your talent pool?

To define your labor market segment, you must first define the proper selling roles for your sales reps and the types of competencies necessary to be effective in those roles. Depending on your product or market strategy and degree of reliance on the sales force, the selling role can take any one of a number of different tracks:

1. Missionary selling
2. Maintaining existing accounts
3. Penetration and leveraging existing relationships
4. Technical selling

Just as the roles for sales reps and for engineers are different, so are the labor markets for each. Therefore, you define the market for sales talent to include companies that could also employ similar sales talent. Often this is a broader group than simply the companies that sell similar products, especially if the market is changing rapidly to meet new customer needs and requirements.

The competitive position that you will take depends on several other business factors. Competitive position is defined by two parameters:

1. Average total compensation—the sum of salary and incentive paid to the average sales rep—which often equates to average W-2 earnings for the sales force.
2. Dispersion of pay within the sales force, which measures both the opportunity for extra pay and the downside compensation risk accepted by the sales rep.

Evolving from this competitive assessment will be your sales force compensation strategy. Examples of such strategies follow:

▪ High-risk/high-reward—used when the sales strategy emphasizes new business development.

▪ Lower risk and reward but high average pay—a combination for a senior relationship manager whose sales cycle is long and whose territory sales volume is irregular.

▪ Stability, experience, and personal qualifications—characteristics of the successful relationship manager.

- Lower-risk compensation/average pay level—a combination often used to attract entry-level sales personnel during their initial period of training and maturing.

- Lower risk and opportunity/higher pay level—the practice of hiring sales reps with superior qualifications. The intent is to move the entry-level reps through the organization as the first step to a management career in marketing, product management, or general management. In all cases, field experience is used as a training ground more than as a proving ground.

Gathering Market Intelligence

As with any other competitive analysis project, there is no universal or even single best source of information to tell you the amount and variability of the compensation paid by your relevant labor market competitors. Each of the various research sources has distinct benefits and limitations. To understand what role a survey has in your research, it may be useful to review each source of data. The most prevalent data sources are published surveys, custom surveys, compensation databases, and recruiting and exit interviews.

Published Surveys

Sales managers and human resources professionals have access to a variety of published surveys, each with its own unique characteristics that may either enhance or reduce its usefulness for your company's analysis.

In evaluating the survey quality, you should answer the following questions:

- Which companies participated in the study?

- What is the sample size for relevant industry clusters? All surveys have certain industry groupings that are stronger than others. Because you intend to use the survey as a snapshot of your entire industry, there is strength in numbers if the companies are relevant competitors.

- Is the survey well documented? A number of widely published surveys do not disclose the participants making up the survey population. It is difficult to draw conclusions on blind data.

- Is compensation variability reported? Several widely used surveys collect data only on the *average* compensation of the respondents' sales forces.

▪ How timely are the data? While some surveys are published only biennially, the labor market is fluid and bonus levels can vary with business cycles. Other surveys have a long time lag in reporting, so that there could be a one- to two-year gap between the year in which incentives were earned and the year in which the survey is published.

Custom Surveys

Often senior management will feel uncomfortable with published surveys because of the age of the data or the questionable relevance of the survey participants. In these circumstances, a custom survey among specific companies may be necessary. A properly conducted custom survey can provide the most timely, verifiable, and accurate data on the labor market. Such accuracy is not without costs, however, and the price a company pays is not always denominated in dollars. The most obvious nonmonetary cost is the time spent in gathering and documenting a compensation survey for both the participants and the surveyors themselves.

Compensation Databases

Several consulting firms maintain compensation databases in which they annually update files on the actual compensation and position scope data for management and professional positions. These firms have recently added a number of sales rep and sales manager positions to their databases.

The database approach can offer the focused selection of participants of a custom study combined with the speed and lower cost of a published survey. For this approach to be practical, the database must include a number of your most relevant competitor companies. You could then choose to run a selective database extraction of the compensation data of those competitors. Alternatively, you might need certain companies whose data are indispensable to understanding your labor market.

This solicitation process requires much less cost and elapsed time than starting a specialized survey from scratch. Industry clusters begin to form over time. When a database is well represented in one segment, such as telecommunications or computer software, then the remaining holdout companies are usually quick to participate.

Recruiting and Exit Interviews

Information from recruiting and exit interviews can give valuable insight about competitor pay practices, although these findings are best used as a secondary source. It is often difficult to determine whether quoted compensation figures are the maximum opportunities, reasonable expectations, longer-term averages, or actual recent results. These sources can all help to verify and reinforce information gained by other means and thus have a place in competitive analyses, but not as the centerpiece.

Determining Competitive Comparisons

Total Market Approach

The aim of this approach is to understand how much total compensation is paid to sales reps and how it is distributed among the universe of reps in the reporting companies. The end product of the analysis can be presented in graphic and tabular formats, as shown in Exhibit 9-8.

The graphic format depicts the distribution of W-2 earnings among all the reps in the reporting companies. An arithmetic mean (average) of total pay has been calculated and printed in the upper left-hand corner of the chart. To determine the pay at any level within the industry, simply scan across the x-axis to the desired segment— say, the eightieth percentile—and then read the y-axis value for the line. The result is that level of W-2 earnings that equals or exceeds the pay delivered to 80 percent of the sales reps in the industry. Put another way, only one in five reps makes more than that amount.

Market Analysis Approach

This second approach is based on the premise that the labor market is not dominated by a collection of individual sales reps but instead is composed of a group of companies that administer their programs to reinforce their own product or market strategies. From year to year, quotas and territories are revised and refined, and compensation policies determine the overall increase in the sales compensation budget. As with professionally published surveys, there are two statistics that are being measured by this method:

1. The overall average compensation cost per sales rep, which is a "managed" number at most companies today, as sales managers set quotas and territories to correspond to a targeted earnings level for the "average" rep.

2. The degree of difference (or dispersion) of actual W-2 earnings within a sales force, which will vary from company to company.

Exhibit 9-8. Cumulative Distribution of Total Cash Compensation Earnings: Sales Representative.

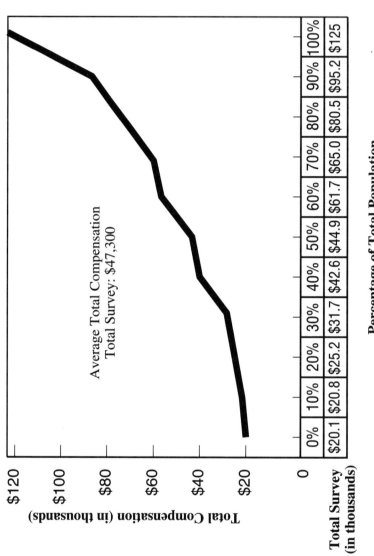

Average Total Compensation
Total Survey: $47,300

	0%	10%	20%	30%	40%	50%	60%	70%	80%	90%	100%
Total Survey (in thousands)	$20.1	$20.8	$25.2	$31.7	$42.6	$44.9	$61.7	$65.0	$80.5	$95.2	$125

**Percentage of Total Population
Earning at or Below Amount**

Total Compensation (in thousands)

This two-step analysis addresses the question of whether a rep can best advance his personal net worth by moving to a higher-paying company or delivering stronger performance. It can be of significant benefit if you are planning a large survey or are in an industry with very large sales forces.

Once again, additional information about automobile and expense reimbursement, benefits eligibility, and use of contests or other awards can improve the quality of the overall analysis.

10

Establishing Guiding Principles

Guiding principles help set the stage for evaluating alternative plan designs and developing a new incentive compensation plan design. They play an important role in summarizing the objectives and philosophy of the compensation program, ultimately helping to ensure that the recommended program is aligned with management's strategic goals.

10.1   Guiding Principles: A Definition

Guiding principles serve to direct decisions on how to design each element of the total rewards program, which includes not just pay, recognition, and benefits but also personal development and work environment. (The total reward package offered to salespeople is discussed in more detail in Chapter 21.) In addition, guiding principles help define how to communicate to salespeople the links among:

1. Individual performance
2. Team and unit performance
3. Company performance
4. Company culture and management's value
5. Employee rewards

Defining guiding principles, a key part of the initial fact-finding effort, draws heavily on both the written and unwritten objectives and the style of senior management. The most valuable source of input is typically interviews and conversations with executives and senior functional managers. Additionally, written documentation, if it exists, on the company's compensation philosophy is extremely valuable input. Often companies do not have a formal, written compensation philosophy, so information on this topic must come from the management interviews. And even if a formal written compensation philosophy does exist, it often is not specific to the sales organization, or the sales organization may have a different compensation philosophy from the rest of the organization. It is important to clarify these points early in the design process.

The principles are important because they help provide a reality check throughout the incentive design process. At each stage in this process—identifying performance measures and assigning weights, determining target total cash compensation levels, developing payout mechanics, defining the frequency of payout, and so forth—the guiding principles allow design team members to ensure that their incentive recommendations are consistent with management's philosophy, goals, and objectives. In addition, when there are several alternative incentive design elements or alternative incentive plans under consideration, the principles help guide the design team in the selection of the alternative that best fits the organization.

10.2   Statements of Beliefs and Direction

Your company's guiding principles should include a relatively short list of statements that provide directional insight but do not jump to conclusions as to what the compensation solutions should be. They provide broad criteria to determine what the appropriate compensation plan design should be.

Documenting a company's guiding principles typically addresses such points as these:

1. Pay plan linkage to company and individual performance
2. Labor markets against which pay is calibrated
3. How much to pay as compared to a defined peer group of companies (for both base salary and incentives)
4. Basis for determining pay: cost of sales or of labor
5. Methods and timing of employee communications about pay
6. Vertical and horizontal alignment of pay plans
7. Related performance management and support programs
8. Career paths and linkages to compensation

Exhibit 10-1 illustrates the varying nature of these principles.

10.3   Integrating Guiding Principles Into the Compensation Design Process

Guiding principles have two key uses in the development of a new sales compensation program. First, they are used on an ongoing ba-

Exhibit 10-1. Examples of Principles and Related Pay Programs.

- *Pay program link to company performance*
  - We will implement pay programs that reward for increasing shareholder value.
  - We will increase market share by rewarding first for increased penetration of existing customers and then for the acquisition of new customers.

- *Pay program link to individual performance*
  - We will measure and pay for quantitative sales results and eliminate subjectivity in the compensation plan.
  - Those with more impact on company performance will have a higher percentage of pay at risk.
  - The sales compensation plan must allow the sales force to easily measure their performance and readily calculate potential rewards.

- *Labor markets and peer group comparisons*
  - We will have a total cash compensation program that is competitive with market comparators in our industry segment.
  - Each sales employee's total compensation for target performance will be equitable in form and opportunity with peers within the company.

- *Basis for determining target pay levels*
  - We will align the pay structure with market and pay base salaries at the fiftieth percentile and target total compensation at the seventy-fifth percentile.
  - We will employ a cost-of-labor approach, not a cost-of-sales approach.

- *Philosophy and approach to pay communications*
  - We will communicate these principles in a clear and open fashion.
  - We will openly discuss the competitiveness of our pay.
  - The sales compensation plan will be aligned to business objectives and will change as objectives change.

- *Alignment with other related pay programs*
  - We will align field employee and field management pay plans.
  - We will align field sales and field service pay plans.
  - We will use long-term incentive mechanisms to increase the retention of experienced, high-performing sales reps with a sense of ownership.

- *Related performance management programs*
  - The sales compensation program will attract, retain, and reward high-performing individuals who have industry experience and both sales and technical competencies.
  - We will use base salary increases to reward for development of defined core competencies.

- *Approach to career paths*
  - We will create a pay progression system that provides for career progression from sales into marketing and, as appropriate, into the field again.
  - Our pay program will have appropriate flexibility to allow individuals to pursue either a management career track or a professional sales career track.
  - We will provide performance development tools and processes that reinforce our business values and the achievement of key results.

sis throughout the design process, where they serve as a tool and a point of reference by the compensation design team. The team should regularly refer to the guiding principles at each stage of the design process, from concept formulation to detailed plan design, to ensure alignment between the recommended plan and management philosophy and goals.

Second, the principles form part of the communication and roll-out of the new program after the completion and approval of the recommended design. The guiding principles should be integrated into the communication message from management to the sales force. In this way, management can more clearly explain the rationale and criteria behind the new compensation plan design. This provides a critically important context within which the sales force can understand how management developed the new plan and what role the sales force needs to play in achieving the overall strategic business objectives. Providing this context can significantly aid in ensuring the field's acceptance of the new plan.

Also design principles often highlight the need for changes in other sales management processes required for the recommended incentive plan to be successful.

11

Selecting From the Menu of Plan Design Alternatives

Up to this point, we have examined the role of the salesperson in the marketing mix, seen how to determine compensation levels relative to the competitive market, and studied the concept of risk as it affects sales behavior and compensation. Now we are ready to turn to the main point of this book: the choices for paying salespeople.

Fortunately (or unfortunately, depending on your perspective), the sales manager has a tremendous variety of choices. The three basic components of compensation—salary, commission, and bonus—can be mixed and matched in numerous ways to create a compensation approach that supports corporate and sales strategy, and motivates and rewards desired sales performance. (As a reminder, we are covering only *cash* compensation in this chapter. Benefits are not generally considered effective in driving salesperson behavior, while noncash incentives are. These and other parts of a total reward program are covered in Chapter 21.)

11.1 Salary-Only Plans

Sometimes straight salary might be the best option, as it is in the following examples:

▪ *Highly technical sales.* A highly technical sales process often requires the vendor to create a customized product tailored to the needs of the customer. Here the sales rep becomes a coordinator of a team of sales, marketing, technical product design, and engineering resources required to execute the sale. In such cases, the salesperson may have very little direct influence over the sale. One example is the sale of steel to automobile manufacturers, where a complex design and testing process is required before orders are placed. The sales rep in this example functions as both project coordinator and relationship manager, while the sales team consists of engineers, chemists, and manufacturing managers. In this situation straight salary may be appropriate because the sales representative has little direct influence (or prominence) on the sale.

- *Extremely large, infrequent sales.* Some products are purchased only after a multiyear sales process due to cost or the strategic implications of the purchase. The commercial aircraft industry provides an excellent example of sales that can range into the hundreds of millions of dollars and take years to complete. The salesperson in such an environment spends much of his time maintaining relationships with both existing and prospective customers so that he will be positioned properly when the next sales opportunity arises. A straight salary approach effectively compensates these salespeople in the long periods between sales and ensures they are not overpaid when major sales occur.

- *Pull-through (demand generation) sales.* Some sales reps concentrate their efforts on creating demand rather than on selling directly to the end user. One example is the agricultural-chemical salesperson, who spends much of her time educating farmers about agricultural chemicals in general, and her company's products in particular. Her role is to increase awareness and influence the resulting demand, but not to close sales. The actual fulfillment of the sale occurs through the distribution channel—in this case, the local farmers' cooperative or agricultural products retailer. Because it is difficult, or perhaps impossible, to link the salesperson's efforts directly to sales of the product in such cases, a straight salary approach may be appropriate.

- *Volatile or unpredictable marketplace.* Sometimes demand does not fit known patterns or is driven by unpredictable, external factors. The steel industry is an example. The volatility or unpredictability of the marketplace makes it difficult to set and allocate goals, or determine the degree of the salesperson's influence on a particular sale. Straight salary helps ensure fair and predictable sales rep earnings in these markets.

- *New or transitioning salespeople.* Salespeople who are new to a company, a job, or a territory may need some time to ramp up their selling performance. Inexperienced, salespeople may need time for training and to acquire a base level of product or service knowledge. A salary-only plan can be used to allow sellers in these circumstances to get up to speed and develop a sales pipeline. To help the transition to an incentive plan after the initial period, the salary may be expressed for a defined time period as a draw against future incentive earnings or in the form of a guaranteed incentive.

Advantages of Straight Salary Plans

- They are simple to understand and administer.
- They encourage customer service, because getting the next sale (and its incentive payment) is not uppermost in the rep's mind.
- They provide salespeople with predictable income.
- They eliminate sales crediting issues, especially in complex team-selling environments.
- Management has maximum flexibility to rearrange territories, reassign accounts, and change salesperson priorities without affecting pay.

Disadvantages of Straight Salary Plans

- They limit management's ability to use compensation as a tool for driving sales force behavior and communicating sales priorities.
- Fixed compensation costs increase, thereby raising the cost of sales when revenue production is down.
- They lower salespeople's incentive to increase sales results dramatically.
- They may attract security-minded (risk-averse) salespeople who may not strive for maximum results.
- They do not differentiate top performers from underperformers; indeed, top performers subsidize the pay of poor performers.

11.2 Cost-of-Sales vs. Cost-of-Labor Philosophies

Before proceeding to the discussion of commission and bonus plans, we must introduce an important concept in determining whether to use commission-based incentives, bonus-based incentives, or a combination of the two. The issue is whether the company adopts a *cost-of-sales* or a *cost-of-labor* philosophy for managing sales force pay.

The cost-of-sales philosophy is predicated on the notion that salespeople should receive a piece of the action or a portion of every dollar they sell, *regardless* of how much they may earn in total relative to other company employees or their peers in the competitive labor market. Simply stated, the sky is the limit when it comes to paying salespeople; management is indifferent about how much they earn as long as sales are significant. Under this arrangement, compensation cost as a percentage of revenue is essentially constant.

By contrast, a cost-of-labor philosophy states that salespeople have a defined dollar value in the labor market regarding a competitive range of pay. The company should not need to vary from this market pay rate in order to attract and retain the desired level of sales talent. Accordingly, for a specified level of performance (often expressed as a target, goal, or quota), the company will provide a specified amount of pay that is competitive with the defined labor market. In other words, the cost-of-labor approach delivers a planned amount of pay to salespeople who deliver a targeted level of performance.

Organizations in markets where the salesperson, not the company, "owns the customer" usually adopt a cost-of-sales philosophy. A good way to determine who owns the customer is to see whether customers follow their sales rep to a different vendor when the sales rep changes employers. Industries where the sales rep is likely to own the customer include insurance (particularly individual, as opposed to corporate, lines of insurance), real estate, and the equity markets (such as stock brokerages). Also, a cost-of-sales approach is often adopted by start-up companies when the key sales and service delivery functions, such as sales, marketing, and customer service, normally present in a more mature company are, in fact, imbedded in the salesperson. As such, the prominence of the salesperson—his ability to influence personally the customer's buying decision—in the overall marketing mix is relatively high. If not for the efforts of the salesperson, little, if anything, would happen.

Companies that believe the organization, not the salesperson, owns the customer most often employ a cost-of-labor philosophy. Most organizations that sell their products and services in a business-to-business environment fall in this category. Correspondingly, a cost-of-labor approach is more prevalent in mature, stable organizations or industries with established marketing, sales support, and customer service functions to reinforce the sales process. As such, the prominence of the salesperson in the overall marketing mix is somewhat diminished, not because she is less effective in her selling role but because there are more resources contributing to the sales process.

The implications of a cost-of-sales versus cost-of-labor philosophy are straightforward. Cost-of-sales firms often pay an incentive ("a piece of the action") in the form of commission-only plans or salary plus commission plans. Conversely, cost-of-labor organizations often use goals or quotas to calibrate their compensation plans, equalize unequal territory sizes, and define performance targets for salespeople. Salary plus bonus plans are best suited to this approach. Combination salary plus commission and bonus plans blend elements of both philosophies by paying both a piece of the action and a bonus for achieving a specific goal. However, combination plans are generally better suited to a cost-of-sales philosophy than to a cost-of-labor philosophy.

11.3   Commissions

A commission is an absolute form of measurement that pays the salesperson a percentage or portion of all the business she generates. The cost-of-sales philosophy provides a rationale for paying salespeople a piece of the action or commission. Commission-based plans come in two forms: commission-only plans (straight commission with no base salary) and salary plus commission plans that pay commission in addition to a fixed salary. The former is relatively uncommon today.

Commission-Only Plans

From the sales rep's point of view, the straight commission plan represents the best opportunity to build a franchise. In its most common form, the straight commission plan is simple in concept: the salesperson receives a percentage of the revenue dollars generated. In a straight commission environment, selling expenses may or may not be reimbursed by the company. If they are not, the commission rate (the percentage of the unit of volume earned) is generally somewhat higher to offset costs incurred by the salesperson. Commission-only plans generally pay incentives from the first unit of sales volume generated.

Two basic variables define the form of a commission plan:

1. *Basis of performance measurement.* The unit of volume against which a commission rate is applied can take numerous forms and should be driven by company objectives, sales and marketing strategy, defined selling roles, and the factors most controllable by the salesperson. Some of the most common bases of measurement for a commission plan include the following:

- x percent of revenue dollars generated
- x percent of gross or net profit dollars generated
- x percent of list price
- $\$x$ per unit sold

2. *Shape of the commission payout curve.* The shape of the commission payout curve is most easily illustrated by plotting the intersection of two variables: performance along a continuum from low to high and the resultant commission payout. There are two basic approaches that lead to variations in the shape of the resulting payout curve. A *flat commission rate* implies a single commission rate (e.g., 3 percent of all revenue sold) regardless of the corresponding performance level. In other words, the slope of the payout curve is a constant line that does not change shape or slope as performance increases or decreases. With a *variable commission rate* approach, commission rates are adjusted upward or downward at various levels of performance to help calibrate earnings and motivate the desired behavior. The slope of the payout curve will vary at key points in the performance continuum (e.g., at a break-even level of sales volume, when quota is achieved, or when a defined level of excellence is attained). A variable commission rate plan may incorporate accelerators (increasing the slope of the payout curve), or decelerators (decreasing the slope of the payout curve), or both. A detailed discussion of this type of commission rate adjuster is provided in Chapter 13.

Very few companies pay only straight commission. Although commission-only plans are consistent with a cost-of-sales philosophy, other conditions should be present. A straight commission approach may be appropriate in the following situations:

1. The sales rep's success can be measured completely and accurately on a short-term basis.

2. The sales cycle is relatively short, allowing frequent performance measurement and incentive payout.

3. Few factors other than the salesperson's personal selling skill and effort determine the success of the sale.

4. No significant nonsales activities (customer training and education, installation support, customer service, receivables management) need be performed by the rep.

5. Cyclicality or seasonality is minimal, so revenues are relatively smooth from month to month.

6. The company makes little investment in its salespeople in the form of training, and salespeople are easily replaced. In short, turnover is not costly.

7. There is no compelling need to control or otherwise manage sales rep earnings to a specified level.

Advantages of Commission-Only Plans

- Management can attract high-performing salespeople who are willing to share the risks of the business.
- Nonperformers are encouraged to leave the organization.
- Compensation costs are completely variable.
- They are easy to understand and administer.
- They encourage maximum sales effort, making them very useful in penetrating new markets.
- They minimize the need for supervision by treating sales reps much like independent contractors.

Disadvantages of Commission-Only Plans

- They severely limit management's ability to direct selling efforts, require nonselling activities, modify or realign territories, communicate and reward desired levels of performance, or promote salespeople into nonselling positions.
- They encourage a short-term orientation, possibly at the expense of longer-term, business-building activities or customer service.
- They allow sales reps to earn a high level of income from mature territories without making new sales or acquiring new accounts.
- All territories are assumed equal in size in order to yield equal commission payouts for equal selling skill and effort (in reality, few territories have equal potential).
- They reward salespeople who pursue the greatest payoff for the least effort (straight commission plans allow reps to set their own performance goals based on their desired level of income).
- They may create conflict between the salesperson's dependence on any and all volume, and the company's need to focus on the most profitable or strategically important products and markets.
- They generate little employee loyalty.

Salary Plus Commission Plans

The salary plus commission approach can be thought of as a joint venture between the salesperson and the company. Through commissions, sales reps share in the business that they help to generate. At the same time, the company pays salespeople a salary that compensates them for personal experience and skills, and also for the nonsales activities management requires them to perform.

The salary plus commission approach is consistent with the cost-of-sales philosophy. A salary plus commission plan is most appropriate in these situations:

1. Barriers to entry require a level of guaranteed income to compete in the labor market.

2. Sales results are directly related to the activities of sales reps but are not fully controlled by them, making it appropriate for the company and salespeople to share the risk. In a cyclical or seasonal market, for example, a salary helps companies retain sales talent through the inevitable downturns.

3. The company enjoys high levels of market and customer awareness of its products and services, decreasing the reps' overall prominence in the sales process.

4. Sales results are important, but management wants to retain some control over the reps' nonselling activities. A salary enables the sales manager to encourage, for example, postsale service, customer education, market or customer research, and other nonselling activities.

The relative weight of salary and the target incentive pay or commission (the pay mix) is primarily driven by the prominence of the sales job and the company's philosophy on risk in the pay plan. However, prevailing market pay practices should also be considered. Generally the more prominent the sales job is, the larger the proportion of the incentive or commission element relative to the level of target total cash compensation. However, in some circumstances, the market may require a high base salary to attract and retain sales personnel.

Advantages of Salary Plus Commission Plans

- They attract sales reps who have skills beyond just pure selling.
- They help retain employees during tough times while maintaining a variable compensation element in the pay plan.
- They help sales management direct salespeople to perform nonsales activities.
- They provide a tight link between pay and performance.
- Companies can begin to construct career paths based on both selling and nonselling skills.

Disadvantages of Salary Plus Commission Plans

• They can become overly complex and therefore difficult to understand and administer.

• The emphasis on the most important results can be diluted when management designs plans that try to micromanage the sales force.

• They increase the level of fixed compensation cost relative to commission-only plans.

• All territories are assumed to be equal in size in order to yield equal commission payouts for equal selling skill and effort.

• They share some of the disadvantages of commission-only plans, including limiting management's ability to realign territories or reassign accounts while rewarding salespeople merely for having large territories.

The salary plus commission plan is popular among both companies and salespeople. The commission element provides companies with a means to motivate and reward desired selling behavior, and the salary element provides management with a lever to help direct nonselling activities. From the salesperson's perspective, the commission element provides significant earnings opportunity while the salary provides a sense of security.

11.4 Salary Plus Bonus Plans

A bonus is a relative form of measurement that pays the salesperson all or a portion of a fixed dollar amount (e.g., 20 percent of base salary or $10,000) for the achievement of a predefined objective or quota. The higher the achievement relative to the assigned objective, the larger the incentive award. The salary plus bonus approach resembles the salary plus commission plan but is more appropriate in the following situations.

1. The company has a cost-of-labor philosophy (as opposed to a cost-of-sales philosophy) and desires to manage pay more closely around predetermined cost objectives.

2. The sales rep has a lower degree of prominence or influence on the sale than commissionable reps.

3. The salesperson has important objectives that cannot be measured or motivated by a volume-only commission plan.

Because of these factors, a bonus is almost never used without a base salary.

A bonus plan can be constructed to resemble a commission by delivering an uncapped, linear payout curve that yields additional earnings for each incremental unit of goal attainment. The key difference is that the slope of the payout curve is driven not just by sales volume alone, but by the percentage of quota or goal achieved. In addition, rather than pay a percentage of the volume generated, the bonus pays a percentage of a target bonus amount (or portion of base salary) for every percentage point of quota achieved.

Although salary plus bonus plans are best suited to companies that meet one or more of the conditions described, it is useful to examine some specific circumstances that may drive the need for salary plus bonus plans:

1. *Results cannot be measured purely in volume terms.* Sometimes a company wants salespeople to help achieve the company's product mix, channel mix, or other strategic objectives in addition to its overall sales goals; in other words, the *quality* of the volume generated is an important consideration. Examples include selling a balanced mix of products or increasing revenue through defined channels of distribution or specific customer segments.

2. *Sales dollar volume is not a direct reflection of the quality of performance.* Some businesses require a specific level of selling effort to close the sale; however, the revenue generated by the rep varies widely from sale to sale. For example, process control systems for paper plants vary tremendously in price, depending on the size of the installation, but the steps and effort required to make the sale are, for the most part, the same for all sales.

3. *New account sales generate relatively low initial revenue but yield significant annuity dollars.* In some cases, acquiring a new account does not yield significant short-term revenue but instead creates a stream of recurring sales with considerable long-term potential. In these cases the primary role of the sales rep may be to identify and acquire new accounts, leaving the account development and primary revenue generation activities to others. The services industry, data processing in particular, does business in this manner.

Advantages of Salary Plus Bonus Plans

▪ Management can equalize unequal territory sizes by predefining a target level of performance (or quota) specific to each territory, which when achieved yields the same predefined target bonus amount among all salespeople.

- Management can reward both the amount (volume) and the quality of the business the salesperson generates.

- Management can direct and reward the performance of important nonselling activities.

- The plan provides the flexibility to balance short- and long-term objectives for the sales force.

- The company can manage variable pay more closely around the achievement of defined objectives.

- Management has flexibility to realign territories or reassign accounts without affecting sales rep pay.

Disadvantages of Salary Plus Bonus Plans

- They rely on the development and administration of effective goal-setting and territory allocation systems, requiring well-defined processes and dedicated resources. Naturally, this increases the cost of plan administration.

- Depending on the performance measures selected, management may not be able to predict accurately the cost of sales compensation as a percentage of sales.

- They tempt management with many possible measurement and payment options. Management all too often succumbs to the temptation by creating plans that are complex, unfocused, and difficult to administer.

- They allow management to create poorly structured plans that reward sellers for performing activities rather than for achieving objective, measurable, and meaningful results.

11.5 Combination Plans

Combination plans, not surprisingly, provide reps with the opportunity to earn both commission and bonus incentives, in addition to a base salary. This approach has the distinct advantage of allowing the company to straddle the philosophical line between cost of sales and cost of labor. It allows management to provide salespeople with a commission on sales while also motivating other complementary behavior that is more suited to bonus plans. Companies most suited to this form of incentive arrangement generally operate in established markets that are either not fully mature or are underpenetrated by the company. For example, a company selling into a mature market but with only a 20 percent market share may want to pay salespeople a commission on new sales and a bonus for managing existing business. Similarly a business with a 60 percent share in a growing market may want to continue to pay salespeople a commission for the business they help build, but may add a bonus to reward selling a broad mix of products. Like bonus plans, combination plans are almost never used without a base salary.

The combination approach provides companies with a flexible management tool but should be used with caution. Many organizations create combination plans by merely adding bonuses to existing commission plans. This rarely drives the desired behavior but almost always increases compensation costs. Companies designing combination plans should consider both the relative weight of incentive dollars paid in commission and bonus as well as the total dollars earned. Although there is no hard and fast rule, generally any bonus that comprises less than 10 to 15 percent of the target total cash compensation usually fails to drive behavior and instead only increases costs.

Combination plans share many of the same advantages and disadvantages as salary plus commission and salary plus bonus plans. Perhaps the biggest danger is creating a combination plan by adding a commission or bonus opportunity on to an existing incentive plan structure without a corresponding decrease in salary to fund the new incentive. This approach usually results in higher costs without motivating the desired behavior.

12

Packaging Compensation Risk

The amount of incentive that a particular sales compensation program contains is related to the amount of risk built into the program. *Risk* is the probability that an expected compensation result will not be attained; as such, it is the inverse of opportunity. Generally expected compensation approximates the competitive compensation level for similar positions.

Although it is obvious that the different compensation approaches vary with respect to risk, it would be wrong to assume that each approach carries a specific and unvarying amount of risk. With the exception of straight salary, plan types can vary considerably in risk, depending on how they are designed. This gives the designer tremendous flexibility in influencing the behavior of the sales representative.

12.1 The Strange Case of Salary Plus Commission Plans

The ever-popular salary plus commission approach has an interesting characteristic: It is effective in both low- and high-prominence situations, but is less effective in between, at middle levels of prominence. Think about this. We look toward straight salaries in low-prominence situations and toward straight commission in very high-prominence situations. What is it about the two that makes for an effective approach? The answer is that a salary plus commission plan can look, from an operational perspective, very much like a straight salary plan or like a straight commission plan. However, we cannot make it look like a salary plus bonus plan, which is what works best for sales situations in the middle of the prominence scale.

12.2 Low-Risk Plans

A low-risk plan is one in which the sales representative is likely to earn close to the expected level of income, regardless of the form in which it is paid. The level of performance required to hit the targeted level of earnings is the critical element here, rather than whether payment is in the form of salary, bonus, or commission. Management backs into a commission rate or bonus schedule based on the targeted earnings level for the position and expected sales results in the territory. Frequently the commission rate is tailored to the territory, resulting in the apparently illogical result that a sale in one territory is worth more or less than the same sale in another territory.

Where sales results are very stable over time, this approach is easy to implement. Where they are not, various rules are constructed to ensure that the sales rep's income stays within acceptable boundaries. The most common example is the use of a cap on incentive earnings, or a windfall clause enabling management to reduce or eliminate credit for sales that do not meet certain parameters (generally loosely defined).

Let's construct a simple example to see how this might be done. Assume that territory volume is expected to be $1.5 million and earnings are targeted at $60,000. Further assume that, based on current prices, territory volume has never been less than $1.2 million or more than $1.8 million. We could pay the rep a salary of $45,000 and a commission of 1 percent of sales (which would be $15,000 on $1.5 million). Based on territory history, the range of earnings is likely to be $57,000 to $63,000. That is not much variation. If we wanted to ensure results within this range, we might cap incentive earnings at $20,000 or $25,000. We have created a low-risk incentive plan.

Why bother with incentive plans that have low risk? There are several reasons:

• The sales rep feels like a contributor to the business. There is no greater source of alienation in business than the feeling that our existence does not matter to the company. Even a small amount of variation in pay based on results will help to maintain a focus on the results.

• Low prominence does not mean no prominence. Focusing the rep's attention on job performance will probably generate some additional results.

• There may be a philosophical reason to use incentives. If the company has other, higher-prominence sales forces or makes substantial use of incentives outside the sales area, it would be an anomaly to have a salaried sales force.

12.3   High-Risk Plans

We frequently think of commissions as high-risk plans, although we just looked at one that carried low risk due to the nature of the territory. When a "stretch" level of performance is required to generate incentive earnings and the base salary alone is insufficient to enable the representative to live comfortably, we have a high-risk plan. Carried far enough, it becomes the equivalent of a straight commission plan.

Let's go back to the example that we used before, but change the incentive element. Instead of paying 1 percent on sales, we pay no incentive below 90 percent of expected sales of $1.5 million. Thus, at $1.35 million, we begin paying an incentive of 10 percent of marginal sales. At the expected sales level, we still pay $15,000 in commissions (the difference between the $1.5 million target and the $1.35 million threshold). But we do not pay any commissions in part of the range of expected performance (between $1.2 million and $1.35 million). At the top end of the historical performance range, $1.8 million, we pay $30,000 in commissions (10 percent of $300,000) for a far different top end of $75,000 total cash. We have just expanded the compensation range to between $45,000 and $75,000 from between $57,000 and $63,000, thus introducing significantly higher risk into the situation. Whether this is appropriate is a separate issue and depends on the sales rep's ability to influence the actual results within that range.

Why not just use a straight commission in this situation? The reason is that high barriers to entry may require a substantial level of fixed compensation to attract personnel with appropriate skills or to hold them in place during short-term slack periods. Further, security-oriented companies may find it culturally unacceptable to use straight commission plans.

12.4   Confusion Over the Pay Mix Percentage

The mix of compensation—that is, the relative levels of salary and incentive in the total compensation package—can be misleading as an indicator of the level of risk. The two examples already provided illustrate this point. Both packages had a salary-to-incentive mix of 75 percent to 25 percent ($45,000 in salary and $15,000 in incentive at the targeted total earnings level). Yet the second package had substantially higher risk than did the first because of the introduction of a high threshold ($1.35 million).

Following through on this concept, we can construct a wide variety of mixes, all having approximately the same degree of risk. Conversely, we can introduce varying degrees of risk into plans using the same mix at the targeted level of earnings. Where risk (downside earnings potential) varies, opportunity (upside earnings potential) must also vary. To impose risk without providing opportunity is irresponsible from a plan design perspective. In the second example, we increased opportunity in direct proportion to the risk introduced.

If the competitive pay level for a sales job is $50,000 and we pay a salary of $40,000 and target incentive earnings at $10,000, we have an 80/20 mix, a mix commonly found in industrial selling situations. If, in a stable growth market in an established territory, we require a 25 percent growth in sales to earn that $10,000, we have probably created a high-risk plan. Presumably we provide very high earnings leverage above that performance level to compensate for the risk. We can shift that mix to 60/40 by paying a salary of $30,000 and targeting incentive earnings at $20,000. If we structure the plan so that the salesperson can earn the $20,000 with an 8 percent increase in sales, we have created a lower-risk plan, even though the mix is weighted more toward the incentive element.

12.5 Dealing With a Disguised Salary

In certain industrial selling situations where the sales job is fairly low in prominence, salary plus commission plans approximate the income consequences of straight salary. In these situations, sales results vary little from predicted results. Product usage can be predicted for each account, and the supplier has an exclusive franchise, or buying patterns are such that one supplier is unlikely to exclude another from an account. The greatest potential for variation in projected volume arises if an account leaves the territory or another one comes in during the year. As in the example in section 12.2, the range of performance across which the incentive is likely to be paid is narrow, resulting in a narrow range of total compensation results. The range of performance shown in that example (plus or minus 20 percent of projected) is actually quite broad compared to many situations. Many companies can project territory volume within 10 percent of actual on a consistent basis. Under such circumstances, any incentive plan targeted to pay a given level of compensation at the projected sales level is little different, in terms of pay result, from a straight salary.

13

Using Mechanics to Fine-Tune a Plan Design

By now you have determined which jobs are eligible for incentive compensation, determined their prominence and used that to define the appropriate pay mix, defined performance measures and their weights, and selected the form of incentive (commission, bonus, or a combination). In this chapter, we will examine the ways in which management can use plan mechanics (linked measures, adjusters, hurdles, caps, and other technical tools) to calibrate payouts and motivate and reward the desired performance.

As a manager, you may want the plan to drive specific behaviors and help salespeople make trade-off decisions. You may also want to find ways to keep the pressure on as sales reps increase their performance during the course of a year (or other measurement period). Finally, you may need to examine ways to protect your company against excessive or inappropriate payouts.

13.1 Linked Measures

Often salespeople must make difficult trade-off decisions. The most common is the trade-off between revenue and profit. After all, one of the easiest ways to increase sales is to offer a discount. This becomes a problem very quickly if sales representatives have pricing authority—the ability to set price, even within predefined limits—with little or no incentive to protect margins. Other examples of trade-offs are revenue and product mix, and revenue and order size, especially in distribution organizations.

Mechanics that link performance measures provide management with a powerful tool to help salespeople make the appropriate trade-off decisions. Properly used, linked measures can communicate management's trade-off priorities directly through the compensation plan.

The Bonus/Commission Matrix

The bonus matrix is among the simplest and most easily understood means for linking two different—and often opposing—performance measures. Bonus earnings are calculated as a percentage of the target bonus amount. Bonus amounts increase from the lower left to the upper right diagonal of the matrix (that is, bonus earnings are maximized by performing well against both measures simultaneously). In addition, the incumbent earns a higher bonus amount for target performance against both measures rather than excellence for one measure and threshold for the other. Exhibit 13-1 shows a bonus matrix.

To use the matrix, find the revenue to quota performance achieved along the left side of the matrix, and then the profit performance achieved along the bottom of the matrix. The bonus earned is at the intersection of the two. A salesperson performing at goal in both revenue and profit will earn a $10,000 bonus. Earnings also increase as performance increases in either measure. If he pulls in over 110 percent of his revenue target, at a margin of over 110 percent of his profit objective, the bonus rises to $25,000. The only way to earn top dollar is to perform well simultaneously on *both* measures; however, in this example, the total incentive earnings are capped or limited at $25,000.

Matrices can also be used for commission purposes. Exhibit 13-2 shows a commission matrix. With the commission matrix, commission rates increase as performance increases. In Exhibit 13-2, the trade-off is made between total revenue and average revenue per order. In this example, the highest possible commission rate is 2.50 percent for total revenue performance over 110 percent of goal *and* with an average revenue per order of $525 or more.

The matrix can be finely tuned. Both commission and bonus matrices can be extended up and to the right, providing an uncapped incentive opportunity. Performance measure weights can also be applied. In the examples shown in Exhibits 13-1 and 13-2, each measure pays out equally. The weighting in Exhibit 13-1 is 50 percent on revenue and 50 percent on profit, while the weighting in Exhibit 13-2 is 50 percent on revenue and 50 percent on average revenue per order. Finally, the matrix can accelerate or decelerate incentive earnings as performance increases.

Advantages and Disadvantages of the Matrix Design

Matrices have several important advantages as a means of linking incentive plan measures. They are:

(text continues on page 160)

Exhibit 13-1. Revenue and Profitability Bonus Matrix.

Revenue vs. Quota	90.0%–93.3%	93.4%–96.6%	96.7%–99.9%	100.0%–103.3%	103.4%–106.6%	106.7%–109.9%	110.0%+
110.0%+	$7,500	$9,000	$10,400	$11,900	$16,300	$20,600	$25,000
106.7%–109.9%	$6,900	$8,300	$9,800	$11,300	$11,400	$16,300	$20,600
103.4%–106.6%	$6,300	$7,700	$9,200	$10,600	$12,500	$14,400	$16,300
100.0%–103.3%	$5,600	$7,100	$8,500	*$10,000*	$10,600	$11,300	$11,900
96.7%–99.9%	$5,400	$6,500	$7,500	$8,500	$9,200	$9,800	$10,400
93.4%–96.6%	$5,200	$5,800	$6,500	$7,100	$7,700	$8,300	$9,000
90.0%–93.3%	$5,000	$5,200	$5,400	$5,600	$6,300	$6,900	$7,500

Profitability vs. Quota

Exhibit 13-2. Total Revenue and Average Revenue per Order Commission Matrix.

Total Revenue vs. Quota	$0–$99	$100–$174	$175–$249	$250–$324	$325–$449	$450–$524	$525+
110.0%+	0.75%	0.90%	1.04%	1.19%	1.63%	2.06%	2.50%
106.7%–109.9%	0.69%	0.83%	0.98%	1.13%	1.44%	1.75%	2.06%
103.4%–106.6%	0.63%	0.77%	0.92%	1.06%	1.25%	1.44%	1.63%
100.0%–103.3%	0.56%	0.71%	0.85%	1.00%	1.06%	1.13%	1.19%
96.7%–99.9%	0.54%	0.65%	0.75%	0.85%	0.92%	0.98%	1.04%
93.4%–96.6%	0.52%	0.58%	0.65%	0.71%	0.77%	0.83%	0.90%
90.0%–93.3%	0.50%	0.52%	0.54%	0.56%	0.63%	0.69%	0.75%

Average Revenue per Order

- An effective, flexible means of linking two performance measures.
- Simple to understand, communicate, and administer.
- Easy to fine-tune to incorporate the changing performance measure weightings, accelerators, decelerators, or cap.

Matrices have one specific disadvantage: Management must define ranges of performance for incentive purposes (e.g., 100 percent to 125 percent of goal). There is no increase in earnings for increased performance *within* the range. Earnings increase only by moving *between* ranges. This problem can be offset somewhat by creating matrices with more, rather than fewer, rows and columns. As a rule, try to use matrices no larger than seven rows by seven columns.

13.2 Multipliers

Multipliers provide a similar means of linking performance measures and helping drive the appropriate trade-off decisions. However, multipliers automatically communicate the priority between the two measures by using one measure to fund the second. In short, multipliers should be used to send a clear message: "Do this *first*. Do that *second*."

Multiplier earnings are calculated as a percentage or portion of the actual earnings from the highest-priority measure. For example, you can link revenue (the first priority) and product mix (the second) by paying a *product mix bonus,* which is a percentage of revenue bonus earnings, calculated as follows:

$$\text{Revenue bonus earnings} \quad \times \quad \text{Product mix multiplier rate} \quad = \quad \text{Product mix bonus earnings.}$$

Multiplier rates used to determine the final bonus amount are generally shown in tabular form. Following is a product mix multiplier table:

Number of Product Quotas Achieved	Multiplier Rate (percentage of revenue bonus earnings)
7+	150
6	100
5	66
4	40
3	15

Number of Product Quotas Achieved	*Multiplier Rate (percentage of revenue bonus earnings)*
2	0
1	0
0	0

Using this table, management can quickly and easily calculate the product mix bonus earnings. For example, assuming that a sales representative earns a $10,000 revenue bonus in the first quarter and achieves five product mix quotas, the product mix multiplier rate is 66 percent. The rep's product mix bonus earnings would be $6,600, calculated using the above formula:

$10,000		66%		$6,600
(revenue bonus earnings)	×	(product mix multiplier rate)	=	(product mix bonus earnings)

Like matrices, multipliers can be finely tuned. The incentive measure weights may be adjusted by changing the rates on the multiplier table. Thresholds, caps, accelerators, and decelerators can also be applied easily, once again, by carefully selecting multiplier rates. In some cases, you may want to penalize sellers for unacceptably low performance on a specific measure. Negative multiplier rates can be used to *take away* incentive earnings should a seller fail to meet minimum performance levels. Naturally, you should use this option with extreme care.

Multipliers have several important advantages as a means of linking incentive plan measures:

- They are an effective, flexible means of linking two performance measures.

- They provide a means of defining the priority between two linked measures.

- They are relatively simple to understand, communicate, and administer.

- They are easy to fine-tune to incorporate the desired performance measure weightings, accelerators, decelerators, or caps.

- Because multiplier rates can be calculated with a formula, there is an infinite number of possible multiplier rates that increase as performance increases. This also eliminates the need to define performance ranges (a disadvantage inherent in the matrix concept discussed earlier).

Multipliers have one specific disadvantage: They are slightly more difficult to understand and communicate than a simple matrix.

13.3   Adjusters

The rate at which incentive pay is earned may be adjusted as performance increases. The four types of incentive earnings rate adjusters—constant, progressive, regressive, and combination—are illustrated in Exhibit 13-3, with their advantages and disadvantages outlined in Exhibit 13-4. Exhibit 13-4 also lists when adjusters are to be used.

Constant, or Linear, Incentive Rate

This is the simplest adjuster. Earnings increase at a constant rate as performance increases (see Exhibit 13-3A). An excellent example of a constant rate plan is a straight commission—for example, 2 percent of all revenue sold. Constant incentive rates are appropriate when performance cannot be predicted with a great deal of accuracy. Volatile markets, start-up companies, and lack of management ability to define meaningful quotas or goals are all good reasons to use constant incentive rates.

Progressive, or Accelerated, Incentive Rate

With this adjuster, the rate of incentive earnings will increase once the salesperson reaches a specified level of performance. Rates may accelerate at a single point (as shown in Exhibit 13-3B) or at multiple points (e.g., at 75 percent, 100 percent, and 125 percent of goal).

Accelerated rates are predicated on the principle that the last dollar of revenue is the most difficult to attain and consequently should carry the greatest reward. This often makes sound business sense, especially since most businesses must sell a certain amount of product in order to cover fixed costs. Accelerated rates can be calibrated to increase payout only after fixed costs are covered. Most important, accelerated rates provide significant incentive to perform. Finally, accelerators reward high levels of performance during each measurement period, thereby encouraging salespeople to close business sooner rather than later.

A potential downside of using accelerated rates is increased pressure to pull forward orders through heavy discounting or other

Exhibit 13-3. Four Types of Incentive Rate Adjusters.

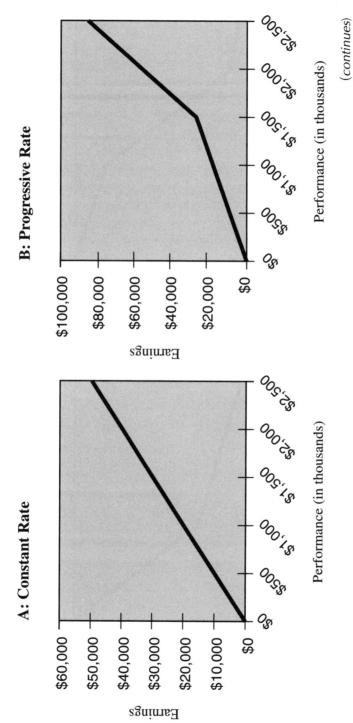

A: Constant Rate

B: Progressive Rate

(continues)

Exhibit 13-3. (*continued*)

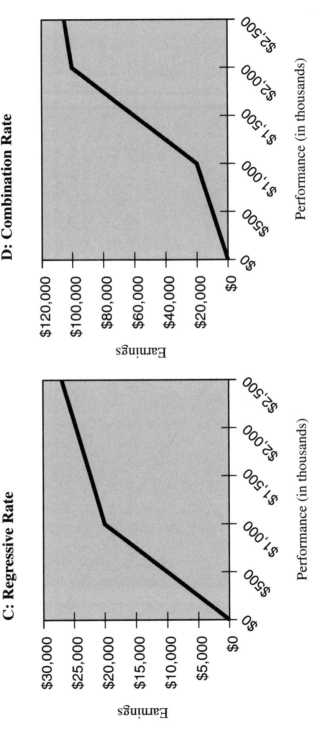

C: Regressive Rate

D: Combination Rate

Exhibit 13-4. Adjusters: Advantages, Disadvantages, and When to Use.

Rate Adjuster	Advantages	Disadvantages	When to Use
Constant rate (none)	• Simple and easy to use • Does not require accurate goals	• Does not provide additional incentive for high performance	• Goal setting is difficult or impossible • Start-ups, highly volatile markets
Progressive rate (accelerator)	• Motivates and rewards high levels of performance	• Requires accurate goals • Can provide an incentive for reps. to "pull forward" orders, causing periodic spikes in business	• Predictable markets, well-developed businesses
Regressive rate (decelerator)	• Protects the company from overpayment	• Requires accurate goals • May demotivate the sales force	• Markets where sales reps have little influence on order size or profit • Extremely large sales are common
Combination rate	• Motivates increased performance and protects against overpayment	• Complex and potentially demotivating when decelerating rates are applied	• Markets where extremely large deals occur, but reps have great influence on small and midsized orders

means. This may both hurt the sales price and cause a recurring spike in order activity (e.g., orders flood in on the last day of the month or quarter) that puts a strain on operations as well. More important, accelerated rates put a great deal of pressure on goal-setting processes. Goals must be set to help determine where the change in rates will occur. Disastrous results may occur if the acceleration points are not set consistently and judiciously. Goals set too low will cause significant incentive overpayments due to accelerated earnings over goal. Goals set too high will demotivate even the best performers in the sales force.

Regressive, or Decelerated, Incentive Rate

Shown in Exhibit 13-3C, this type of rate adjuster is the least popular. Nevertheless, there are circumstances in which its use is appropriate. As the name implies, decelerated rates decrease the rate of incentive earnings once a specific level of performance is reached. A primary reason to use decelerated rates is in circumstances where, beyond a certain level of personal performance, salespeople have declining direct influence on subsequent sales. A classic example of this is *blue bird sales*. (A *blue bird* is a very large order that was unexpected; it came out of the blue.) It would be inappropriate to pay a salesperson top incentive dollar for large sales he did not influence. Another circumstance where decelerated rates may be appropriate is when sales representatives have a high influence on securing the order but very little influence on its size or profitability. Finally, regressive incentive rates may be used in circumstances where an exceptional number of orders may strain manufacturing capability.

Of course, the major disadvantages of decelerated rates are their potential to demotivate the sales force and the pressure their use puts on the goal-setting process.

Combination Rate

This adjuster incorporates both accelerated and decelerated features into a single plan; these are illustrated in Exhibit 13-3D. Combination rates are used when sales representatives have a high degree of influence on sales up to a point beyond which their influence drops off. The advantages of combination rates are that they motivate and reward increasing performance when sales representatives influence the sale, while protecting the company from overpayment when the sales representatives' influence is low (for example, at very high levels of goal achievement which probably indicates a windfall). A company might want to use a combination plan in a market where most revenue is driven directly by salesperson influence, yet extremely large deals are fairly common. Disadvantages of combination plans lie in their complexity and the potentially demotivating use of the regressive rate.

13.4   Hurdles

Some objectives are so important that companies will not pay incentives until those objectives are met. The practice of withholding incentive pay on one performance measure until a specific goal is achieved on a separate performance measure is called a *hurdle*—for example, achieving quota in two product lines to receive commission payout on any product line sold or selling to five new accounts to receive payout on the profitability bonus.

Hurdles can be a powerful means of communicating priorities and objectives to a sales force. Like matrices and multipliers, they can provide management with a means of linking performance on one measure to performance on another, essentially creating a gate through which the salesperson must pass in order to receive incentive payouts. The advantage of the hurdle is its ability to get the sales force's attention. A major drawback is the extreme pressure they put on the goal-setting system. If hurdles are set too high, salespeople suffer a tremendous blow to their earnings, and management's credibility suffers. As a general rule, 90 to 95 percent of salespeople should clear the hurdle.

13.5   Thresholds and Caps

The last two tools commonly used to fine-tune a plan design are thresholds and caps. A *threshold* is a designated level of performance below which it is inappropriate to pay incentive to the sales force. Thresholds are often expressed as a percentage of goal (that is, commission earnings begin once the salesperson exceeds 70 percent of quota). Thresholds focus salespeople on the range of performance (above threshold) that they have the most influence on, and they also allow a company to cover its fixed costs by specifying a minimally acceptable level of performance before paying sales incentives. Like hurdles, thresholds are heavily dependent on the company's ability to set accurate goals. If thresholds are set too high, the sales force can be unfairly penalized and may become demoralized.

As you might expect, incentive caps or limits are the least popular of all incentive plan mechanics. A *cap* is a predefined maximum level of incentive payout. Caps are the source of much friction between management (particularly financial management who favor caps as a means to protect the company against overpayment) and sales.

Caps may be appropriate for sales positions where prominence is relatively low. In general, they should be used only to ensure against overpayment for sales where the salesperson did not have significant influence. Using a cap exclusively to eliminate the chance of paying salespeople large sums is not sufficient reason to limit incentive pay.

Caps need not be absolute. They may be applied to only one part of a salesperson's pay, leaving other parts of the incentive plan unlimited. An excellent example of such a *perforated cap* is a limitation on incentive payout per individual sale. This protects companies against overpayment for the blue bird sales by limiting the payout on any given deal without limiting the total incentive opportunity.

Caps may demotivate the sales force and have a negative impact on morale. A salesperson who hits the cap is in danger of shutting down his selling efforts (and working on his golf game). However, if used judiciously and under the appropriate circumstances, caps can be a useful tool in managing sales force pay and costs.

14

Analyzing the Cost of the Plan

When designing sales compensation plans, presume that the incentive design should be cost neutral; that is, the total amount of compensation earnings for a given group of salespeople should stay constant and the aggregate performance of the salespeople should increase. Thus, sales compensation design is a revenue-enhancement tool. No recommended compensation plan should be presented to management without testing to determine whether the sales incentive plan is cost neutral; or if the design increases compensation costs, whether the amount of cost increase is offset by a related increase in sales force productivity.

Often an incentive plan is modified as a result of this analytical exercise. Therefore, early communication of the design to management or the sales force is inappropriate.

14.1 Benefits of Analyzing Costs

A cost analysis informs management of the cost implications of the new sales plans for various levels of aggregate and personal performance. Proper costing will give you:

1. The necessary tools to determine if the new sales incentive plan design meets anticipated budget constraints.
2. Insight into what the new plan pays at target performance, less than target performance, and above target performance.
3. An indication of what the plan pays based on the prior year's performance (and therefore how personal historical earnings may vary from projected earnings under the new design).

With this information, you can make better-informed decisions about whether to proceed with the proposed incentive plan designs.

Selling a revised compensation plan to the sales force, even when you are convinced that the new plan offers better compensation opportunities, is often a daunting task. Sales reps typically fear that any change will be for the worse. In fact, whenever a new sales incentive plan is implemented, sales reps become increasingly anxious over the impact the new plan will have on them. Be aware that most sales reps will immediately calculate their projected pay from the new incentive plan based on prior year's performance (assuming consistent performance measures). It is critical to anticipate this situation and determine which reps will have significant pay changes under the new plan. A cost analysis on a person-by-person basis will inform you of such major pay swings. Then you can determine if these differences are acceptable, and if so you can develop appropriate responses to anticipated sales rep concerns. Communicating to the sales force that the new incentive plan was diligently tested adds a strong measure of credibility that it offers reasonable opportunities and that all flaws were eliminated during test runs.

14.2   Incentive Plan Costing Analyses

Three types of cost analyses are typically used when determining the financial impact of a new sales incentive plan: aggregate, distributional, and individual salesperson costing.

Aggregate Cost Analysis

An aggregate cost estimate is the simplest cost model to develop. A par, best-case, and worst-case performer analysis is often completed when gross estimates of the new plan are sufficient for budgeting purposes. Also, you might want to develop this aggregate cost model to determine quickly total salary or incentive compensation costs as a percentage of sales. One of the biggest challenges with this cost model is that the par-performer analysis only estimates the aggregate salary and incentive costs. Therefore, this is the least useful of the three types of analyses.

An example of par-performer cost analysis is shown below. Assume that the following target compensation and performance numbers apply for ABC Company:

Number of sales reps:	20
Average territory revenue achieved:	$5,050,000
Average territory goal:	$5,000,000
Average annual salary:	$60,000
Target annual incentive:	$40,000

Exhibit 14-1. Components for Cost Calculation.

A. Aggregate Par-Performer Cost Estimate

Average annual salary	$ 60,000
Average actual incentive earned	42,400
Average total cash earned	$ 102,400
Number of sales reps	× 20
Total compensation cost	$ 2,048,000
Total sales	$101,000,000
Compensation as a percentage of sales	2.03%

B. Aggregate Best-Case/Worst-Case Performer Cost Estimate

	Best-Case Scenario	Worst-Case Scenario
Average annual salary	$ 60,000	$ 60,000
Average actual incentive earned	76,000	20,000
Average total cash earned	$ 136,000	$ 80,000
Number of sales reps	× 20	× 20
Total compensation cost	$ 2,720,000	$ 1,600,000
Total sales	$115,000,000	$90,000,000
Compensation as a percentage of sales	2.37%	1.78%

Further, assume that the incentive compensation is based on a sales revenue bonus plan that starts paying at 80 percent to goal (the threshold) and accelerates at goal:

Performance	Ranges of Year-to-Date Percentage of Revenue Quota Achieved	Payout per Percentage Point
Excellence	125% or greater	5.5%
Target	100% to 124%	6.0%
Threshold	80% to 99%	5.0%

Based on the assumptions, we see that the average sales rep achieved 101 percent of the average territory revenue goal ($5.05 million versus $5.0 million). Using the revenue bonus rates, we determine that the average sales rep earns an annual incentive of $42,400 ($40,000 target incentive, plus one percentage point times the 6.0 percent bonus rate times the $40,000 target incentive). Exhibit 14-1A illustrates an aggregate par-performer cost estimate.

Par-performer cost estimates are often supplemented with best-case/worst-case performer estimates. Using these other scenarios, management can become better informed about the range of possible aggregate payouts to the sales force.

Exhibit 14-1B shows an example of a best-case/worst-case estimate. Assume an average territory revenue of $5.75 million achieved for the best-case scenario and $4.5 million achieved for the worst-case scenario. Based on these assumptions, we see that the best-case sales reps achieved 115 percent of goal ($5.75 million versus $5.0 million), and the worst-case sales reps achieved 90 percent of goal ($4.5 million versus $5.0 million). Using the given revenue bonus rates, we determine that the best-case sales reps earn an award incentive of $76,000 ($40,000 target incentive, plus 15 percentage points times the 6.0 percent bonus rate times the $40,000 target incentive), and the worst-case sales reps earn an annual incentive of $20,000 (10 percentage points times the 5.0 percent bonus rate times the $40,000 target incentive).

Distributional Cost Analysis

A distributional cost model is typically used for sales forces with a large number of personnel. It is commonly employed where there are 30 or more incumbents in the sales position to which the new sales incentive plan applies. The model assumes that defined numbers of these reps reach differing levels or categories of performance.

The first step in developing this cost model is to break the performance levels into a number of performance categories—for example, threshold, below target, target, above target, and excellent. Next, determine the percentage of the group or number of sales reps who perform at each of the category levels. This process should be accomplished for each performance measure. History often shows that performance is bell shaped; thus, select a bell-shaped performance distribution for the sales force as a starting point for this analysis. However, you might also use the prior year's (or a three-year average) performance distribution.

One advantage of this model is the ease with which you can perform sensitivity analyses. You can simply modify the performance distribution assumptions to evaluate their subsequent impact on the expected plan cost.

Now let's see how this model works. Assume that the ABC Company sales force has 100 sales reps and that management has recently redesigned the sales incentive plan for the par performer.

Management also knows that last year's revenue distribution for these sales reps was as follows:

Performance Category Reached	Portion of Sales Force Reaching Performance Level
Threshold	5 percent
Below target	25 percent
Target	40 percent
Above target	20 percent
Excellence	10 percent

Recall that the average annual salary is $60,000 and the target annual incentive is $40,000. Here again is the sales revenue table for the incentive plan:

Performance	Ranges of Year-to-Date Percentage of Revenue Quota Achieved	Payout per Percentage Point
Excellence	125% or greater	5.5%
Target	100% to 124%	6.0%
Threshold	80% to 99%	5.0%

The complete distributional costing for the new incentive plan is presented in Exhibit 14-2.

Individual Cost Analysis

The acceptability of a new sales incentive plan often depends more on its favorable comparison with the old incentive plan than with external benchmarks. Thus, management must sell the new incentive plan to the sales force as a plan that is equal to or better than the one it is replacing. Ideally, the majority of the sales force (especially the better performers) should be convinced that the new plan presents an opportunity to improve their earnings. Cost modeling, especially incumbent-based cost modeling, with multiple simulations based on various performance levels goes a long way in selling the new incentive plan to the sales force.

You must project precisely the income each member of the sales force can expect to earn under the new plan. Then compare those projections with the individual incentive earnings that could be earned under the existing sales plan. The sales reps will undoubt-

(text continues on page 183)

Exhibit 14-2. Example of Distributional Cost Analysis.

Pay and Performance Assumptions

Job Title	Number	Prior Year Median Total Compensation	Current Year Target Total Compensation	Prior Year Median Sales Revenues	Current Year Target Sales Revenue	Mix Base	Incentive
Sales rep	100	$96,000	$100,000	$4,500,000	$5,000,000	60%	40%

Sales Rep Compensation Assumptions

Number	100	
Target total compensation	$100,000	
Mix		
Base	60%	$60,000
Incentive	40%	$40,000

Sales Force Performance Distribution Assumptions

	Level Performance (revenue vs. goal)					
	Threshold	Low	Target	High	Excellence	Total
Number of reps	10	20	40	20	10	100

(continues)

Incentive Payout Projections per Individual

	Level Performance (% of quota achieved)				
	Threshold (80%)	Low (90%)	Target (100%)	High (113%)	Excellence (125%)
Payout level	$0	$20,000	$40,000	$70,000	$100,000

Note: For low performance, the incentive payout equals incentive compensation opportunity ($40,000) times the weight (100 percent) times the level bonus rate (5.00 percent) times the level percentage points achieved (actual achieved [87.5] minus threshold [75.0]). Similar calculations are completed for the target, high, excellent, and threshold performance levels.

Incentive Payout Projections (under distribution assumptions)

	Threshold	Low	Target	High	Excellent	Total	Average per Incumbent	% of Target
Payout level	$0	$400,000	$1,600,000	$1,400,000	$1,000,000	$4,400,000	$44,000	110.0
Projected total incentive compensation						$4,400,000	$44,000	110.0
Projected total compensation (including base salary)							$104,000	104.0
Prior year median total compensation							$96,000	
Projected total compensation as a percentage of prior year total compensation							108.3%	

(continues)

Exhibit 14-2. (*continued*)

Individual Sales Rep Assumptions

Number	100
Target revenues	$5,000,000

Performance Measure

Revenue bonus	100% Weighting

Sales Force Performance Distribution Assumptions

	Level Performance (revenue vs. goal)					
	Threshold	*Low*	*Target*	*High*	*Excellence*	*Total*
Number of reps	10	20	40	20	10	100

Revenue Projections per Individual

	Level Performance (% of quota achieved)				
	Threshold *(80%)*	*Low* *(90%)*	*Target* *(100%)*	*High* *(113%)*	*Excellence* *(125%)*
Revenue versus goal	$4,000,000	$4,500,000	$5,000,000	$5,625,000	$6,250,000

Incentive Payout Projections

	Threshold	Low	Target	High	Excellence	Total	Average per Incumbent	% of Target
Revenue versus goal	$40,000,000	$90,000,000	$200,000,000	$112,500,000	$62,500,000	$505,000,000	$5,050,000	101.0
Projected sales revenue achieved						$505,000,000	$5,050,000	101.0
Prior year median sales revenue achieved							$4,500,000	
Projected sales revenue percentage of prior year sales revenue							112.2%	

Incentive Compensation Plan Costing Analysis Summary

	Prior Year Pay Levels			Current Year Projected Pay Levels			Variance From Current Pay Levels			
				Average per			Total		Per Incumbent	
Job Title	Median Total Compensation	Number	Total Compensation	Incumbent	Number	Total Compensation	$	%	$	%
Sales rep	$96,000	100	$9,600,000	$104,000	100	$10,400,000	$800,000	8.3%	$8,000	8.3%
Total	$96,000	100	$9,600,000	$104,000	100	$10,400,000	$800,000	8.3%	$8,000	8.3%
Prior year projected with current incentive plan						$9,984,000	$384,000	4.0%		
Projected cost/(savings) increase under new incentive plan[a]						$416,000				

[a]Based on an estimated average compounded annual increase in cash compensation expense of 4.0 percent.

(continues)

Exhibit 14-2. (*continued*)

Projected Sales Revenue Summary

	Prior Year Sales Levels			Current Year Projected Sales Levels			Variance From Current Sales Levels			
							Total		Per Incumbent	
Job Title	Median Total Sales Revenue	Number	Total Sales Revenue	Average per Incumbent	Number	Total Compensation	$	%	$	%
Sales rep	$4,500,000	100	$450,000,000	$5,050,000	100	$505,000,000	$55,000,000	12.2%	$550,000	12.2%
Total	$4,500,000	100	$450,000,000	$5,050,000	100	$505,000,000	$55,000,000	12.2%	$550,000	12.2%
Prior year projected sales given current incentive plan						$481,500,000	$31,500,000	7.0%		
Projected increase/(decrease) in sales under new incentive plan[a]						$23,500,000				

[a]Based on an estimated annual increase of 7.0 percent sales in current year.

Compensation as a Percentage of Sales

	Prior Year	Projected Year	Marginal Increase
Total compensation cost	$9,600,000	$10,400,000	$800,000
Total sales	$450,000,000	$505,000,000	$55,000,000
Compensation as a percentage of sales	2.13%	2.06%	1.45%

Exhibit 14-3. Example of Individual Cost Analysis.

Pay and Performance Assumptions

	Prior Year Target Total Compensation	Projected Number	Projected Target Total Compensation	Mix	
				Base	Incentive
Job Title					
Sales rep	$96,500	10	$100,000	60%	40%

Sales Rep Compensation Assumptions

Number	10	
Target total compensation	$100,000	
Mix		
Base	60%	$60,000
Incentive	40%	$40,000

(continues)

Exhibit 14-3. (*continued*)

Incumbent Model

Sales Rep	Current Base Salary	Annual Revenue Achieved[a]	Annual Revenue Target[a]	Annual Revenue % to Goal	Total Revenue Incentive	Total Earnings
Adams	$59,000	$4,900,000	$5,000,000	98.0%	$36,000	$95,000
Brown	$57,500	$5,000,000	$5,000,000	100.0%	$40,000	$97,500
Cramer	$58,000	$4,945,000	$5,000,000	98.9%	$37,800	$95,800
Douglass	$61,000	$4,532,000	$5,000,000	90.6%	$21,280	$82,280
Espinoza	$60,500	$5,980,000	$5,000,000	119.6%	$87,040	$147,540
Faragamo	$60,000	$5,678,000	$5,000,000	113.6%	$72,544	$132,544
Gugliotta	$59,000	$5,180,000	$5,000,000	103.6%	$48,640	$107,640
Howard	$63,000	$4,302,000	$5,000,000	86.0%	$12,080	$75,080
Isle	$61,500	$5,230,000	$5,000,000	104.6%	$51,040	$112,540
Jones	$56,000	$4,890,000	$5,000,000	97.8%	$35,600	$91,600
Projected sales rep compensation		$50,637,000	$50,000,000	101.3%	$442,024	$1,037,524
Average per sales rep					$44,202	$103,752
Percentage of target					110.5%	103.8%
Current target total compensation						$96,500
Projected total compensation as a percentage of current target total compensation						107.5%

[a]Annual revenue achieved and annual revenue target input data represent actual historical performance.

Current Target Total Compensation/Performance Relative to Projected Compensation/Performance (at prior year performance levels)

Name	Job Title	Current Target Total Compensation	Projected Pay Level	Variance From Current Target Pay Levels	
				$	%
Adams	Sales rep	$96,000	$95,000	($1,000)	−1.0%
Brown	Sales rep	$94,500	$97,500	$3,000	3.2%
Cramer	Sales rep	$95,000	$95,800	$800	0.8%
Douglass	Sales rep	$98,000	$82,280	($15,720)	−16.0%
Espinoza	Sales rep	$97,000	$147,540	$50,540	52.1%
Faragamo	Sales rep	$97,000	$132,544	$35,544	36.6%
Gugliotta	Sales rep	$96,000	$107,640	$11,640	12.1%
Howard	Sales rep	$100,000	$75,080	($24,920)	−24.9%
Isle	Sales rep	$98,500	$112,540	$14,040	14.3%
Jones	Sales rep	$93,000	$91,600	($1,400)	−1.5%
Total		$965,000	$1,037,524	$72,524	7.5%
Prior year projected with current incentive plan			$1,003,600	$38,600	4.0%
Projected increase/(decrease) under new incentive plan[a]			($33,924)		

[a]Based on an estimated average compounded annual increase in cash compensation expense of 4.0 percent.

(continues)

Exhibit 14-3. (*continued*)

Name	Job Title	Prior Year Sales	Projected Sales	Variance From Current Target Sales Levels	
				$	%
Adams	Sales rep	$4,672,897	$4,900,000	$227,103	4.9%
Brown	Sales rep	$4,672,897	$5,000,000	$327,103	7.0%
Cramer	Sales rep	$4,672,897	$4,945,000	$272,103	5.8%
Douglass	Sales rep	$4,672,897	$4,532,000	($140,897)	−3.0%
Espinoza	Sales rep	$4,672,897	$5,980,000	$1,307,103	28.0%
Faragamo	Sales rep	$4,672,897	$5,678,000	$1,005,103	21.5%
Gugliotta	Sales rep	$4,672,897	$5,180,000	$507,103	10.9%
Howard	Sales rep	$4,672,897	$4,302,000	($370,897)	−7.9%
Isle	Sales rep	$4,672,897	$5,230,000	$557,103	11.9%
Jones	Sales rep	$4,672,897	$4,890,000	$217,103	4.6%
Total		$46,728,972	$50,637,000	$3,908,028	8.4%
Prior year projected sales with current incentive plan			$50,000,000	$3,271,028	7.0%
Projected increase/(decrease) under new incentive plan[a]			$637,000		

[a]Based on an estimated average compounded annual increase in sales of 7.0 percent.

Compensation as a Percentage of Sales

	Prior Year	Projected Year	Marginal Increase
Total compensation cost	$965,000	$1,037,524	$72,524
Total sales	$46,728,972	$50,637,000	$3,908,028
Compensation as a percentage of sales	2.07%	2.05%	1.86%

edly do these calculations once they receive the new sales incentive plan!

As before, let's assume that the ABC Company sales force is ten sales reps and that management has recently redesigned the sales incentive plan to mirror the one already presented for the par performer (see Exhibit 14-1A). Recall that the average annual salary is $60,000 and the target annual incentive is $40,000. The sales revenue bonus table was set out on page 171. An example individual costing for the new incentive plan is presented in Exhibit 14-3.

15

Plan Documentation

After you have designed the new incentive plan and determined its cost, you should provide the sales reps with a written description of its mechanics. This part of the implementation and communication process is vital to the success of the program. The plan document will serve as a permanent record of the new incentive plan, readily available as reference to the sales reps.

A comprehensive description of the new incentive plan, the plan document is intended to serve an audience of sales, sales management, and sales administrative personnel. It typically includes a summary of plan structure, a statement of corporate compensation philosophy, a detailed description of the plan's components, incentive calculation examples, and relevant administrative policies.

15.1 Compensation Plan Overview

Typically the first section in a plan document, the overview captures the essence of the new incentive plan in a single page. It highlights the plan objectives, the plan principles, the mix of compensation, the plan components, and the performance measures. Often the corporate compensation philosophy is included in this section of the document.

Exhibit 15-1 contains a sample compensation plan overview section. In this example, we assume that the new incentive plan has a 70/30 percent pay mix and is based on two performance measures: revenue versus quota and product mix. Paid monthly, the revenue measurement is in the form of a bonus that reflects performance each month on a year-to-date basis. The product mix measure is a multiplier that measures performance year to date. It is calculated and paid quarterly.

15.2 Plan Description

The second section of a typical plan document is the detailed plan description. As the title suggests, it describes the mechanics of how the new sales compensation plan works.

Exhibit 15-1. Sample Compensation Plan Overview Section.

Plan objectives	This incentive compensation plan has four important objectives: 1. Promote the achievement of revenue goals. 2. Ensure a balanced selling emphasis across all products. 3. Motivate the sales force to sell what is right for the customer. 4. Reward exceptional performance with outstanding incentive earnings opportunities.
Plan principles	The key principles of the incentive compensation plan are: 1. Clearly identify performance objectives and the keys to success. 2. Link compensation to performance in areas that sales reps can directly influence. 3. Reward sales reps for performance that supports the company's objectives.
Pay mix	Pay mix is the split between base salary and the target incentive amount, both expressed as a percentage of target total cash compensation at expected levels of performance (quota). Generally the mix of incentive compensation is 70 percent base salary and 30 percent incentive pay, assuming planned or 100 percent quota performance.
Plan components	The incentive compensation plan consists of three elements: 1. Base salary. 2. Monthly revenue bonus. 3. Quarterly product mix multiplier.
Performance measures	The two performance measures reps can directly affect are: 1. Revenue versus quota. 2. Product mix.

The first segment of this section describes how the base salary will be paid. Here you might wish to explain briefly the rationale behind base salary adjustments, if included in the plan design, and management's expectations for performance reimbursed by the salary.

Next comes the description of the incentive portion of the compensation plan. In this segment detail the incentive plan structure for each performance measure. Describe the incentive formula type (e.g., commission, bonus), the performance methodology (whether the plan component pays out on a discrete or cumulative basis over a specified time period), the payout frequency, and how incentive earnings are calculated (as a percentage of sales dollars, like a commission, or as a percentage of the annual component incentive amount, like a bonus). Also include an incentive rate table in this section, highlighting the accelerator and decelerator points in the incentive plan.

Typically the next segment highlights how to calculate incentive earnings for the designated time period. This is often best communicated in two forms: describing the calculation in words and then pictorially detailing how the incentive earnings are calculated. The final segment in this section describes how to calculate the total incentive earnings for the designated time period. This too should be communicated in both the written and pictorial formats. Exhibit 15-2 illustrates the various segments of a sample plan description.

15.3 Incentive Calculation Examples

The third section of a typical plan document provides examples detailing how the new incentive plan works. This section is typically the lengthiest of the plan document. If the final document appears too long, it may be placed in an appendix.

Throughout the year, the sales reps will use this section frequently. The first part contains a list of target incentive and performance assumptions, which are the basis for determining the sales rep incentive earnings in the various examples. Next, the incentive example shows how to calculate the incentive earnings based on the given assumptions. The example should be presented in a sequential step format. For instance, the incentive calculation example for the incentive plan described in Exhibit 15-1 should involve a number of steps showing how to determine the year-to-date percentage of revenue quota achieved for each month, how to use this information and the bonus revenue charts to determine monthly revenue bonus earnings, how to calculate the year-to-date percentage of quota achieved for each product mix category for each quarter, and, finally, how to use the product mix information and the quarterly product mix multiplier schedule to determine product mix multiplier earnings.

A step-by-step calculation example for the incentive plan described in Exhibit 15-1 follows. It illustrates the incentive calculation steps for the monthly revenue bonus and the quarterly product mix multiplier. Key assumptions include:

Exhibit 15-2. Sample Plan Description.

Base salary. Base salary is paid biweekly. Annual performance evaluations provide the opportunity for base salary increases, but they are not guaranteed for each year.

Monthly revenue bonus. The monthly revenue bonus is based on performance against a revenue quota. Revenue versus quota performance is measured on a year-to-date (cumulative) basis. Bonus earnings are calculated as a percentage of the annual target revenue bonus amount.

Bonus rates are expressed in a bonus schedule format. Bonus earnings increase as performance against the year-to-date revenue quota improves. The performance range (e.g., year-to-date percentage of quota achieved) and the bonus rates differ for stable and growth markets. The monthly bonus schedule is as follows:

Year-to-Date Percentage of Quota Achieved		Bonus Rate (% target bonus per % goal achieved)	
Stable Markets	Growth Markets	Stable Markets	Growth Markets
125.1%+	140.1%+	6.0%	4.0%
100.1–125.0%	100.1–140.0%	7.2	4.5
75.1–100.0%	70.1–100.0%	4.0	3.3

Monthly revenue bonus earnings. To determine the bonus rate to be used each month, calculate the year-to-date percentage of revenue quota achieved. The bonus rate is found on the row of the bonus schedule corresponding to the year-to-date percentage of quota achieved. The bonus schedule is incremental. For example, in a stable market, for revenue performance between 75.1 percent and 100.0 percent of quota, 4.0 percent of the target bonus is earned for each percentage point of revenue quota achieved within that level; for revenue performance between 100.1 percent and 125.0 percent of quota, in addition to the 4.0 percent earned in the first level, 7.2 percent of the target bonus is earned for each percentage point of revenue quota achieved in this second level; and for revenue performance over 125.0 percent of quota, in addition to the 4.0 percent earned in the first level and the 7.2 percent earned in the second level, 6.0 percent of the target bonus is earned for each percentage point of revenue quota achieved in this third level.

To calculate each month the year-to-date revenue bonus earnings, multiply the bonus rate as determined on the schedule by the quota percentage points achieved for each level of performance, and then by the year-to-date target bonus amount. Finally, subtract the bonus earnings already paid in previous months. Here is the formula:

$$\text{Bonus rate} \times \begin{matrix} \text{Quota} \\ \text{percentage} \\ \text{points for} \\ \text{each level of} \\ \text{performance} \end{matrix} \times \begin{matrix} \text{Year-to-date} \\ \text{target bonus} \end{matrix} - \begin{matrix} \text{Previous} \\ \text{month's} \\ \text{bonus} \\ \text{earnings} \end{matrix} = \begin{matrix} \text{Monthly} \\ \text{revenue} \\ \text{bonus} \\ \text{earnings} \end{matrix}$$

(continues)

Exhibit 15-2. (*continued*)

Quarterly product mix multiplier. Quarterly earnings are driven by performance against a product mix objective. This is measured as the simple average percentage of quotas achieved by the sales rep for all four product categories combined during the quarter. Other product categories may be added at any time, as appropriate. Performance against the four category quotas is measured on a year-to-date basis.

Multiplier earnings are calculated as a percentage of the year-to-date revenue bonus earnings. Multiplier rates increase as overall product mix performance improves. To be eligible for any multiplier earnings, your performance must be at least 70 percent of quota for each product category. To be eligible for upside (over-target) multiplier earnings, your performance must be at least 95 percent of quota for each product category.

Quarterly multiplier earnings. To determine the multiplier rate to use each quarter, calculate the year-to-date average product mix percentage of quota achieved for all four product categories combined. The multiplier rate to use is found on the row of the multiplier schedule corresponding to the average percentage achieved:

Average Percentage of Combined Product Quotas Achieved	Multiplier Rate (% of quarterly revenue bonus earnings)
120.0%+	42.9%
110.0–119.9%	38.0
100.0–109.9%	33.3
87.5–99.9%	20.0
75.0–87.4%	10.0

To calculate the quarterly multiplier earnings, multiply the quarterly revenue bonus earnings by the multiplier rate as determined on the schedule, and then subtract the multiplier earnings paid in previous quarters:

$$\begin{matrix} \text{Quarterly} \\ \text{revenue bonus} \\ \text{earnings} \end{matrix} \times \text{Multiplier rate} - \begin{matrix} \text{Previous} \\ \text{quarters'} \\ \text{multiplier} \\ \text{earnings} \end{matrix} = \begin{matrix} \text{Final quarterly} \\ \text{multiplier} \\ \text{earnings} \end{matrix}$$

Total incentive earnings. To calculate the total incentive earnings for the year, add the sum of monthly revenue bonus earnings to the four quarterly product mix multiplier payouts:

$$\begin{matrix} \text{Sum of monthly} \\ \text{revenue bonus} \\ \text{earnings} \end{matrix} + \begin{matrix} \text{Sum of quarterly} \\ \text{product mix multiplier} \\ \text{earnings} \end{matrix} = \begin{matrix} \text{Total annual incentive} \\ \text{earnings} \end{matrix}$$

Target total cash compensation:	$75,000
Plan pay mix:	70/30%
Base salary:	$52,500
Target incentive:	$22,500
Sales market:	Stable

The sales rep's target incentive and actual performance assumptions for this example are presented in Exhibit 15-3, with the full calculation of incentive earnings in Exhibit 15-4.

15.4 Administrative Policies and Practices

No plan document would be complete without a section that delineates the sales incentive plan administrative provisions. It is important to have a written record of these items so that the sales rep can refer to them at any time. The written record also virtually eliminates the subjective nature of some policy interpretation. When a rep has concern over the interpretation of a certain policy, this section should answer most questions that may arise.

Prior to publication, this section (and perhaps the whole document) should be reviewed thoroughly by the legal department to ensure that the plan policies are in accordance with the intent of the law. This section also serves as a legal document if a sales compensation dispute arises between the company and a current or former sales rep.

Several key topics should be covered in this section. It is imperative to state when the plan goes into effect and the length of the plan. Base salary and incentive payment timing and administration procedures should be highlighted, informing the sales rep how and how often each component of the compensation plan will be paid. The segment should detail those who are eligible for sales incentive payments. Items concerning actual incentive plan payments, such as overpayments and guarantees, need to be explicitly stated so as to avoid future confusion over these topics. This section should highlight management's policies on sales crediting, returns, changes, terminations, and pay advances. If management chooses to reserve the right to amend or modify the sales incentive plan at any time, this section should include this statement of fact.

The topical list shown in Exhibit 15-5 is by no means exhaustive, but it does include some of the items found in most sales incentive plan documents.

(text continues on page 198)

Exhibit 15-3. Incentive Calculation Assumptions.

Target Incentive Assumptions

Incentive Component	Weighting	Target Monthly Bonus	Target Quarterly Bonus	Target Annual Bonus
Revenue	75%	$1,406	$4,219	$16,875
Product Mix	25%	NA	$1,406	$5,625
Total	100%	$1,406	$5,625	$22,500

Revenue Performance Assumptions

Performance Period	Year-to-Date Revenue	Year-to-Date Revenue Quota
January	$140,000	$125,000
February	$275,000	$260,000

Product Mix Performance Assumptions

Performance Period	Product Category 1		Product Category 2		Product Category 3		Product Category 4	
	YTD Revenue	YTD Quota	YTD Revenue	YTD Quota	YTD Revenue	YTD Quota	YTD Revenue	YTD Quota
First quarter	$310,000	$300,000	$55,000	$50,000	$12,000	$12,500	$13,000	$12,500

Exhibit 15-4. Step-by-Step Incentive Earnings Calculation Example.

Step 1. Calculate the year-to-date percentage of revenue quota achieved for January.

January year-to-date revenue achieved		January year-to-date revenue quota		January year-to-date percentage of quota achieved
	÷		=	
$140,000		$125,000		112.0%

The January year-to-date percentage of revenue quota achieved is 112.0 percent.

Step 2. Using the revenue bonus schedule, determine the bonus rate for January year-to-date quota performance of 112.0 percent.

Monthly Revenue Bonus

Year-to-Date Percentage of Quota Achieved		Bonus Rate (% target bonus per % goal achieved)	
Stable Markets	*Growth Markets*	*Stable Markets*	*Growth Markets*
125.1%+	140.1%+	6.0%	4.0%
100.1–125.0%	*100.1–140.0%*	*7.2*	*4.5*
75.1–100.0%	*70.1–100.0%*	*4.0*	*3.3*

For January year-to-date quota performance of 112.0 percent, the bonus rate is 4.0 percent for the 75.1–100.0 percent level, and 7.2 percent for the 100.1–125.0 percent level.

Step 3. Calculate the percentage points achieved in each performance level.

January year-to-date target/actual percentage of quota achieved		Threshold percentage of quota		Level 1 percentage points achieved
	−		=	
100.0%		75.0%		25.0

January year-to-date excellence/actual percentage of quota achieved		Target percentage of quota		Level 2 percentage points achieved
	−		=	
112.0%		100.0%		12.0

The January year-to-date level 1 percentage points achieved are 25.0, and the January year-to-date level 2 percentage points achieved are 12.0.

(*continues*)

Exhibit 15-4. (*continued*)

Step 4. Calculate the January revenue bonus earnings.

January year-to-date target bonus		Level 1 percentage points achieved		Level 1 bonus rate		Level 1 January revenue bonus earnings
$1,406	×	25.0	×	4.0%	=	$1,406

January year-to-date target bonus		Level 2 percentage points achieved		Level 2 bonus rate		Level 2 January revenue bonus earnings
$1,406	×	12.0	×	7.2%	=	$1,215

Level 1 January revenue bonus earnings		Level 2 January revenue bonus earnings		Previous month's bonus earnings		January bonus earnings
$1,406	+	$1,215	−	$0	=	$2,621

The January total revenue bonus earnings are $2,621.

Step 5. Calculate the year-to-date percentage of revenue quota achieved for February.

February year-to-date revenue achieved		February year-to-date revenue quota		February year-to-date percentage of quota achieved
$275,000	÷	$260,000	=	105.8%

The February year-to-date percentage of revenue quota achieved is 105.8 percent.

Step 6. Using the revenue bonus schedule, determine the bonus rate for February year-to-date quota performance of 105.8%.

Monthly Revenue Bonus

Year-to-Date Percentage of Quota Achieved		Bonus Rate (% target bonus per % goal achieved)	
Stable Markets	*Growth Markets*	*Stable Markets*	*Growth Markets*
125.1%+	140.1%+	6.0%	4.0%
100.1–125.0%	100.1–140.0%	*7.2*	4.5
75.1–100.0%	70.1–100.0%	*4.0*	3.3

For February year-to-date quota performance of 105.8 percent, the bonus rate is 4.0 percent for the 75.1–100.0 percent level and 7.2 percent for the 100.1–125.0 percent level.

Step 7. Calculate the percentage points achieved in each performance level.

February year-to-date target/actual percentage of quota achieved	−	Threshold percentage of quota	=	Level 1 percentage points achieved
100.0%		75.0%		25.0

February year-to-date excellence/actual percentage of quota achieved	−	Target percentage of quota	=	Level 2 percentage points achieved
105.8%		100.0%		5.8

The February year-to-date level 1 percentage points achieved are 25.0, and the February year-to-date level 2 percentage points achieved are 5.8.

Step 8. Calculate the February year-to-date target revenue bonus amount.

Target annual revenue bonus	÷	Number of months in a year	×	Number of months transpired	=	February year-to-date target bonus
$16,875		12		2		$2,813

The February year-to-date target revenue bonus amount is $2,813.

Step 9. Calculate the February revenue bonus earnings.

February year-to-date target bonus	×	Level 1 percentage points achieved	×	Level 1 bonus rate	=	Level 1 February year-to-date revenue bonus earnings
$2,813		25.0		4.0%		$2,813

February year-to-date target bonus	×	Level 2 percentage points achieved	×	Level 2 bonus rate	=	Level 2 February year-to-date revenue bonus earnings
$2,813		5.8		7.2%		$1,175

(continues)

Exhibit 15-4. *(continued)*

Level 1 February year- to-date revenue + bonus earnings	Level 2 February year- to-date revenue − bonus earnings	Previous month's bonus earnings (January) =	February bonus earnings
$2,813	$1,175	$2,621	$1,367

The February total revenue bonus earnings are $1,367.

Step 10. Calculate the February year-to-date revenue bonus earnings.

January bonus earnings	February bonus earnings	February year-to-date total revenue bonus earnings
$2,621 +	$1,367 =	$3,988

The February year-to-date revenue bonus earnings are $3,988.
   Assume the March total revenue bonus earnings are $1,972; therefore, the March year-to-date revenue bonus earnings are $5,960.

Step 11. For March, calculate the year-to-date percentage of quota achieved for each product category.

March year-to-date product category 1 revenue achieved ÷	March year-to-date product category 1 quota =	March year-to-date percentage of quota achieved
$310,000	$300,000	103.3%
March year-to-date product category 2 revenue achieved ÷	March year-to-date product category 2 quota =	March year-to-date percentage of quota achieved
$55,000	$50,000	110.0%
March year-to-date product category 3 revenue achieved ÷	March year-to-date product category 3 quota =	March year-to-date percentage of quota achieved
$12,000	$12,500	96.0%
March year-to-date product category 4 revenue achieved ÷	March year-to-date product category 4 quota =	March year-to-date percentage of quota achieved
$13,000	$12,500	104.0%

For March year-to-date, product category 1 quota performance is 103.3 percent, product category 2 quota performance is 110.0 percent, product category 3 quota performance is 96.0 percent, and product category 4 quota performance is 104.0 percent.

Because quota performance for all four categories is above the 75 percent threshold, the sales rep is eligible for quarterly multiplier earnings. Because quota performance for all four categories is above the 90 percent threshold, the sales rep is eligible for quarterly upside (over target) multiplier earnings.

Step 12. For March, calculate the year-to-date simple average percentage of quota achieved for product mix.

March year-to-date percentage of product category 1 quota achieved		March year-to-date percentage of product category 2 quota achieved		March year-to-date percentage of product category 3 quota achieved		March year-to-date percentage of product category 4 quota achieved		Number of product mix categories		March year-to-date simple average product mix % of quotas achieved
103.3%	+	110.0%	+	96.0%	+	104.0%	÷	4	=	103.3%

The March (quarter 1) year-to-date simple average product mix percentage of quota achieved is 103.3 percent.

Step 13. Using the product mix multiplier schedule, determine the appropriate multiplier rate associated with the March year-to-date average percentage of product quota achieved of 103.3 percent.

Quarterly Product Mix Multiplier

Average Percentage of Combined Product Quotas Achieved	*Multiplier Rate (% of quarterly revenue bonus earnings)*
120.0%+	42.9%
110.0–119.9%	38.0
100.0–109.9%	*33.3*
87.5–99.9%	20.0
75.0–87.4%	10.0

The multiplier rate is 33.3 percent.

(*continues*)

Exhibit 15-4. (*continued*)

Step 14. Calculate the March (quarter 1) product mix multiplier earnings.

March year-to-date revenue bonus earnings	×	March year-to-date multiplier rate	−	Previous quarter's multiplier earnings	=	Quarter 1 year-to-date product mix multiplier earnings
$5,960		33.3%		$0		$1,985

The first quarter product mix multiplier earnings are $1,985.

Step 15. Calculate the year-to-date total incentive earnings through March (quarter 1).

March year-to-date total revenue bonus earnings	+	Quarter 1 year-to-date product mix multiplier earnings	=	March year-to-date total incentive earnings
$5,960		$1,985		$7,945

The March year-to-date total incentive earnings are $7,945.

Exhibit 15-5. Suggested Administrative Provisions.

- Eligibility provisions

- Definitions of key terms and glossary

- Plan start date and duration
    —Timing of payments

- Employment changes
    —New employees
    —Termination (voluntary and involuntary)
    —Retirement
    —Death

- Status changes
    —Transfers to new position or promotions
    —Sales territory changes
    —Disability
    —Vacation provisions
    —Leaves of absence

- Handling of account changes and events
    - —House accounts
    - —Unexpected windfalls
    - —Account transfers and hand-offs to others

- Business expense reimbursements

- Adjustments to incentive calculations
    - —Crediting a sale for incentive purposes
    - —Order cancellations, returns, and corrections
    - —Credit sharing and splits

- Linkage with other programs
    - —Performance management
    - —Merit pay
    - —Benefits (retirement, health, 401(k), etc.)
    - —Noncash recognition

- Quota and goal setting and adjustment procedures

- Plan modification and periodic review

- Adjudication and authority for changes
    - —Handling of exceptions

Exhibit 15-6. Sample Administrative Provisions.

Various plan administration issues affect the payout and administration of the incentive compensation plan. These administrative issues are detailed below:

Base salary administration. Base salaries will be administered in accordance with the company's standard salary administration policies.

Incentive payment timing. The monthly revenue bonus and the quarterly product mix multiplier earnings will be paid within one month after the close of the performance period.

Incentive eligibility. Sales reps who are employed in this job are immediately eligible for the monthly revenue bonus. Sales reps are eligible for quarterly product mix multiplier earnings in a given quarter if they have been employed in a territory for at least sixty calendar days.

Incentive overpayments. In the event of a monthly, quarterly, or year-end incentive overpayment under the monthly revenue bonus or the quarterly product mix multiplier, the amount of the overpayment will be deducted from future bonus or multiplier earnings.

(continues)

Exhibit 15-6. *(continued)*

Management discretion. Management will establish the performance ranges for the monthly revenue bonus and quarterly product mix multiplier at its sole discretion. Management reserves the right to amend or change the incentive compensation program at any time.

Guarantee. For the first six months of employment and participation in this plan, the participant is guaranteed a minimum of 50 percent of the monthly target revenue bonus as calculated from the territory agreement. During this guarantee period, revenue bonus calculations will be made as usual. The revenue bonus amount will be compared to the guarantee amount; the greater of the two amounts will be paid. The guarantee is not a draw against future revenue earnings.

Revenue. The monthly revenue bonus will be paid on both new sales and renewals. The monthly revenue bonus is based on the individual revenue achieved versus quota.

Sales credit. Each sales rep will be paid the revenue bonus on all sales booked in his or her territory. Sales credit will be at the order price minus discounts or distributors' commissions. Each sales rep will also be credited based on assigned accounts. Exceptions can be determined at any time during the plan year and are documented separately.

Returns. Any amount credited back to the customer will be deducted from the responsible sales rep's sales when the customer credit is granted.

Advances. The company will pay no advances against future bonus earnings.

Changes to the plan. Changes, additions, or exceptions to this sales incentive compensation plan require written approval of the Vice President of U.S. Sales. Changes to any territory agreements require the agreement of two levels of management. Any such change will be communicated to the participant and acknowledged by him or her in writing. Unless otherwise specified, amendments will be effective immediately but will not apply retroactively. If an employee wants to appeal the implementation of the sales incentive compensation plan, the appeal should be made to the Vice President of U.S. Sales.

Termination. In the event of a participant's termination of employment, the company will pay the participant's salary and incentive earned through the date of termination. Bonus and multiplier earnings will be calculated on credited sales, net of any deductions, through the final day of work.

General provisions. Participation in this plan is not a guarantee of employment for any specified period of time, and the company reserves the right to dismiss or discharge any participant at any time. Participants may not sell products or services for any other company or individual in connection with any transaction in which this company may be involved.

Effective dates. Prior pay arrangements for the sales reps will terminate and this plan will go into effect on April 1, 1999. The plan will remain in effect until further notice.

Continuing with our illustrative incentive plan, Exhibit 15-6 shows a portion of the actual administrative policies for that plan.

15.5 Territory Agreement

When you give the sales rep a copy of the plan document, schedule a meeting to discuss the details of the plan, specifically concentrating on plan description and examples. At the end of the meeting, inform the sales rep of his or her annual quotas. To show acceptance of the sales quotas (and of the provisions of the sales incentive plan), many companies develop a territory agreement document for the sales manager and the sales rep to sign. This territory agreement allows space for both the annual quota and the annual target incentive for each incentive component, so there is no confusion on the part of the sales rep over the expected performance levels for the measurement period and the amounts to be earned if quotas are reached.

16

Implementing the Sales Compensation Program

Communication and implementation of a new sales incentive plan is one of the most critical aspects of an effective program. While management may take several months gathering facts and analyzing background information, interviewing key internal stakeholders, conducting market-pricing analysis, and developing incentive plan recommendations, these design efforts may be in vain if the rollout of the plan is not clearly thought out and well implemented. Here are the key elements in the implementation phase:

1. Developing a master plan to guide implementation activities related to the rollout of the new incentive plan: a detailed work plan, time line, key milestones, and accountabilities.
2. Formally documenting the technical specifics of the new incentive plan for each position.
3. Packaging the key messages into compelling communication and presentation materials:
    —Executive overview of the new plans.
    —Train-the-trainer presentation to equip sales managers to deliver the details of the incentive plans to the direct sellers.
    —Detailed breakout session presentations for sales managers to deliver to their subordinates.
    —Anticipated questions with appropriate responses.
    —Earnings calculation worksheet for each position incumbent.
4. Defining the system programming requirements used by company personnel to ensure accurate and timely incentive plan administration.
5. Training the sales managers and incentive plan administra-

tion personnel in the specifics of the new plans by developing the required training materials.

16.1 Work Plan Summary

The first step in communicating and implementing the new sales incentive plan is to develop a *work plan summary*. It provides the framework for implementation and helps focus the work team on the expected results, key project milestones, and anticipated completion dates. Exhibit 16-1 shows a suggested work plan summary, with expected results.

16.2 Employee Focus Groups

The success of the transition from an old to a new incentive plan largely depends on management's ability to convince the sales reps that the new program can provide a "better deal." In this regard, communicating the plan means *selling* the plan to the sales force.

One of the best ways to do this is to conduct a number of employee focus groups prior to creating the final plan documentation and communication materials. At this time, you can solicit the sales reps' and sales managers' opinions of the new incentive plan and gather an understanding of the potential responses to questions about it. (Later, when communicating the new plan, you will indicate that sales force input was used in analyzing the old plan and considering alternative designs.) You can also use the focus group as a way to refine the implementation plan. In this way, the new plan offers a potentially "better deal" in that it reflects the sales force's perceptions and comments.

During the focus groups, discuss the strategic rationale behind the new incentive plan. Sales reps often feel that their sales compensation plan was developed in a haphazard way. Communicating to them that the new plan is based on the company's business and marketing strategies improves the chances that they will view the plan as a realistic enforcement of those goals.

Communicate as well that management modeled and tested the new plan as part of the development process. The testing included a sensitivity analysis to evaluate potential incentive payouts at various performance levels. Communicating to the sales force that this step was included adds a strong measure of credibility that the new plan

Exhibit 16-1. Suggested Work Plan Summary.

1. Develop master implementation plan.
   a. Detailed work plan steps
   b. Time line
   c. Identification of key milestones
   d. Assignment of accountability for each key deliverable

2. Conduct employee focus groups.
   a. Understanding of range of potential responses to and questions about the new incentive plans
   b. Refined implementation plan to account for focus group feedback

3. Develop incentive plan documentation to serve as stand-alone reference documents for the new plans.
   a. Statement of corporate compensation philosophy
   b. Detailed incentive plan description
   c. Incentive calculation examples
   d. Administration policies and practices
   e. Territory agreements

4. Develop communication materials, including presentations and training aids.
   a. Executive overview presentation
   b. Train-the-trainer presentation
   c. Detailed breakout session presentation
   d. Question and answer document
   e. Earnings calculation worksheet

5. Conduct implementation team meetings.
   a. Progress updates on all aspects of the implementation plan
   b. Review of draft plan documentation and communication materials

6. Conduct information technology meetings.
   a. Programming of systems to administer sales incentive plans

7. Hold senior management meetings.
   a. Approval of implementation approach and communication materials

8. Initiate train-the-trainer sessions.
   a. Sales managers and sales incentive plan administration personnel trained on the specifics of the new incentive plans
   b. Sales managers prepared to train their assigned sales personnel on the new plans

9. Develop checklist of key items to assist in postimplementation audit.
   a. Corporate and sales personnel equipped with the appropriate tools to conduct the audit, including a checklist to assess the effectiveness of the implementation effort and an understanding of the analyses used to determine whether plan modifications are required

provides reasonable earnings opportunities and that flaws have been removed during the test runs.

16.3   Incentive Plan Documentation

The sales reps should receive a copy of the written plan document at the beginning of the fiscal year. Intended to be the standard reference for sales, sales management, and sales administrative personnel, the plan document typically includes a summary of the plan structure, a statement of corporate compensation philosophy, a detailed description of the plan's components, incentive calculation examples, and relevant administrative policies.

A compensation plan overview summarizes the essence of the new incentive plan into a single page. The overview highlights the plan objectives, the plan principles, the mix of compensation, the plan components, and the performance measures. Often the corporate compensation philosophy is included in this section of the document. The plan description section describes in detail how the new sales compensation plan works, and the incentive calculation examples show the sales rep how to calculate the incentive earnings based on the given assumptions. The example should be presented in a sequential step format. No plan document would be complete without a section that highlights the administrative provisions. It is important to have a written record of these items so that the sales rep can refer to them at any time. Chapter 15 detailed the components of the incentive plan document.

16.4   Training Materials

At the very least, provide the sales force with a printed incentive plan document, describing the new plan and its mechanics. Supplement this information with presentations and training materials to facilitate the communication effort and ensure field commitment to the new incentive plans.

Executive Overview Presentation

The executive overview presentation gives the overall perspective on why the incentive plan has changed and what specifically is different. The presentation should provide background information for management to reference when they are performing some of the tangential functions for the new sales incentive plan, such as territory allocation and goal setting. Some of the potential topics that you might want to cover during this presentation include:

- Pay plan design process and participants
- Rationale for change
- Overview of the new plan, including concepts, components, and sample calculations
- Pay transition plan
- Implications for sales management (including cost estimates)

The executive overview should include a summary of the key findings about the current plan from the fact-finding effort. You should inform the audience about how the new incentive plan was designed (such as using a compensation committee or whether an external consultant was hired), how competitive pay levels were analyzed, whether field interviews were conducted, and how field management review and approval was obtained. To help build commitment for the plan, the presentation should state who was on the compensation committee and who provided input for the new plan, and you should also inform your audience why the new pay plan was designed (perhaps there is a new organization structure or the external environment has changed).

The executive overview should detail the similarities between the new and old plans and point out the main differences in the new plan. A key concept to be included is that the plan is designed to reinforce the business direction and objectives and will help the sales force attain specific strategic and sales management goals.

The next section of the executive overview should help educate the audience on the mechanics of the new incentive plan. First review the components (base salary and incentive pay) and the performance measures (revenue, gross margin and growth) of the new plan. Next, review some of the key compensation concepts to educate the audience on the meaning of compensation terms. Note all of the concepts used in the design of the new plan, including definitions for target total cash compensation, base salary ranges, incentive component weights, commissions, bonuses, and multipliers. Show tables depicting the incentive plan measures, weights, and payout timing for each position. Follow this information with a simple example of how each component of the new incentive plan works.

The last segment of the overview should detail the pay transition plan and the implications for sales management. Explain how the transition will occur, including the key objectives for transition.

Discuss too how the new pay plan will change the way sales managers will manage in the field. For example, if the new plan requires precision goal setting, inform the audience how the company will support new goal-setting procedures, such as using improved market potential information or revising the goal adjustment policies and practices. Then show the audience the expected implementation time frame and planned sequence of events. The final section should summarize the pros and cons of the plan and explain the need for and the benefits of change.

Train-the-Trainer Presentation

The objective of the train-the-trainer session is to teach the first- and second-level sales managers about the fundamentals of the new sales incentive plan. Once they have a proficient knowledge of the sales incentive plan mechanics, they will be better equipped to communicate the plan to their direct reports. Rely on them to be the principal standard-bearers for the new pay plan.

During the implementation period, the sales managers should expect an onslaught of questions from the field, and they must be prepared to answer them.

The training session should inform the sales managers that their role is critical to the success of the overall implementation effort. To that end, expect them to perform a number of crucial functions in the implementation process, including, but not limited to, the following:

- Conducting a sales incentive compensation training session for their direct reports.
- Assessing territory potential and setting goals for their area.
- Conducting individual planning sessions with each of their direct reports.
- Responding to inquiries from employees not participating in the sales incentive plan.
- Channeling ongoing constructive feedback to the appropriate resources.

The training session should cover a number of key topics pertaining to the new incentive plan, including:

- The rationale for creating the new sales incentive plan.
- The process used to develop the sales incentive plan.
- The incentive plan details, including target and upside incen-

tive earnings levels, performance measures, and incentive plan mechanics.

- A detailed incentive plan calculation example.
- The next steps in the implementation effort.

The train-the-trainer session should inform the managers about the rationale for implementing the new incentive plan. A couple of possible reasons might be that the current reward structure lacks a comprehensive incentive plan that rewards sales personnel for their contributions or that a comprehensive sales incentive plan is needed to remain competitive with the prevalent market sales compensation practices. After describing the reason for designing the plan, reiterate the goals for the project. Sample goals might include developing a higher-performing sales organization, rewarding salespeople for their contributions to the success of the company, and supporting the company's primary business objective (for example, promoting profitable revenue growth). At this time you should also remind them that the sales incentive plan represents only one piece of the puzzle. Sales managers should view the sales incentive plan as but one of the many tools they can use to drive and reinforce desired behavior and results.

As with the executive overview, the train-the-trainer materials should state who was on the compensation committee and who provided input to the new plan. They should also show which positions were in the scope of the new incentive plan design project and outline the process involved in the project. Before presenting the incentive plan details, the session should address the definitions of the key incentive design elements, such as target total cash compensation, target incentive compensation, mix, leverage, performance measures, payout frequency, performance measurement methodology, and performance range. Next, the presentation should address plan mechanics and provide an incentive plan example, both of which should have more depth than the executive overview document.

Other Communication Aids

Additional supporting communication materials include a detailed breakout session presentation, a question and answer document, and an earnings calculation worksheet.

The breakout presentation is a detailed incentive plan training aid that sales managers can use in personal meetings with each of their direct reports. Such materials make it easier for the sales managers to teach their reps about the new plan in a consistent, accurate manner. The question and answer document is a prepared list of anticipated questions and appropriate responses that may arise during the rollout effort. This document should also be reviewed with the sales reps during the breakout sessions. The earnings calculation worksheet is a hands-on spreadsheet to enable the sales reps to become familiar with the calculation of the incentive earnings under the new plan. It allows for each sales rep to see how his performance in prior years would generate pay under the new plan. Many companies automate the worksheets so sales reps may also predict earnings on the basis of assumptions about how their territories will perform.

16.5   Implementation Team Meetings

Implementation team meetings are critical to the communication and implementation effort. Such meetings should be used for progress updates on all aspects of the implementation plan and perhaps to review draft plan documentation and communication materials.

It is imperative that you nominate an implementation project manager, who will have the responsibility of coordinating the various communication and implementation efforts. The project manager should create a work plan for each key section of the implementation process, with the project steps and their associated tasks, the due date for each task, and the person responsible for each task. Exhibit 16-2 shows a sample work plan.

16.6   Change Management

Whenever a new sales incentive plan is introduced, you can expect the sales reps to experience anxiety. Depending on their individual responses to the key issues, they will feel either great relief or deep frustration. They will probably focus on several issues:

- Why was the plan changed?
- How much can I earn? What is in it for me?
- What is my individual quota or commission rate? How was it established?
- Are any provisions from the old plan being grandfathered?
- Will the cash payment terms of the new plan cause any tempo-

Exhibit 16-2. Sample Implementation Work Plan.

Implementation Team: Plan Communication and Rollout

Project Step	Task	Timing	Responsibility
1. Define communication strategy.	1. Define key messages and themes targeted at specific audiences: sales, operations, company-wide.	12/1	J. Smith
	2. Select a name for the program.	12/1	Change management team
	3. Create a logo for the program.	12/4	Change management team
2. Finalize outstanding incentive plan issues.	1. Confirm system measurement capabilities.	12/1	F. Jones
	2. Develop alternate incentive plan designs.	12/1	F. Jones
	3. Finalize incentive plan designs.	12/4	F. Jones
	4. Confirm recommended excellence level.	12/8	F. Jones
3. Develop incentive plan documents.	1. Produce first draft plan.	11/25	G. Brown
	2. Review draft plan.	12/1	Task force
	3. Finalize plan document.	12/6	G. Brown
	4. Produce other plan documents based on this template.	12/8	G. Brown
4. Develop communication and training material.	1. Produce first draft train-the-trainer document.	11/29	A. White
	2. Review train-the-trainer document.	12/1	Task force
	3. Finalize train-the-trainer document.	12/4	A. White
	4. Produce first draft Q&A document.	12/1	B. Carp
	5. Review Q&A document.	12/4	Task force
	6. Finalize Q&A document.	12/6	B. Carp
	7. Produce first draft executive overview presentation.	12/8	A. White

Project Step	Task	Timing	Responsibility
	8. Finalize executive overview presentation.	12/15	Task force
	9. Product first draft breakout session.	12/15	Q. Dwyer
	10. Finalize breakout session.	12/19	Task force
5. Manage miscellaneous communication events.	1. Draft invitation to national sales meeting.	12/8	F. Jones
	2. Write company newsletter article.	12/15	B. Carp
	3. Develop postcard series to build anticipation for national sales meeting.	12/22	F. Jones
6. Coordinate incentive plan training schedule.	1. Schedule date for each group.	12/8	I. Smith
	2. Select location for each group.	12/15	I. Smith
	3. Identify training session leader for each group.	12/15	I. Smith

rary cash flow problems? If so, does the plan provide a transition from the old to the new?

Recognizing that reps will fret over these questions, you would be well advised to provide sufficient time before finalizing the plan to prepare written responses to these concerns.

Seriously consider employing a change management team to deal with the culture shock issues. The responsibility of this team is to define the messages, scope, and communication strategy for the overall effort; coordinate all focus group sessions; synthesize focus group feedback into the implementation effort; and coordinate the communication effort. In carrying out its responsibilities, this team focuses on the enablers of change:

1. *Leadership.* Help employees develop a compelling vision of a more desirable future state; model the changes desired in others; provide continuous feedback on progress; provide ongoing coaching and remove obstacles.

2. *Information.* Help employees understand the rationale and re-quirements for change; develop communication channels.

3. *Involvement.* Engage the workforce in the process of change; build a network of sponsors, champions, and change agents to support the change effort; build critical mass of support.

4. *Change competencies.* Provide employees with the knowledge, skills, and tools they need to participate and maximize their contribution.

5. *Measurement and reinforcement.* Develop balanced indicators of change representing realization of the vision; provide information on progress to all employees regularly; recognize individual and team contribution.

16.7   Timing of Plan Introduction

When a new or significantly revised sales incentive compensation system is implemented, one question always arises: "Should we introduce the program all at once, phase it in over time, or introduce it on a trial basis to secure participant acceptance?" The answer is, "It depends on a number of external and internal factors affecting each company's situation."

External Factors	*Internal Factors*
Industry characteristics	Degree of change from past
Company's competitive position	Company and sales force culture
Competitors' response level	Information systems limitations
	Cost to implement
	Clarity and direction of marketing and sales plans
	Cost of sales position

Immediate Introduction

Introducing a new sales incentive program all at once could be appropriate if one or more of these internal conditions exist:

- The changes to the current incentive plan are not major. In essence, the incentive plan is being fine-tuned slightly to reflect today's sales and marketing situation better.

- Management wants either to shift the sales force's behavior to a new marketing and sales orientation or to begin to lower a perceived high-cost-of-sales position by focusing attention on achieving additional sales volume.

- The culture of the company is such that changes are always fully announced and quickly implemented, with the sales force able to accommodate all that this may entail.

- The systems needed to measure, track, record, and communicate performance against the new sales incentive program are already in place (or management is willing to invest heavily to ensure they are).

With regard to external factors, the immediate introduction of a new sales incentive plan can be undertaken if:

- The industry in which the company competes is not highly cyclical. Picking the wrong part of the cycle for introduction could demoralize the sales force.

- The company is not dominant in its primary markets and the response level of competitors to its sales strategy change is not immediate. Given these conditions, introducing the entire plan at once can help build marketing position while competitors are not paying attention.

Recently a company that had just undergone a leveraged buyout from its parent introduced a new incentive program. The management of the buyout was interested in immediately redirecting the efforts of the sales force to stress certain high-margin, hard-to-sell product lines. Considering its internal and external situation, the company felt comfortable in introducing the new incentive program all at once.

Phasing In a New Plan

If your industry is evolving due to such factors as deregulation, global competition, or domestic consolidation, you should probably introduce a new sales incentive plan gradually. With respect to internal factors, a phase-in approach should be considered if:

- The anticipated plan changes and behavior modifications are considerable and significant.
- Management sees limited need to shift the sales strategy (and sales force behavior) dramatically in the short run.

- The company's culture is to proceed slowly and cautiously and with periodic reviews of new programs or systems.
- The sales force is not normally accustomed to undergoing quick, major changes or is slowly making the transition to a new organizational structure.
- Needed support systems will not be fully in place for an indefinite period (possibly due to cost considerations).

The deregulation of the energy utility companies represents a situation requiring a phase-in approach. In many countries, the industry is undergoing massive changes in the marketplace. Utility companies face a Brave New World full of competition and opportunities, but also full of major transitions, as well as new sales and marketing programs, new sales positions, and redefined profiles for their salespeople. Moreover, all of this change is occurring within a conservative culture that values caution and technical excellence. Full-scale, total implementation of new sales incentive programs is unwise for most companies.

Trial Introduction

Testing a new sales incentive compensation system to secure participants' acceptance is not frequently done, but it does merit serious consideration if the industry is seasonal, the company is the dominant leader, or competitors are quick to respond to its moves. The reason is that the downside risks of immediate implementation may be too costly from a market share perspective if every aspect of implementation does not proceed well.

In considering internal factors, testing should be undertaken when the company's culture or that of the sales force is one of thoroughly testing new programs. In addition, if the new plan requires either a major reeducation of sales management or considerable additional resources, testing may provide the time and proof required for all affected parties to feel comfortable with these changes.

The correct approach for any company depends on a thorough analysis of both external and internal factors. But moving too slowly in implementation may be just as damaging as moving too quickly.

16.8   Considerations in Implementing New Plans

In introducing a new sales incentive compensation program, try to anticipate problems concerning its design and administration and

establish responses before communicating the plans to the field. Here are some issues likely to arise:

Issue	*Discussion*
Payout period	If the new program has a different payout period, you may need a transition policy to avoid creating cash flow problems for reps.
Definitions for new performance measures	Including a new performance measure for incentive purposes is not uncommon. Make sure that you define the measure clearly (e.g., for new account volume, what qualifies as a new account?).
Quota-setting procedures and processes	When an incentive plan includes the first-time use of quotas, spell out the whole process and all procedures for the sales force. Doing so helps the sales force commit to the new program and perceive it as straightforward.
Handling house accounts	In most instances, house accounts are managed, serviced, and "sold" by management rather than by the field sales force. In some companies, however, house accounts may be transferred back to individual sales reps, possibly with an accompanying increase in incentive earnings potential. Management must carefully describe how such a transfer will be handled for incentive purposes.
Crediting orders	Generally orders can be credited when the order is secured, the order is shipped, the invoice is submitted, or payment is received. With respect to incentive plans whose design accelerates incentive earnings after a quota is fully attained, defining the exact point at which orders are credited can be important to sales performance, motivation, and company cost.
Splitting credits	Companies often split credits when a

	customer places an order in one location for shipment in another. Generally companies use a fifty-fifty split between the two sales reps involved. In some selling situations, however, a more detailed approach may be required. For example, in the sale of building products, one sales rep may be involved with the architect, another with the owner-developer, and a third with the contractor at the building location.
Employee benefits	Addressing the question of how the sales force's benefit plans may be affected by the incentive plan is important. The concern is how the earnings base for benefit purposes will be computed.
New employees and sales trainees	When a new employee will be eligible for participation in the incentive plan and whether a sales trainee will participate at all are important questions. In most cases, sales trainees are not included in incentive programs until they are promoted from trainee status.
Reviewing and modifying the incentive program	Companies should clearly define who will have authority to review and modify the program incentive plan and who will adjudicate windfall and shortfall situations (in which broad economic factors rather than the sales rep create sales). In some companies, a committee of three (representing the finance, sales, and human resources functions) is used to convey a sense of fairness and balance in these situations.

The treatment of such issues may suggest a constantly changing incentive plan. Nevertheless, management should assure sales reps that although emphasis points (e.g., measurement weightings) may change to support the company's marketing strategy, the fundamental program remains constant.

16.9   Transition Approaches

Although a new plan can be phased in gradually, sales managers frequently have to make immediate behavioral changes. In our culture, however, it is very difficult to reduce base salaries. How, then, can you accomplish the transition? More important, how long can you (and your supervisor) wait for the necessary changes to occur? The most extreme situation you are likely to face is one in which your sales force is compensated on a straight salary basis.

In these circumstances, you are asking sales reps to adopt a new mind-set—one that contains more risk than they had previously encountered in their job. Keep in mind, though, that there was risk in that all-salary position. Depending on the time frame and management process, an individual's entire compensation could be lost if he or she failed to deliver the performance level expected. However, few individuals view that consequence with the same immediacy as they would a compensation program that cut their base salaries 15 percent (even if the program gave them the opportunity to earn more through incentives).

One way to ease the transition is to assure sales reps that if they attain quota, they will earn no less than they would have under the prior compensation scheme. Instead of instilling confidence in the appropriateness of the new compensation plan, however, this approach may leave the sales force questioning your confidence in the plan's design. Another solution is to permit a draw against incentive payments equal to some portion of the difference between the new base salaries and the prior compensation levels. You then have the problem of recapturing the draw if performance doesn't meet expectations. Moreover, if the individual's compensation is not variable, you are forgoing an important motivational opportunity.

The key to this dilemma is to maintain the individual's cash flow over the immediate short term, with a phasing in of the variable component and the associated impact on an individual's total cash compensation.

Your objective is to start to align the sales force's perceptions of their compensation with the eventual configuration of the compensation program. At the same time, assure them that over the near term, their cash flow will not suffer if they attain the desired performance criteria. With this objective in mind, and assuming that the reps will attain your desired incentive and base salary relationship in three years (admittedly a long time, but cited for simplicity's sake), Exhibit 16-3 illustrates the makeup approach you could take. Instead of cutting base salary and then putting in the full incentive

Exhibit 16-3. Calculation of Makeup Bonus.

Year	Base	Incentive	Makeup Bonus	Total	Pay Mix (at target performance)
A. Sales Targets Attained					
1	$28,600	$ 0	$1,400	$30,000	95%/5%
2	27,200	1,400	1,400	30,000	90/10
3	25,800	2,800	1,400	30,000	80/15
4	25,800	4,100	0	30,000	85/15
B. Sales Targets Exceeded					
1	$28,600	$ 0	$1,400	$30,000	
2	27,200	2,800	1,400	31,400	
3	25,800	5,600	1,400	32,800	
4	25,800	8,200	0	34,000	
C. Sales Targets Not Attained					
1	$28,600	$ 0	$1,400	$30,000	
2	27,200	0	1,400	28,600	
3	25,800	0	1,400	27,200	
4	25,800	0	0	25,800	

opportunity, phase in the incentive opportunity while reducing the base salary until the desired mix of base and incentive is attained.

Assume that the accounting system won't provide enough information to determine the actual incentive award until after the performance period has ended. In this situation, you should offer a "makeup" bonus to maintain cash flow during the transition period, with the actual incentive payment being made in the period following the actual performance. The makeup bonus remains constant during the phase-in, while the actual incentive payments reflect the sales rep's performance. Exhibit 16-3A assumes that an individual attains the sales targets, thus substantiating his or her incentive award at the desired level. Exhibit 16-3B assumes that an individual exceeds the sales targets, thus doubling his or her incentive award from the desired norm. And Exhibit 16-3C assumes that an individual fails to attain the sales targets, thus yielding no incentive award.

Because the remaining cash flows reflect individual performance, the first bonus payment represents the real "cost" of this type of phase-in. On the other hand, there are significant benefits to be gained, principally that the sales reps' motivation is maintained because their standard of living will not be disturbed (assuming they attain targeted performance). More important, the phase-in approach increases the motivational impact of the plan by demonstrating to those who fear they may be unable to cope with an incentive environment that they can improve their economic standard with better performance. Finally, by slowly lowering compensation for those who cannot meet performance expectations, the plan encourages them to seek other employment opportunities.

If your organization has not used incentives in the past, its goal-setting process is not likely to be as strong as it would have been if compensation depended on performance against established goals. Therefore, the phase-in helps reduce the impact of weak goal setting on compensation levels.

Of course, you may discover that your current compensation levels are competitive with the base salaries of other competitors who employ incentive compensation plans. In this case, if the adoption of a competitive total compensation level would create your desired mix between base and incentives, then you merely have to add the incentive to your existing compensation program.

Finally, if competitive norms indicate a relatively low level of incentive opportunity, you may consider freezing base salaries and transferring the base salary increase into an incentive opportunity. In a sense, this is the reverse of the salary reduction approach.

16.10   Adding Participants

Companies sometimes expand incentive eligibility to incorporate groups not previously included in the program. Such a decision usually relates to changes in the sales and marketing strategies and the realization that other members of the sales organization can influence sales success. The adoption of an at-risk element in the compensation of nonsales employees can be an important recognition of this fact but must be done carefully to meet both the company's and the participants' expectations.

Before deciding to increase participation, consider whether you will be able to quantify the impact of the new group on some aspect of the sales process. This assessment will ensure that an expansion is appropriate and indicate the performance measures that you should consider in the new incentive plan.

Changes in marketing strategy can often mandate the inclusion of additional participants in a sales compensation plan, especially when one objective of such an action is to change the participants' behavior and attitudes. For example, a company with a well-established customer service operation wants to increase the time available to the field sales force for prospecting. One way to accomplish this objective is to reduce sales force involvement in fulfilling routine orders and tracking delivery problems. Currently, however, the customer service group is not organized along customer lines, nor does it view itself as anything more than an order expediter. Nevertheless, this group represents the staff resources for freeing field sales force time.

Clearly much has to be done if this strategy is to prove effective. At the very least, a portion of compensation should be put at risk for individuals who have not had a specific customer orientation and have not been evaluated against sales-specific performance expectations. For such an approach to be successful, you must train the customer service personnel in their new role, and they have to develop the skills and orientation necessary to align their activities with their customers.

Incentive compensation can provide an important reinforcement to this change, but this step by itself is unlikely to represent the catalyst for change in the overall organization. Although the change may mandate a reevaluation of the position's worth, you may find that the addition of an incentive element may be enough to reflect the increased responsibilities and accountabilities of the revised role. If this is the case, the transition will be relatively easy. On the other hand, you will have a different challenge if you find that current base salaries are competitive with total compensation levels and you want to add an incentive element. Cutting back base salaries is the only alternative, and this, as we have seen, must be done carefully.

Adding participants to an existing program can be dangerous if the available funds are diluted or if standards applicable to the existing group are not readily transferable to the new participants. The following lists highlight the considerations to be addressed: perspective of plan design, organizational design, information management, and compensation and benefits design.

Plan Design

- What are the key performance factors for the existing sales compensation plan?
- Are they appropriate for the new sales compensation plan participants? For a particular group of customers or territory? Over a different time period?
- Are there subordinate measures that would more accurately

align the sales compensation plan with participants' responsibilities?

Organizational Design

- Do the incumbents possess the skills necessary to accomplish their new role? If not, can they be trained?

- Do existing recruitment and career paths represent an appropriate source for future hiring needs?

- Are you trying to create a career hierarchy within the position, or will someone's career naturally take him or her out of the department to a position ineligible for incentive compensation? If this is the case, will your plans be thwarted because the compensation plan (in concert with base salary) is providing earnings that are equivalent to the higher position?

- Is there a union contract in place that will require negotiation of the incentive formula?

- Do supervisors possess the skills required to administer an incentive compensation program?

- Is the nature of the sales environment such that the plan will work only if it is team oriented?

- Can you differentiate among levels of individual contribution within the team environment?

- Will employees accept such a differentiation?

Information Management

- Will the new program base incentives on individual or team performance?

- In the information system, can you link customers with the responsible employees?

- Will employees have access to customer information so that they can assess the impact of their actions?

- How will the organization control the inflow of new customers and allocate opportunities across the group of employees?

- Are there customer characteristics (e.g., central purchasing but dispersed distribution) that require a service team?

- Will the participants control pricing within an allowable range, and should profitability be a factor in the incentive compensation plan?

• Are the participants responsible for allocating product resources throughout the customer base? If so, there may be a need to resolve potential conflict among sales reps.

Compensation and Benefits Design

• Do you employ a percentage-of-sales criterion for the total sales compensation costs that will limit your ability to add participants?

• Will the participants remain in the salary administration program, or will all of their increases be incentive driven?

• Will there be a single salary rate for the position?

• If an employee is promoted to a nonincentive position, will his or her salary and increase be determined from his or her current salary (influenced by the existence of the incentive plan), or will the total compensation form the basis for the salary associated with the promotion?

• Are benefits determined from an employee's base salary? If so, does the existence of an incentive plan create a situation in which the employee's benefit plan participation is adversely affected? Do W-2 earnings make more sense?

• Is there so much volatility in earnings from year to year that some type of averaging must be employed for determining the compensation base for benefit purposes?

You can add participants to a plan in a number of ways, depending on their role, impact on the sales function, and compensation.

Clearly, the easiest transition is one in which the new participants have a direct impact on a specific segment of the organization's sales and their current base salary levels do not require reduction. In this circumstance, you merely add the incentive opportunity to the base salary, communicating the performance expectations, measuring the eventual outcomes, and calculating the incentive payments.

The most difficult situation may be one in which current base salaries are above competitive norms, and some type of reduction must be effected if you are to accomplish your objective without increasing compensation costs.

Depending on the particular details, you can align base compensation with competitive norms by cutting base salaries, either immediately or in steps, while increasing the incentive elements or by decreasing base salaries for new employees while treating the "excess" salary paid to current employees as a guaranteed advance against incentive payments.

The techniques for making the transition from an all-base salary to a base-plus-incentive mix are important. More important, however, is the communication of the transition, so that participants understand all aspects of the new plan:

- What activities relate to sales success.

- What the economic benefits (risks) are under the new approach.

- What new career steps are possible.

- Why employees are being included in the incentive plan, how they should modify their interactions with customers, and how they can maximize their incentive opportunity (assuming, for instance, that the new plan participants have an indirect sales support role, such as customer service).

- What type of training or experience an employee must acquire to become eligible for promotion. Is there a greater degree of career risk, and are quantitative and qualitative performance standards now in place?

Consider the following case involving the realignment of a customer service group. In the past, this group responded to questions from the field or from customers concerning product availability, back-order status, pricing, and so on. The sales force handled all sales responsibilities, but in many instances acted as an "information broker" between the customers and customer service. Sales rep utilization was lower than it should have been because a significant part of the reps' time was spent "taking care of the orders."

Management recognized that the customer service group could assume more responsibility. It assigned senior members to a large corporate account and gave them the responsibility for coordinating product shipments, order execution, and so on with the sales force. Concurrent with a customer segmentation strategy, the company established a telesales unit to act as the principal contact with the company's lower-volume customers. In view of these changes, management decided that the base salary approach might not be the most effective way to reinforce the new sales strategy. By creating a modest at-risk element in the compensation plan, it sought to develop a proactive customer service group. Furthermore, a higher at-risk portion would motivate the telesales unit to stay in touch with its customers and increase sales volume.

Although the compensation program was the smallest element of this strategy, it was perceived as the glue that would bind the program elements together. Unless participants saw the plan's introduction as a dramatic departure from past practices, they might not develop the desired combination of energy and new vision.

Management understood that it was more important to create heroes than it was to identify poor performers, and that the short-term cost of overpaying was far less significant than the potential of long-term erosion in share and continued erosion in margin that could be attributed to the old system. So with a clear vision of its objectives and acceptance of the phase-in approach, the company developed an implementation strategy that had broad performance spectrums with an award scale that rapidly accelerated (or decelerated) only at the extremes of the performance spectrum. Thus, in the beginning, most participants felt that they were meeting objectives.

16.11   Eliminating Participants

When an individual ceases to be a participant in the sales incentive compensation plan, a company's approach to the change should reflect sound business judgment. The nature of the termination of plan participation will dictate the appropriate approach, as shown in Exhibit 16-4.

The approaches suggested are guidelines that should be perceived as fair and equitable in most situations, but there are always exceptions. Your company can use whatever approach seems to make good sense in context; the most important thing is to be sure that the rules are spelled out in advance and understood by all plan participants. In general, make the rules as tough as possible within reason. For example, it is reasonable to deny incentive pay to those who terminate before the end of the measuring period. If in a particular case, you wish to be more generous (for example, if a sales rep is accepting a position with a major customer), it is much easier to liberalize the rule interpretation than to do the reverse.

16.12   Handling Employees in Transition

It is inevitable that some employees will evolve into a different status during the performance period. Promotions, terminations, and other circumstances present challenges in changing compensation for

Exhibit 16-4. Payment of Incentive Upon Termination of Employment.

Reason for Termination of Plan Participation	Appropriate Approach to Determining Incentive Earned	
	Incentive Period Completed	Incentive Period Not Completed
Voluntary termination of employment	Paid as soon as practicable.	Forfeited; completion of incentive period should be condition of earning award.
Involuntary termination of employment	Paid as soon as practicable.	Forfeited as above; amount accrued could be paid as part of (or in addition to) severance benefits.
Promotion or transfer to a position not eligible for any incentive compensation	Paid. If a long-term sales cycle, employee could continue to receive awards for a period of time (e.g., six months to two years).	At least the amount earned to date of transfer should be paid. Participant would continue to end of current period (even longer if a long-term sales cycle) to facilitate transfer.
Promotion to a position eligible for a different bonus plan (e.g., executive incentive plan)	Paid for incentive period completed. Participant then terminates.	Same as above, except that awards from sales plan (if any) following transfer date could be deducted from executive incentive award earned for that period.
Retirement (normal to early)	Paid as soon as possible.	Pro rata accrual share paid as soon as practicable.
Death	Paid to estate as soon as practicable.	Pro rata accrued share paid to estate as soon as practicable.
Long-term disability	Paid as soon as practicable.	Pro rata share paid as soon as practicable.

these personnel in transition. You will find the following questions helpful in assessing your options:

Promoted Employees

- Is it reasonable to continue some forms of sales incentive in the new position? If not, are other variable compensation techniques viable, for example, stock options or corporate incentive plans (short or long term)?

- If no incentive compensation is viable, where should the employee's salary be placed in the new salary range?
    - —Equal to her prior year's W-2?
    - —At some percentage of her former total compensation, for example, 80 percent?
    - —At the level that would be generated if she met quota (performance objectives)?
    - —At some average of the past several years?
- If the sales process has a long time frame for completion, will the employee receive all, or a portion, of the sales incentives for sales that close after her transfer?
- If the sales rep has had access to a company car, will you provide a one-time bonus to purchase the vehicle? Should the promoted rep retain the vehicle or the cash car allowance?
- Is there a net gain to the employee that should be factored into the termination discussions? For example, if the definition of earnings is base salary, and not W-2 income, will moving to a higher salary significantly improve the former sales rep's total compensation?
- Does the transfer represent a desired change in life-style, for example, no travel or a different career path, that should not be considered in the termination process?
- If an entire group of employees is being removed from plan participation, do their base salaries require adjustment to realign their no-risk compensation with other comparable jobs in the organization?

Retiring Employees

- What will be the residual, if any, paid for sales that close after the individual's retirement date?
- How long should residuals be paid?
- Is there any benefit in having the retiring employee involved in introducing the new sales rep to the customer base?
- Should the retiring sales rep receive a portion of the new sales rep's incentives if he is responsible for influencing a smooth transition?

Terminated Employees

- Does the employee receive payments for sales that close or ship after the termination date?
- If the employee has a deficit in his draw, will any severance payments be reduced by the amount of the deficit?

- If incentives have been earned but are unpaid, will payment be deferred pending compliance with any noncompete clauses?
- Will payments be withheld until the terminated employee returns company sales literature, keys to the company car, company computer, and so on?
- Will the treatment vary if the termination is for poor performance or for violation of a company policy?

Employees Still in the Sales Force—Plan Terminated

- If an employee is doing the same job, will his base salary represent the average of prior years' total compensation?
- For how many years will performance be used to calculate the average?
- Will the payment be based on each individual's past performance or the average earnings for individuals in the same job?
- Will there be any other form of incentive that will influence the calculation?
- Will benefit participation be enhanced because the employee has a higher base salary?
- Are compensation levels such that no increase in current base salaries is warranted?
- If past compensation levels are such that the employee's compensation is above the new base salary range, will you:
  - —Reduce salary to the range maximum? Red-circle salary and allow increases only when salary falls into the range sometime in the future?
  - —Continue to allow salary increases but only at a percentage of range movement?

16.13   Postimplementation Audit

A properly designed sales incentive plan will communicate sales priorities to the field. More likely than not, however, some confusion over plan elements will remain. Therefore, plan to provide an ongoing, sustained communication program to ensure understanding and bring about the desired behavioral changes.

After the initial communication, determine if your messages were understood and if any areas of uncertainty exist. In this regard, the field management team can prove invaluable, especially if they were instrumental in the plan introduction. To assess the need for further communications, gather information concerning the types of questions asked during and after the introductory meetings. Using a checklist to assess the effectiveness of the implementation effort and the plan itself should help gather the needed information.

Consider the attitude of the sales force. Are they charged up as a result of the new plan? Or are they so filled with fear or anger that they are not selling? If the latter is the case, you have a serious problem. On the other hand, if the sales environment has changed substantially and you need a sales force with a different risk profile, the sales compensation program can complement other management programs designed to transform the characteristics of the sales team.

Because of the qualitative nature of sales force attitudes, don't hesitate to discuss the plan with a spectrum of sales employees. Don't introduce bias into your information by talking only with the high performers; you need to consider the attitudes of both the good performers and those who are not meeting expectations.

With the results of this work in hand, plan the activities necessary to ensure the success of the program—for example, informational and skills training, more coaching on the part of sales management, and regular communication to share sales strategies and successes. Alternatively, you may conclude that further action above and beyond the normal sales management process is unnecessary. Although consistency in leadership direction is necessary to instill confidence on part of the sales force, don't be doctrinaire in your planning. If new information indicates that changes must be made, communicate this fact as quickly as possible, along with the changes you seek.

16.14 Midyear Audit

If the incentive plan changes are significant, assess the impact on sales force performance after a reasonable period of time. Because most sales goals are set on a yearly basis, a midyear review will allow you to use the information as part of the goal-setting process that typically begins during the third quarter.

First determine whether any part of the sales process is cyclical and whether you can project annual sales performance from year-to-date (YTD) results. Or, it might be better to contrast performance to the prior year's YTD results.

After making this decision, assess the plan's impact on your sales force:

- Have the desired behavioral changes occurred (either activities or actual sales results)?
- Has the desired impact on compensation been achieved?
- Have you lost any key reps to competitors?
- Has the plan design encouraged less productive sales force members to seek nonsales careers?
- Is the targeted level of compensation being achieved?
- Is the distribution between the highest-paid and the lowest-paid employee appropriate?
- Are the outcomes influenced by any windfalls or unanticipated broad-based changes?
- Are you attaining your desired cost-of-sales targets?
- Are the right customers receiving appropriate attention?
- Are the right products or services receiving enough emphasis?

Finally, given the fact that not enough time may have passed for a sound quantitative analysis to be made, how do you *feel* about the changes? Is your intuition saying that your decision was correct, or are you beginning to second-guess the plan design?

Based on the information you develop, you should consider some communication to the sales force on the status of the plan and your anticipated approach for the coming year.

17

Setting Reasonable Goals

17.1 Why Goal Setting Is Important

Sales reps are among the most goal-oriented people. What makes a sales job so exciting is the fact that the rep is out there alone, with just the customer, a goal, and (of course) the incentive plan.

With all sales jobs, some measurement of sales performance always exists, whether it is based on a period of time (monthly, quarterly, or yearly), volume, or some other factor. It may be called quota, target, or expectation—but it's still a goal.

If you ask a cross-section of your reps to list their goals, the responses might surprise you. Some reps will mention one or two areas without being specific. Others will be very specific. Still others will list the company's stated goals and some personal goals. Most, however, will probably cite goals whose achievement is rewarded by the compensation program.

Whenever a company announces a new sales compensation plan and assigns territories, reps can usually determine at once how they feel about the plan. Goals and performance help shape their response. Some plans (often bonus plans) explicitly set goals, whereas others (often commission plans) provide inherent, unstated goals that depend on the income aspirations of the sales reps.

A sales compensation program provides the means by which you can establish and reinforce the organization's goals. You can set goals in as simple or as complex a fashion as your sales managers, information systems, and communications systems can handle. As a general guideline, more than three or four distinct goals in a given time period will diffuse sales focus, but these goals (and their relative incentive plan weights) can vary by territory. Other goals over and above any incentive directives (e.g., teamwork, paperwork, service level) can be incorporated into the overall system if meaningfully communicated and treated as part of the overall assessment at the time of a salary review.

To be effective, however, goals must be meaningful and fair, and they must be clearly communicated. Management must strive for goal clarity, so individuals know what is expected of them and how their roles fit within the company's strategy. Too often organizations ignore these guiding principles, creating confusion or discontent among the sales force. In setting and stating goals, consider the consequences carefully.

17.2 Illustrating Explicit Quotas

Sales managers can incorporate sales goals, frequently called quotas, into a field sales compensation program through base salary validation, thresholds, commission accelerators, or quota "kickers." Base the precise form of the sales quota on the objectives you are trying to accomplish with the sales force and, of course, the ability of your management processes and measurement systems to support the plan's design.

Base Salary Validation

Base salary validation provides the easiest method of setting sales goals. Assume that you have two sales reps whose respective base salaries are $56,000 and $48,000 per year and you want to pay them a 4 percent commission after they attain a minimal level of acceptable sales performance. If you set an equal sales goal for both reps (for example, $1,000,000), you might be criticized for inappropriately determining equitable performance standards, for one might assume that the sales rep with the higher base salary is more experienced and more able to carry a higher level of expected performance. By dividing their base salaries by the commission rate, you can convert their compensation to an equivalent level of sales performance, thus setting a sales goal that represents an equal relationship between expected performance and compensation. For example, the sales rep earning $48,000 would have a $1,200,000 quota, and the one earning $56,000 would have a $1,400,000 quota. (Whether you should consider such a mechanical approach to quota setting is an issue discussed later in this chapter.)

This approach to quota setting creates a disguised commission, in that the base salary represents a more stable element of the compensation program. In some ways, it resembles a draw. Unlike a commission plan, however, the base salary would not have to be recaptured if the sales rep did not attain the required sales. Over the long run, sales management would have to weed out unacceptable performers from the sales force rather than have the commission plan eliminate those who couldn't meet the sales challenge.

Thresholds

Thresholds represent another way to set sales quotas. In some ways, thresholds parallel the base salary validation approach but without the direct link to a rep's earned compensation. For example, you might provide no incentive for the first $500,000 of sales, 10 percent on the next $500,000, 8 percent on the next $1 million, and 5 percent on all sales in excess of $2 million.

Commission Accelerators

Commissions can accelerate with higher levels of sales performance or the introduction of new product lines or expansion into new customer bases. Suppose that you want to encourage rapid introduction of a new product line that will require your sales force to direct more time and energy to nontraditional customers. In addition to the introduction of a new product commission schedule, you might also consider an additional commission on sales of existing product lines, once some level of new product sales is attained. For example, you might say that in addition to the commission for the new product, a sales rep who attains new product shipments of $300,000 by the first quarter (net of returns and allowances) will receive an additional 5 percent commission on all other product sales for the year. If she attains $300,000 in new product sales by the second quarter, she will receive an additional 2.5 percent commission on all other product sales for the year. Furthermore, there will be no additional commission for new product shipments during the last half of the year, except for the basic commission associated with the product.

Quota "Kickers"

In some industries, the need to achieve balanced line sales in each territory is paramount. Instead of merely setting individual product line quotas and related commissions and hoping for the best, the sales compensation plan can achieve this objective through a commission kicker based on quota attainment in each line.

Assume that you are paying a graduated commission on three product lines, with each commission rate representing the underlying profitability and difficulty of the sale. To reduce the inclination to sell only the product with the highest close rate, you could develop a plan with an additional commission payment at year end if aggregate quota attainment exceeds 100 percent (and each product line has at least 75 percent quota attainment). Clearly, this approach requires great confidence in your quota-setting process (if it is to be perceived as equitable), and sales reps must have confidence that they can attain some additional award. Furthermore, setting too low a quota in one product line can result in more volatility in the comparison of performance, allowing sales reps to play off the various plan elements to their economic advantage.

Quotas and Commissions

The issue of quota setting strikes at the heart of the commission-setting process. Because quotas integrate opportunity (as defined by territory characteristics) and performance (as measured by sales results), you have to be wary of performance assessments based solely on an individual's compensation. Absent specific information concerning territory characteristics (e.g., number of potential opportunities, concentration of customers, size, and business characteristics), you may be operating on the assumption (perhaps mistakenly) that all territories are equivalent and, therefore, a uniform commission structure will accurately represent individual performance.

On the other hand, your management task will become infinitely more complicated if you try to set individual quotas, in effect "handicapping" each member of your sales force by setting different rates to yield equivalent compensation for performance that is perceived to be "equivalent." Such an approach is time-consuming, and your sales force will quickly perceive that you are managing compensation rather than performance. Unless weak performers are removed, this can have a chilling impact on motivation; employees who are managing large territories or accounts see their compensation opportunities equivalent to those of other members of the sales force with lower performance.

Consequently, in setting commission quotas, evaluate the outcome in the light of the interaction of the commission rates and the nature of the territory. Sometimes the nature of the business is so long term that the measurement of results (and hence the determination of an annual commission) can be misleading. This is especially true when the development cycle is long, product specification is a critical task, and, once accomplished, current year's sales results are more a result of the health of the customer's business than the sales rep's efforts. In these instances, the compensation plan should have a more long-term focus. For example, the sales rep's base salary range could be related to the nature of the territory volume and product mix as measured over a rolling time period. Some sales managers may view this technique as lacking, in that the retrospective focus in the compensation plan may result in a gradual erosion in performance.

17.3   Implicit Quotas

Although not all plans incorporate sales quotas explicitly, all plans contain implicit quotas. The implicit quota is represented by any of the countless patterns of performance results that, if accomplished, enable the rep to exceed targeted (or comfortable) income levels. The danger inherent is quite apparent. The company has inadvertently promised to overpay (versus targets or average) under certain patterns of performance. If the sales rep can achieve that income comfort level while concentrating on certain aspects of the sales task to the exclusion of others, then the purpose of the plan is defeated. The sales rep can be expected to take the path of least resistance toward the highest possible income. The company must ensure that an unreasonably easy path cannot be selected.

17.4   "Typical" Quota Setting

One of the most frustrating responsibilities for sales and marketing managers is setting equitable and realistic sales quotas in relation to corporate strategies. Even as simple a tactic as distinguishing, via the incentive plan, between selling to new customers and selling to existing customers goes unused by many companies.

Part of the problem is that in pursuit of simplicity and fairness, a sales manager may either divide up the regional sales quota, assigning an equal portion to each rep, or tie every rep's quota to his or her sales results from last year. These approaches may be simple, but they are rarely fair or effective.

To reflect territorial and other differences, assign to each rep a customized set of objectives (volume, product line, accounts, profit) along with a strategy for attaining them. This makes quota setting more complicated, but not too complicated, for the average rep to understand. Some managers worry that reps will see their increased involvement in goal setting as a chance for negotiation and will share only as much information as will strengthen their hand. These obstacles can be overcome, however, and the results are well worth the effort.

Start with the assumption that if you pick a single number as a dollar volume quota, that number will probably be wrong. It gives the illusion of precision but is based on a variety of assumptions and subjective judgments. You and the sales rep, however, can probably agree on a range of assumptions—regarding prices (yours and those of your competitors), production levels, interest rates—that represent the spectrum from worst case to best case, with the most likely case equaling the dollar volume quota. Incentive payments will usually rise steadily from the minimum (probably resulting in zero incentive payout) to the maximum.

Naturally, this combination of a top-down/bottom-up process lives or dies by the amount of information available. Given sufficient information about the market, the territory, and your corporation's plans, however, you and the sales rep can establish an equitable range of quotas for each territory, thus creating effective motivation for each rep.

17.5   Top-Down Quota Allocation

The quota-setting process typically involves the fragmentation of a large, random number and the arbitrary allocation of a manufacturing forecast among sales territories. Let's consider the motivational implications of such an approach and evaluate the effectiveness of this method in accomplishing your principal objective: to ensure organizational success by selling customers products that generate a fair return on shareholders' investment.

Unfortunately, in the planning scenario, last year's sales represent the foundation for the planning process, and pricing decisions are based on last year's sales figures and the increase in costs. This number crunching creates a financial model for the organization, but does it represent market realities?

Faced with a projection of sales volumes that, for example, have increased in aggregate 10 percent from the prior year, the challenge now is to allocate this "nut" to the regional and district sales managers. Furthermore, the financial model may have been predicated on a specific product mix, which must also be distributed among the sales personnel if the corporation's overall goals are to be met.

So the quotas come cascading down from on high. The allocation can take many forms: equal distribution by sales rep, allocation based on last year's performance, a push into specific market segments, or allocation on the basis of sales reps' compensation. (Let's say the rep makes x in base with a y percent commission; he or she will have to sell z million to make target compensation.)

But where do the customer and your competitors enter into this equation? Because the model was manufacturing driven, you're selling what you're making. Unfortunately, your competitors have redesigned their products in response to a market shift, and you haven't gotten your company past the tooling stage. Or perhaps you're leading your competitors into the market with a new product but allocating only 30 percent of production capacity to the new line. Sales demand is brisk, and your sales force is forced to go on allocation, spreading out the supply so everyone is at least a little bit happy. This tactic, however, prevents you from supplying several dominant customers.

The list of what-ifs is endless, but the message is the same: Top-down quota setting is fraught with peril, because it separates you from the most important source of information concerning your customers: your sales force. Who else spends more time in contact with the most important element in the success of your business? Who can tell you more about what the market is requiring, both now and in the future?

Unfortunately, rather than viewing the sales force as an ally, sales management often views it as an adversary. For example, management may suspect that wily sales reps "underestimate" product demand ("sandbag") to get low quotas, or management may believe that the reps' job is limited solely to getting "this year's numbers, . . . so we'll let the marketing staff worry about two years out."

To do the job right, sales management needs information—lots of it. On the basis of customer demand and buying patterns and shifts in competitive pricing, the sales force can provide a bottom-up forecast of what can be sold and at what price. You should then factor in this point of departure into the manufacturing plan to verify whether the company's financial goals can be met.

With this approach in hand, the sales force can strive to increase market share and profitability by selling what your customers want, rather than what you think they want. Customer-driven sales plans have a greater opportunity for success than do manufacturing-oriented programs.

17.6   Is a Dollar Equal to a Dollar?

Andy Salesengineer closed the year with $2 million in bookings, while Sarah Fieldsales finished with $3 million. Who had the better year, and who deserves the higher pay?

Unless Andy and Sarah are selling to the same type of customer,

Exhibit 17.1. Sales Volume vs. Compensation Market Value for Regional, Distributor, and National Sales.

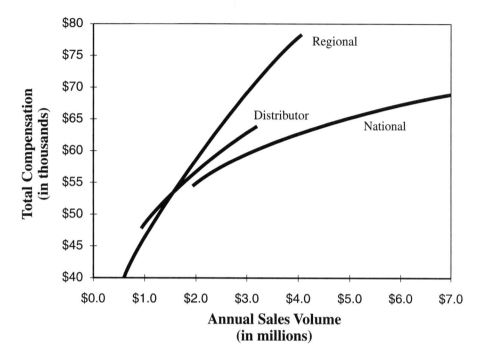

you couldn't even begin to tell. Even if they did have similar sales roles, a single year's sales results might not be meaningful. If everything else were equal and the nature of the job made one year's sales relevant, Sarah had the better year. But these conditions occur less often than you might think. Let's examine these points more carefully.

Exhibit 17-1 shows sales compensation versus volume for a fictional company with three different sales jobs. One force sells to major national accounts, a second to regional accounts large enough to merit direct sales coverage but not quite national in scope, and a third to distributors (the distributor has its own sales force, marketing a wide variety of products to small accounts). To get items quickly, large accounts also buy from distributors on occasion.

The exhibit shows three distinct curves, all representing different linkages of sales dollars to compensation. The national salespeople manage a long-term account relationship. That curve starts higher, because higher levels of selling and technical knowledge are required. The curve, however, is fairly flat. Once the relationship is established, further sales are driven more by the national account's own successes. Regional sales reps do not need as much experience to undertake the job, but if they are good, they can have a dramatic influence on results through prospecting and penetration. Hence, the regional curve is steepest. The distributor sales role falls between that of national and regional roles, as does the distributor curve.

Is a dollar equal to a dollar? No. In this company's business, $3 million of sales requires selling skills commanding approximately $58,000 through national accounts, $63,000 through distributors, and $69,000 through regional accounts. Moreover, an extra dollar of sales is worth more in regional and distributor accounts and less in national accounts.

These relationships vary from industry to industry. In some, the national and regional curves might be closer (or perhaps even reversed). So don't revamp your compensation systems to match these curves without first understanding the sales skills required in each role. But the basic point remains: A dollar of sales in one job isn't necessarily equal to a dollar in another.

All sales dollars aren't equal for another reason: Volume doesn't always provide the best way to measure results. For example, in the national sales job, you would find a fairly wide dispersion of pay versus sales volume, even in an organization where the best-paid salespeople are also the best performers. Why? Because selling national accounts is generally a long-term business, and the accounts most difficult to sell (and therefore requiring the highest selling skills) aren't always the largest. Other things being equal, more sales deserve more dollars, but things are equal less often in the national sales role than in most others. Conversely, the regional role would probably have a tighter relationship of sales volume to performance, and the sales reps within the distributor organization would probably have the closest relationship of all.

The bottom line is that sales effectiveness can't always be measured in dollars. Some situations, per dollar of revenue, simply cost more to sell. And why not? We don't expect the ratios of R&D, advertising, or many other expenses to sales in the business world to be the same across different industries. Why should sales (which may sell related products, but to customers in different industries) be any different? Certain dollars of revenue indicate selling accomplishments better than others do.

17.7   Planning vs. Compensation Functions

One company faced the problem of dwindling sales. A corporate strategic planner offered her solution to the division general manager: "We must spend more on marketing and improve our product quality. Furthermore, the sales force has been too complacent this year. It must sell more. With dedicated sales efforts, an improved product, and a bigger marketing budget, we must sell $100 million this year with $8 million net income. Actually, we ought to be able to sell $110 million!"

"Eight million net!" exclaimed the general manager. "We did only $4 million last year."

"Nonetheless, we must strive for $110 million, or at least $100 million," said the planner. "There is no other way."

After considering the planner's advice, the divisional head decided to carry out the plan. He realized, however, that the company couldn't simply increase margins and marketing and product development expenses at the same time. Therefore, he trimmed 20 percent from the expense budget. Convinced that the sales organization really had been lax, he concluded that if he needed $100 million in sales, he'd better ask for $110 million.

The general manager called a meeting with his top sales managers to explain the situation. He concluded by telling them, "We've got to get $110 million in sales, and here are your quotas."

You know the rest of the story. The sales managers met with their sales reps, and each divided up the group's sales quota. The process continued until each dollar was allocated down the line.

Put yourself in the shoes of a rep who has managed to reach $1 million in sales the past year (an increase of 50 percent over the prior year). Her share of this year's quota is $1.5 million. Below $1.4 million she gets no incentive pay at all.

Other than increased anxiety among the field staff, what has been accomplished? A poor sales performer might be forced to work a bit harder. But does it make sense to treat the entire sales organization this way? Field sales is usually the first to know when trouble is coming. By the time the corporate rain dance starts, the average field organization is working as hard as it is going to.

All that has been done is to tell the field to "go sell." *They know that already.* To get them to sell more effectively, you must tell them more about what to sell and how to sell it. Let's review the process.

We began with $100 million, a figure of questionable validity (some studies suggest that corporate strategic plans tend to overestimate actual results). We then took this probably optimistic figure and reduced the odds of attaining it by cutting the investments on which it was based. We next increased the $100 million by 10 percent to make sure that we would get what we really needed. And then, worst of all, we allocated the result to the field, holding people accountable for the same narrow range of results (plus or minus 10 percent) we did at the corporate level.

Because of the law of large numbers, this last point is the coup de grace to a constructive goal-setting process. If you've got a random event with a central tendency, the more events observed, the more accurate the estimate of what's likely to occur. That's one theory behind conglomerates: When division A is down, division B will be up, and we will all survive. The same logic applies in reverse. If plus or minus 10 percent of $100 million is a reasonable range of performance, mere statistics suggest that the range around $10 million must be greater than 10 percent, and the range around $1 million greater still.

Ironically, we've accomplished the exact opposite of our intentions. Sales reps within the performance band—a small group, because it's a narrow band—do have an incentive to do better: They're "in the game." But those below (and with little chance of earning anything) might as well coast or look for another job. Those above might just as well coast too—or do the minimum to ensure they get the sales they know they can realize.

The goals and objectives developed for corporate planning purposes can serve a constructive purpose. But if blindly applied to the selling situation, these measures can actually hurt. Unlike a corporate manager who can hire additional people and add other resources, the sales rep's resources are fixed. Sales reps have about two thousand hours to work with in a year. To improve their effectiveness, they must apply those hours in a better way. If the message from the top is, "Do more," but with no guidance as to what to do, the best you can expect is no change, and the result might well be detrimental. If you want your sales force to sell more, you have to tell them how.

17.8 Limits of Revenue Accounting

Although it is a fact of life in business, traditional revenue accounting measures paint an incomplete, and possibly misleading, picture of effectiveness. Sales is a continuous process; revenue accounting recognizes only discrete twelve-month periods. Sales reps usually have their greatest influence on bookings, yet revenue accounting recognizes shipping and billing, at which point the sales rep's job may have been over for months. Furthermore, many sales rep activities affect future sales, or sales in other territories, or sales that will occur if other conditions (such as price competitiveness) are also met.

For these reasons, revenue accounting measures must usually be supplemented by measures that are closer to the control of the sales rep. Suppose that you have two reps and that each has landed a major account in the same industry. Both accounts need the part that you supply. Both reps have worked hard to be sure the customer has exactly what it needs: the right product specification, the necessary customizing, and so on. And both reps have great bookings to show for it.

The only trouble is that two years later, when your customers' products hit the market, one customer's product has a feature that sends sales through the roof, to the detriment of the other customer. One will now have to cancel shipments; the other will have to increase them. Except for some minor troubleshooting with regard to setting up delivery, your sales reps have both moved on to other prospects, secure in the knowledge that they have done a good job. Although both *have* done an excellent job, the revenue accounting system will show that one has terrific billings while the other is in a slump.

In fact, the key performance criterion—getting the product specified—is not captured in the current accounting system. The revenue accounting system becomes increasingly flawed as a measure of sales success when the product development or specification cycle is greater than the calendar year. In these instances, effective sales management mandates an activity-based performance system to supplement the accounting system. For example, identifying sales prospects, obtaining bid opportunities, closing the bid, and managing subsequent execution would more accurately represent the factors that should be measured to differentiate sales success.

One might conclude that in short-cycle sales processes (a short time between the purchase decision and shipment), the revenue accounting system is not flawed. As is often the case, the answer is, "It depends." If territory design has created balanced territories, then this indeed may be the case. On the other hand, consider the differences in performance measurement if one territory is made up of a group of customers concentrated in a small geographic area, and the other is dispersed over an area that requires four times the amount of travel to reach all customers. Clearly, the sales rep in the latter territory is going to have fewer opportunities to meet with her customers. Consequently, her sales level, measured by the revenue accounting system, may not be as noteworthy as those of her colleague.

Notwithstanding the problems of accurately differentiating levels of sales performance, revenue accounting systems can be even more misleading if you hold sales reps responsible for pricing and you are not able to track the gross margin of the products your sales reps are selling. If this were to occur, you could give away the store and not realize it. For example, if the accounting system tracks revenue, large volumes of business could be perceived as representing excellent sales performance. Unfortunately, if the outcome derives from inappropriate pricing, you may be on the road to financial disaster.

17.9   Nonrevenue Goals

The revenue accounting statement cannot acknowledge any sales event, no matter how important, that does not immediately generate short-term revenue. Yet in many sales jobs, sales impact is best reflected by nonrevenue results. One way to capture this important aspect of performance is through special or key account goals that focus attention on accomplishing definite objectives with significant accounts and prospects. Goals should be selected for their importance to profitable sales and territorial growth, through either immediate increase or laying the groundwork for future growth.

When the manager and sales rep meet to set goals, each account and prospect should be thoroughly reviewed and analyzed. This review should address two fundamental questions: What do we really want to accomplish? and How can we do it?

The answer to "What?" comes from thorough analysis of the competitive sales situation. Here are some helpful questions to explore in this analysis:

- What new requirement does the prospect or account have that we can address?
- How can we address it?
- What are the steps we must take?
- How can we help the account sell?
- Are there any implications for marketing, product development, or some other area?
- How can we increase volume?
- Who is the competition?
- What are the needs of the account?
- How can we meet these needs?
- Where are competitors weak?

- What new developments are occurring?
- What are possible matches between developing product lines and future customer requirements?
- Where can we increase profits?
- What new products or programs provide opportunities?
- Which prospects are the most attractive?

The answer to "How?" then becomes the specific goal. To the extent possible, tentative goals should be listed for every account of consequence. After each has been analyzed, the list should reviewed and the most important opportunities (from a profit-making perspective) selected. For these, a specific goal that satisfies these criteria should be formulated:

1. The goal is important. It relates to overall company strategies and is worth stating.
2. It is accomplishable given what we know about the account. (If it is not, but still worth trying, what would have to happen to make this a good objective for the next period?)
3. It is clearly stated and verifiable, so the sales manager and sales rep can agree about whether it has been accomplished.
4. It builds on prior goals and can support new ones in future periods.

Setting sound goals is difficult. Impossible goals are self-defeating; goals that are too easy don't accomplish anything and can demoralize top performers. It's generally best to have the sales rep select the goals and have the manager approve and refine them. This approach also helps build commitment to attaining the goals. Other ways to strengthen the goal-setting and performance relationship include:

- Using shorter performance periods (e.g., six months, four months, or a quarter).

- Building in a means to revise, reweight, and substitute goals (especially when required due to changes in company priorities).

- Allowing recognition, where warranted, of "nonprogrammed" goals (events you couldn't have known about in the past but could get credit for recognizing and exploiting).

Not all of these steps are appropriate in every circumstance, but they're worth considering in volatile sales environments.

In all situations, the key to success is using the program to es-

Exhibit 17-2. Territory Volume Goal Sheet.

Territory _____	Sales Engineer _____		Account Manager _____		Year and Quarter _____		
		Volume History				*Estimated Volume This Quarter*	
Account	Prior Quarter Volume	Last Year's Volume	Volume to Date	Volume This Quarter Last Year		Most Likely	Highest Possible
_____	_____	_____	_____	_____		_____	_____
_____	_____	_____	_____	_____		_____	_____
_____	_____	_____	_____	_____		_____	_____
_____	_____	_____	_____	_____		_____	_____

tablish rapport at all levels in the sales organization. Through program documentation, communication, and training, make sure that the process is consistently and equitably applied.

17.10   Account Analysis Worksheet

Each account and important prospect should be analyzed to determine likely future volume. One approach is to use a worksheet completed by the sales rep and reviewed in a discussion between the rep and sales manager.

Exhibit 17-2 illustrates one possible worksheet format. The volume history columns show product sales last year, this period last year, this year to date, and the most recent period. The estimated-volume-this-period columns would be filled in jointly, after consideration of such relevant field conditions as changes in other products and services that would affect sales of this product line; market acceptance due to changed business conditions; changes in prices, advertising policies, and other elements of the marketing mix; and the competitive climate.

The totals of the most likely estimates and the highest possible estimates from the territory volume goal worksheet then become judgment points used to establish final volume goals for each territory.

Exhibit 17-3. Territory Report of Incentive Earned.

Territory _____ Sales Engineer _____ Account Manager _____ Quarter _____

Volume Goal and Results:	Volume Goal Range _____ to _____	Actual Volume	Assigned Points	Points Earned

Account Goal and Results: Key Account/Prospect		Assigned Points	

Total Points Earned
Time Point Value   × $ _____
Incentive Earned   _____

17.11   Worksheet for Computing Awards

A final step in the goal-setting process is to summarize the goals established and track progress in achieving them. This can be a powerful communication and motivational tool.

Exhibit 17-3 shows a form that can be used to track progress and calculate final incentive payouts. It combines both sales volume and key account goals. The "accomplishment" part of the form would be filled out by the sales rep as the year progressed and goals were met. The form would be reviewed from time to time by the sales rep and manager. At the end of the year (or incentive period, if shorter than a year), the results would be evaluated, points assigned, and payments made.

18

Designing Plans for Specialized Selling Roles

How simple your life would be if customers bought in ways that allowed you to credit each sale to a specific salesperson. The buying process would be more orderly and predictable, and sales crediting issues would be nonexistent. Unfortunately, multiple buyers who need all sorts of information and support across many geographic sites are a part of a normal business-to-business selling proposition. In addition, certain types of customers—for example, government or indirect channel accounts—often require specialized selling roles to meet their unique needs.

At one time or another, most sales forces face situations that do not fit the norm. Incentive plan designers should not let the fact that certain markets are different deter them from adopting a sales compensation program to manage selling resources better; fundamental compensation design principles will still apply to specialized selling roles.

In this chapter we will explore a variety of specialized selling roles and the unique challenges they present in designing rational and compelling incentive plans.

18.1 Government Account Manager

Sales to government entities—federal, state, local, and foreign—frequently require skills and degrees of prominence far different from those employed in sales to the private sector. Sales to governments typically involve a process of competitive bidding that begins with a request for proposal (RFP) and concludes with the selection of a vendor from among a list of final contenders. Selling is often a team effort, requiring a variety of skills, several of which may be required of a single sales rep. The sales process generally includes two phases:

1. Obtaining information from sources in government, allowing the vendor to respond to the RFP on the basis of an understanding of the factors that will influence the selection.

2. Presenting and revising the proposal, and redefining the scope of the project to meet the customers' needs.

Sales to governments are predictable in one sense: the date that a contract will be awarded is often known far in advance. These sales, however, do not follow predictable chronological patterns and do not occur at regular intervals. Therefore, in most months, no current sales will be recorded, but work in various stages of the proposal process will be under way to secure future sales. Conversely, sales results in a given month simply reflect the date a contract is awarded, not the sales activities undertaken in that month to improve the chances of securing contracts to be awarded in the future.

Most conventional approaches to sales compensation do not fit government sales for these reasons:

- Conventional plans assume that there will be results within a year, but government sales often take more than twelve months to complete.

- Given the big-ticket, random incidence of sales, sales goals cannot be set with any degree of confidence. Selling skills may influence whether a sale is made, but the timing and size of the sale are almost entirely beyond the influence of the sales rep.

- Any measure of results must await the awarding of the contract. However, one can see why an incentive based on current sales would be at best incomplete and at worst a misleading measure of sales effectiveness. The principal accomplishments of the government sales force in a given month relate not to contracts awarded that month but to work on upcoming contracts in various stages of completion.

Because conventional compensation measures are inappropriate for government sales forces, you might consider pay plans for dedicated government sellers that include straight salary (a common approach even when commercial salespeople are rewarded), a higher proportion of salary in the mix of fixed and variable pay, or a cap on the incentive to be earned from any one transaction to avoid "lottery ticket" overpayments when a big sale occurs.

With respect to government sales, two other specific compensation approaches recognize that the calendar has less meaning than does the event of the sale: *event-driven* and *line-of-credit* pay approaches.

The incentive period of the event-driven approach is neither a year nor a quarter, but rather the life of the contract. The sales rep receives "simulated equity" in the contract itself. He could receive a front-end bonus for securing the sale, paid at the time the contract is awarded. This approach could be applied to award incentive payments *before* the sale as well, based on achieving key, definable milestones that signify progress toward securing the final contract. Or he could receive a continuing share of revenue or profit if he played a significant role in defining the scope of the project secured from the contract, with awards paid on anniversary dates of the contract's acquisition.

The line-of-credit approach recognizes that a rep may have no sales in a particular month or year, but that eventually some revenue must be generated. Therefore, he receives a salary, part or all of which is treated as an advance against a compensation line of credit. For example, the salary may be $80,000 per year and the credit limit $300,000. Whenever a sale is made, part of the line of credit is repaid, according to the plan's commission schedule. Accumulated commission in excess of the accumulated salary is paid to the individual on a quarterly or annual basis. Thus, all sales are credited toward earnings, but the timing of sales has no impact on compensation. Should the accumulated excess of salary over commission exceed the credit line, the rep would likely be informed that his productivity no longer justifies the high salary or (perhaps) his continued employment.

The line-of-credit approach applies the commission principle in a nonchronological, event-driven context. As with any other commission approach, its validity rests on a close linkage between sales prominence and revenue results. There is often a very distant relationship between the sales rep and the revenue in government sales. In such cases, plan designers might use the line-of-credit approach in those relatively few situations where the sales rep can parlay his unique skills or personal relationships with government decision makers into government contracts.

18.2   Distributor or Agent Sales Representative

Selling to distributors can also require specialized selling skills. For example, the sales rep can function as a consultant to the distributor in all facets of the latter's business, including inventory control and the management of the distributor's sales staff. Orchestrating a mutually beneficial relationship between a manufacturer and its distributors can be a delicate balancing act, yet it can be reinforced using conventional compensation techniques for both the rep specializing in managing distributors and the distributor sales organization itself.

Distributor Sales to End Users

A manufacturer either sells direct through dedicated sales reps or through an indirect channel of distribution. Manufacturers that sell through an indirect channel of distribution, including distributors, agents, and value-added resellers, typically do so as a means of gaining access to a customer segment that cannot be captured profitably through direct channels. Therefore, the role of the distributor is analogous to that of the commissioned sales rep whose influence over sales volume is so pervasive, if not exclusive, that current sales volume is an accurate and potentially complete measure of worth. Hence, a commission approach, historically the preeminent way distributors pay their sales staff, is appropriate in this context. While distributors may use variants of the commission approach in dealing with their salespeople, in all cases, current sales volume (or production) should be the primary metric by which they measure performance.

Another measure of importance may be profitability, particularly if the distributor sales rep has pricing authority. In this case, the margins on the volume generated by the rep are at least partially controlled by the sales force. As such, a measure of gross margin dollars or gross margin percentage may be appropriate to balance what may otherwise be a pure volume orientation. If so, employing a design technique to link compensation mathematically with *both* imperatives can avoid overly rewarding the seller for excellent performance on but one of the two measures.

Finally, product mix may represent another strategic performance measure of relevance if the distributor sells a broad array of products, if certain product lines are significantly more profitable, or if some lines are strategically more important to the distributor. Once again, linkages can be used to reward the most desirable volume and appropriate product mix. (Mathematical tools to link multiple performance measures to compensation were discussed in detail in Chapter 13.)

Manufacturer Sales to Distributors

The role of the individual who is responsible for sales to distributors is more multifaceted than that of the distribution rep, but it can normally be accommodated by a conventional sales compensation program. Such an individual functions as an overall business adviser to the distributor, helping the distributor manage its sales force and, in the process, obtaining a greater "mind share" among the distributor reps for the manufacturers' products. The manufacturer rep may also aid in selecting, motivating, and training distributor sales and service personnel. At times, the responsibilities of the manufacturer rep may even extend to recruiting, selecting, and replacing distributors.

Although all of these functions relate more to business management than to selling, they are nevertheless undertaken for a single purpose: to maximize the flow of the manufacturers' goods through the distributor organization. This volume can be measured on a *sales-in* basis (the volume of sales made to the distributor organization) or a *sales-out* basis (the volume of product that flows through the distributor to its end-user customer). A sales-in measure is more directly tied to the manufacturer sales rep's individual control and influence. However, when using a sales-in measure of volume, steps must be taken to avoid channel loading—pushing more product into the distributor than what is demanded in the market or what can be reasonably sold by the distributor. Conversely, a sales-out measure of volume provides less line-of-sight to the individual seller's influence, but more clearly reflects the actual demand for the product in the marketplace as well as the effectiveness of the distributor's sales staff in moving it. As with the selection of any other performance measure, the sales-in versus sales-out question must be answered within the context of the desired selling role of the manufacturer sales rep. That being the case, a compensation arrangement based on volume secured from assigned accounts (perhaps relative to goal) should determine a significant amount of the incentive compensation for the distributor sales rep.

18.3 Technical Support Representative

Technical support personnel lend a depth of technical expertise to support the customer and the vendor's sales personnel during the sales process. Technical support reps are more commonly used when the product being sold (or the markets into which the product is being sold) requires significant technical expertise beyond what is normally expected of the sales rep. In such an environment, the sales rep with whom the technical support rep is selling may be considered more of a generalist who provides market or customer expertise to complement the support rep's technical depth.

Technical support reps are typically based in the field, and they may support the sales reps on a presale or a postsale basis, or both. Presale support activities often include conducting product demonstrations, participating in joint sales calls with the sales rep, and helping the customer to test the vendor's product in a simulated use environment. Postsale activities often include product installation support, customer training, and even ongoing account maintenance work. Technical support reps are usually deployed into defined teams of sales reps or float across geographic regions or market segments supporting multiple salespeople.

Because of their interdependence with the sales rep in executing the sales process and their significant customer contact and potential influence, technical support reps are commonly eligible to participate in a sales compensation program that is similar to or linked with the incentive arrangement for the sales reps they support. Indeed, a high degree of interdependence with salespeople in executing the sales process provides a compelling argument for sales incentive eligibility.

Consistent with their sales involvement, technical support reps are often teamed with salespeople for performance measurement and incentive compensation purposes. The most common measure of team performance is the combined results from the selling efforts of all the sales reps they support. This is often expressed as an aggregate measure of sales volume achieved by the team or as the overall average percentage of goal achieved by the individual salespeople they support. The logic in this approach is that if the support rep performs her assigned role well, the sales team as a whole has an increasing chance of achieving its selling goal.

Other common performance measures include key milestones in the sales process that indicate an increasing likelihood the sale will occur, such as the number of product demonstrations conducted or successfully completing a product qualification test. For a postsale technical support rep, the number of training sessions held is an example of this type of activity measure. Such milestone or activity measures should be used sparingly, with more focus being placed on the volume- or production-oriented measures that closely reflect the success of the business. Placing less emphasis on activity measures avoids the pitfall of paying for events that may yield little or no results.

18.4   Field Product or Market Manager

Like the specialized expertise of the technical support rep, the field product or market manager has a deep level of expertise in the assigned product line or market segment. Such a specialized selling role is needed when the product or market in question places significant demands on the knowledge, expertise, and experience that the vendor's selling resources bring to the table. A frequent response to these demands is a sales resource dedicated to the product or market in question. Unlike the technical support rep, the field product or market manager typically owns a base of accounts with responsibility to achieve an individual sales goal. In addition, he may or may not be supported by a technical sales support resource.

Conventional sales compensation techniques apply to these specialized selling roles with some slight changes in the selection of performance measures. A basic measure of sales productivity still applies, such as sales or revenue volume; however, the volume should be expressed and measured in terms of the specific assigned product or market (e.g., product line X or market segment Y sales volume compared with a goal). In addition to a basic volume measure, secondary strategic performance measures might be used to reward the specialized nature of the role more specifically.

For the field product specialist, a measure of product mix is often used. It indicates how effectively the salesperson is selling the breadth of the product line. It is especially relevant if there are multiple product lines assigned or multiple categories within the assigned product lines, each with its own sales goal. A common approach to measuring product mix is to compute the combined simple average of the goal achievement percentage for all product line goals. The challenge is that superior performance in one product line can more than make up for completely neglecting another product line. To drive balanced selling across multiple product lines or categories, a hurdle can be employed. For the salesperson to be eligible for incentive earnings, the product mix incentive opportunity may be based on the average goal performance for all product lines combined, but a hurdle might require a minimum level of performance (e.g., 80 percent of goal) for all assigned product lines.

For the field market manager, a measure of market share in the assigned market is often a compelling complement to the fundamental measure of sales volume. Market share is simply a measure of the vendor's share of the customers' expenditures (actual or potential) for the defined product or service. A common challenge is the lack of available, statistically sound market share data. Because most vendors are not the sole-source provider of the given product or service to their customers, they typically own less than 100 percent of the customer's budgeted purchases for that product. The vendor is then forced to estimate the total size of the customer's product budget, including the amount spent on that product with the competition. This often requires customer reporting of such information to the vendor, but customers are often reluctant to share this information in the interest of retaining some advantage in the sales and buying process. If the information is provided, it may become a point of negotiation for additional customer concessions on the part of the vendor. However, if captured, market share data can yield a compelling metric of the field market manager's success in penetrating the targeted market segments.

18.5 National Account Manager

The role of acquiring, developing, and retaining "national" accounts often requires skills that are very different from those needed to manage smaller local or regional accounts. As such, the national account manager (NAM) position is often the most senior individual contributor selling position, with the major accounts NAMs manage being viewed as assets of the company.

A national account is typically defined as a customer with a national or even global presence, translating into large-scale volume selling opportunities for the vendor. The NAM assigned to the account is responsible for coordinating the selling activities to the account across all its locations. Thus, NAMs are typically responsible for a limited list of named accounts rather than a geographic territory of accounts.

Selling to national accounts (often termed corporate, major, or global accounts) is typically characterized by long, complex selling cycles involving multiple decision makers and points of influence. One of the keys to determining the level of prominence for national account sales is the extent to which the key buying decision is made centrally with a corporate buyer or locally with a local or regional buyer. The location of the key buyer commonly takes one of two forms:

▪ *Central sanction, central buy.* In this scenario, the corporate-office-domiciled buyer makes the buying decision, which is then imposed company-wide, requiring local sites that may have their own purchasing function to conform to the corporate mandate. In such cases, the NAM is highly prominent in acquiring the original sale but then must rely heavily on local selling resources to ensure effective order fulfillment and after-sales service. However, local sales reps may significantly influence future buying decisions made at the corporate level with the level and quality of local service support they provide.

▪ *Central sanction, local buy.* In this case, the corporate buyer approves vendors from whom local buyers can procure goods and services; however, it is left to the local buyer to chose the vendor with whom they will do business. The NAM is key to getting the vendor on the approved vendor list, either formally or informally, and in maintaining a presence with the corporate entity. It is the local sales rep, however, who ultimately influences the local buying decision.

In either scenario, a great deal of teamwork and coordination between NAM and local selling resources is required to respond to the many potential points of influence and to execute the sales and service delivery process.

Pay implications for NAMs are fairly straightforward. Because of the high level of skill and experience required for the position, NAMs usually command a premium in terms of target total cash compensation relative to local or geographic sales reps. While the NAM may be highly prominent in the sale, the long sales cycles often moderate the amount of pay placed at risk. Therefore, if a NAM and local sales rep position are deemed equally prominent relative to their respective selling tasks, the NAM may have more fixed pay and less variable pay. However, the leverage (or amount of upside incentive offered for excellent performance) is the same for the two positions relative to the amount of pay each has at risk.

In addition to differences in pay mix, the NAM may be subject to performance measures driven by team as well as individual performance. The intent of a team measure is to gauge the NAM's effectiveness in coordinating the contingent of selling and support resources that serve the national account at its various decentralized sites. Depending on the role played by local selling resources, it may be appropriate to measure local sales reps on their success in supporting a national account as a separate measure of their performance. Finally, because the NAM is often tasked with strategic imperatives that are difficult to measure in gross volume or profitability terms, it is not unusual to tie a portion of variable pay to what might be called performance objectives (also termed strategic sales objectives) or key sales objectives. Examples of these NAM objectives include successfully negotiating a new long-term contract, achieving exclusivity with the account, improving overall account share, or raising an externally validated measure of account satisfaction. The intent of such an incentive component is to complement the core productivity-oriented measure, thereby more accurately measuring the NAM on true success with assigned accounts.

18.6   Channel Manager

The role of channel manager is similar to the role of a manufacturer sales rep selling to a distributor as described earlier in this chapter. The channel manager is tasked with managing an indirect channel of distribution and maximizing the sale of the vendor's products or services through the assigned channel(s). Examples of indirect channels of distribution vary by industry but include wholesale distributors, resellers, VARs (value-added resellers), VADs (value-added distributors), and major retailers. Key activities undertaken in support of a channel are varied, often going beyond pure selling to fall under the heading of general business adviser to the channel partner. Some of these critical activities include:

- Acquiring new channel partners
- Planning and executing joint advertising and promotional campaigns
- Coordinating jointly developed products or services of interest to channel partners
- Training of channel partner salespeople
- Providing in-store merchandising support for retailers
- Providing inventory planning and management support
- Representing vendor and channel partners at key industry events and trade shows

As with the manufacturer sales rep selling to distributors, the question of measuring a channel manager's performance on the basis of sales-in to the channel versus sales-out of the channel must be addressed. Again, the answer lies in the vendor's definition of the channel manager's key selling roles. Ultimately, issues such as channel manager degree of control and influence; potential for channel loading; and revenue measurement, tracking, and recognition capabilities must be considered in determining the most appropriate measures of performance. However, as is the case with the national account manager, a volume-oriented measure alone is often an insufficient gauge of a channel manager's contribution. Again, more strategic measures of performance such as channel partner penetration, product mix, channel profitability, and acquisition of new productive channel partners may be appropriate. The more these strategic measures of performance focus on results (such as volume increase resulting from joint promotions) rather than activities (such as launching three joint promotions), the better.

Because the channel manager typically has little to no contact with the end user of the vendor's product or service, the position is often found to have little prominence in the sale. Other variables in the marketing mix such as advertising and promotions and the strength of channel partners' selling resources often play a larger role in influencing the ultimate purchase decision. Therefore, the channel manager's mix of fixed and variable pay is skewed toward guaranteed income. Additionally, the form of incentive is typically a bonus rather than a commission.

18.7   Telesales Representative

The use of telephone-based selling clearly signals a vendor's strategy to deploy a low-cost direct channel of distribution. A telesales function can be extremely effective at penetrating market segments that cannot be accessed profitably using field-based sellers because of the size or location of the accounts in question. Because it is still a direct channel, the vendor retains more control in the sales process than can be maintained by selling through an indirect channel.

The prominence of a telesales rep may vary significantly depending on how the channel and the role are structured. A key factor is the extent of inbound versus outbound calling activity. There are three primary forms:

▪ *Inbound only.* An inbound telesales function only responds to incoming customer calls in support of field-based selling efforts. There is no outbound calling to existing or prospective customers. Inbound telesales reps may engage in little or no active selling if they simply fulfill orders or execute a customer service role. They may, however, have an active role in "up-selling" inbound customers to additional or different products or services than the customers originally had in mind.

■ *Outbound only.* An outbound telesales rep is often a prominent selling role with explicit independent selling responsibility. An outbound telesales role may be defined principally as a support for field sellers' efforts with their assigned accounts with no individual account ownership or as an independent seller with ownership of a geographic territory or named account list. In either case, an outbound telesales rep position is more prominent in the sale than his inbound counterpart.

■ *Inbound and outbound.* Rather than performing one role or the other exclusively, a combination inbound and outbound telesales rep is a common selling role. This combination telesales rep answers inbound calls in an effort to fulfill orders and service customers stimulated by direct in-field selling activity. Yet, the rep also actively places outbound calls in a direct selling role. A key to managing and compensating this combined role is clearly defining the desired balance between inbound and outbound calling activity.

Because of the clear differences in role and prominence of inbound versus outbound telesales reps, implications for incentive pay are fairly clear. The inbound telesales rep performing only an order fulfillment or customer service role is often paid only a base salary or hourly wage with no performance-based variable compensation. To the extent that the inbound telesales rep engages in up-selling activity, a modest amount of variable pay may be appropriate. The variable opportunity would be based either on the sales performance of the overall telesales team or on the performance of the entire sales organization (field and telesales). This team measure of performance is appropriate because inbound telesales reps have no influence in creating selling opportunities; they simply respond to and maximize each customer contact opportunity they have.

For the outbound telesales rep or the combination telesales rep, a slightly to significantly more aggressive mix of pay is typically warranted. If the telesales rep is responsible for penetrating a base of accounts or geographic territory, the role is undoubtedly more prominent than if the telesales rep simply supports the field-based sales rep who has formal ownership of account relationships. In the former situation, an individual measure of sales performance, as would be used for a field-based sales rep, is appropriate. In the latter situation, the telesales rep is more appropriately rewarded on the basis of the collective selling success of the team of field sellers and telesales reps. Accordingly, the mix of fixed and variable pay, as well as the upside leverage, would be more aggressive for the telesales rep with his own base of accounts than they would be for the telesales rep supporting field-based salespeople. For the combination telesales rep, a combination of team and individual measures of volume contribution is usually appropriate.

19

Measuring and Rewarding Team Selling

19.1　A Case for Team Selling

Look inside most companies today, and you'll find a veritable smorgasbord of teams—from continuous improvement teams to crossfunctional product development teams to leadership and client relationship management teams. Management has come to the realization that in many situations, individuals working together can drive performance to a higher level than the same individuals working independently. This concept applies to the sales force as well.

In many selling situations, selling teams can attain higher levels of performance than individuals working independently. For example, an electrical products manufacturer found that selling teams of sales engineers, design engineers, and manufacturing managers were able to increase sales, profitability, and customer satisfaction by tailoring products for their most important customers. A publishing company found that sales process teams made up of sales, operations, and customer service personnel were able to improve efficiencies and reduce customer complaints by better understanding each function's requirements in the process. A pharmaceutical company learned that regional selling teams composed of sales representatives from the same geographic area improved effectiveness due to an increased sharing of market information and local best practices. In all three cases, the increased communication and trust among the functions represented on the team increased efficiency and effectiveness, improved the organization's ability to learn, and ultimately led to better sales results.

Sales teams differ from other types of teams in a number of important respects, largely because the selling operation itself typically differs in culture, organization, and systems. These differences have a major impact on the way management must compensate sales teams. Traditionally, selling has been an individualist's game, best played by solo practitioners accustomed to setting their own pace, making their own decisions, and being rewarded largely in proportion to their efforts. Although most sales reps understand that their individual sales goals roll up to a cumulative organizational goal, their focus generally remains on their specific, personal objectives. That's why the shift to a team focus poses some special challenges for a sales organization. In fact, there is a natural tendency for sales reps to resist team selling:

"What if I get stuck with a loser teammate?"

"Will I be supporting a free rider?"

"How will team membership affect my compensation?"

"Will I lose my independence?"

"How do we resolve conflict?"

"Who is my boss?"

Given the challenges associated with creating selling teams, it is imperative that you first clearly demonstrate a compelling business case for using them. Without clear logic and evidence that team selling is required to reinforce the business strategy, teams will fail. It must be clear that teams will drive strategic results to a higher level than is possible when individuals work apart.

19.2   What Sales Management Systems Must Be in Place?

Compensating selling teams is only one of several management issues that must be addressed to implement team selling. In addition to rewards, factors such as clear tasks and goals, supportive culture, appropriate human resources processes, and organizational structure play an important role in effective team selling.

Research shows that sales reps are motivated by having clearly defined sales tasks. Similarly, selling teams must have clear role definitions to operate effectively. In fact, these definitions are more critical in team selling to avoid duplication, omissions, and degradation of selling tasks. Worse, confusion arises when team members have different goals, plans, budgets, and management direction. For team selling roles to be clear, the following points must be defined and communicated:

1. Who the members of the team are.
2. What accountability part-time and full-time members have.

3. What the relative importance is of the team objective versus individual objectives.
4. How team conflict will be resolved.

Further, an organization's culture must also reinforce team selling for it to succeed. This requires senior management to walk the talk. This cultural shift can be particularly difficult for managers who grew up in an environment where sales staff were lone rangers, working independently. There must be a culture of cooperation, not competition. Many sales organizations have intentionally promoted some, if not significant, internal competition to drive results between sales staff from different regions or divisions. This competition can be an obstacle to the effectiveness of team selling. Managers must continuously reinforce the importance of team selling, work well with their counterparts from other divisions, and resolve conflicts objectively. In the end, management must set the example.

In many sales organizations, the selection criteria for sales reps include attributes such as independence, being motivated by money, and willingness to accept direction. The products of these criteria are people who do not like working on teams, prefer much of their pay to be based on their individual performance, and do not deal well with ambiguity. Therefore, if an organization commits to a team selling approach, the selection criteria often must be changed to recruit team-oriented skills. Additionally, training systems should be implemented to develop team competencies among the existing sales force.

Pooling information, resources, contacts, and tasks is essential to teamwork, but sometimes contrary to individual selling. Getting sales reps to share ideas fully and consistently can require a fairly significant cultural shift. While team-building training and the right reward program can go a long way toward eliminating barriers, a sound, full-circle performance management system can also be a critical ingredient in the mix.

The full-circle evaluation approach is, by definition, a group exercise, requiring participation from virtually everyone involved in the selling process. Under this approach, customers, co-workers, subordinates, and supervisors provide performance feedback and commentary on an individual or a team's performance, or both. Although this approach is not viable in all selling situations, it can be effective in organizations where sales reps work closely with co-workers and customers.

Organizational silos between functions or divisions often impede communications and prevent effective team selling. "In interviews, salespeople repeatedly cited more communication as the one thing that could most improve teamwork on shared accounts" (Frank V. Cespedes, Stephen X. Doyle, and Robert J. Freedman, "Teamwork for Today's Selling," *Harvard Business Review*, March–April 1989). To assess whether a reorganization is required to support team selling, ask:

1. Are teams able to form across functional or divisional lines?
2. Do reporting relationships get in the way of effective teamwork?

19.3   What Performance Measures Make Sense?

Team measures, like individual measures, must reflect and reinforce your organization's business strategy and objectives. Beyond that, measures must be objective, quantifiable, relevant to and controllable by the team, and have balanced representation of short-term and long-term success factors.

There is a straightforward, four-step approach to selecting performance measures for individuals on selling teams:

1. Develop performance measures for each level of the organization, including cross-divisional and cross-functional teams and individual metrics. (See Exhibit 19-1.)
2. Assign team measures to individual team members. (See Exhibit 19-2.)
3. Merge team measures with individual measures to derive combined performance measures for each salesperson. (See Exhibit 19-3.)
4. Weight the measures according to their importance to each role. (See Exhibit 19-4.)

Once performance measures are selected, ensure that:

- Priorities, weighting, and goals are shared across team members to ensure fairness and to minimize redundancies.
- Weights accurately reflect individuals' roles on the team.
- Individuals have no more than five performance measures.
- The performance tracking system is tested for at least one tracking cycle prior to using it for reward purposes.

Setting team goals is different from setting individual goals. After all, teams must be formed out of necessity to achieve a higher

Exhibit 19-1. Setting Performance Measures for All Organizational Levels

Individual Measures	Individual Salesperson			
	Rep A	Rep B	Rep C	Specialist Rep
Individual Territory Sales	✔	✔	✔	✔
Territory Sales - Product A	✔	✔		
Territory Sales - Product B	✔	✔		✔
Sales Activities	✔	✔	✔	✔

District

Cross-Divisional Team

Territory

Performance measures are determined for each territory and specialist rep, while metrics are also defined for each organizational level above the territory sales force. For example, the performance of territory rep A will be measured against four norms, while territory rep C's performance will be assessed on only two measures.

level of performance than individuals could achieve working independently. "Walk over" or easily achieved team goals serve to eradicate the need for teams.

19.4 The Right Balance Between Individual and Team Results

Three decades of organization research demonstrate that well-designed reward systems increase motivation by 20 to 30 percent when certain conditions are in place:

Exhibit 19-2. Team Member Assignments.

Team Measures	District Team			
	Rep A	Rep B	Rep C	Specialist Rep
District Sales	✔	✔	✔	✔
District Productivity			✔	

Team Measures	Cross-Divisional Team			
	Rep A	Rep B	Rep C	Specialist Rep
Team Sales - Product A	✔	✔		
Team Sales - Product B	✔	✔		✔

Two separate teams are formed. While the territory reps retain their responsibility for territory-level results, they will also participate in the two teams and be measured for their respective team performances as well. The metrics used to measure the success of both teams are shown in the far left-hand column of the two tables above.

1. The rewards are valued.
2. Personal control over performance is high.
3. Salespersons believe that effort leads to rewarded results.
4. Feedback is timely and accurate.

However, rewards based on team performance may adversely affect the existence or level of these conditions. For example, sales reps accustomed to being measured on their individual sales results may feel that their personal control over results is diminished if their performance is going to be based on a team's sales results. They may also feel that their personal effort is less likely to lead to rewarded results since they must depend on others to be successful.

Several practices can mitigate the adverse consequences of team rewards:

Exhibit 19-3. Merging of Team and Individual Performance Measures.

Team Measures	District Team			
	Rep A	Rep B	Rep C	Specialist Rep
District Sales	✔	✔	✔	✔
District Productivity			✔	

Team Measures	Cross-Divisional Team			
	Rep A	Rep B	Rep C	Specialist Rep
Team Sales - Product A	✔	✔		
Team Sales - Product B	✔	✔		✔

Combined Measures	Individual Salesperson			
	Rep A	Rep B	Rep C	Specialist Rep
Individual Territory Sales	✔	✔	✔	✔
Team Sales - Product A	✔	✔		
Team Sales - Product B	✔	✔		
Sales Activities	✔	✔	✔	✔
District Sales	✔	✔	✔	✔
District Productivity			✔	

In the end, each salesperson's performance will be measured on the basis of several measures, some reflecting individual territory results and others reflecting the performance of the teams on which the individual participates. The next step is to determine the relative emphasis or importance among the assigned measures.

Exhibit 19-4. Assigning Weights to Each Performance Measure.

Combined Measures	Individual Salesperson			
	Rep A	Rep B	Rep C	Specialist Rep
Individual Territory Sales	20%	30%	30%	20%
Team Sales - Product A	25%	15%		
Team Sales - Product B	15%	25%		
Sales Activities	10%	10%	20%	40%
District Sales	30%	20%	40%	40%
District Productivity			10%	
Total	100%	100%	100%	100%

1. Team members must understand the business case for team selling.
2. Team members must be actively involved in team decisions.
3. The probability of individuals' receiving at least target or planned incentive payout levels should not be diminished with team rewards.
4. There must be proportional financial consequences for both high team *and* low team contributions.

The incentive design options for selling teams range in emphasis from primarily individual performance oriented to primarily team performance oriented (see Exhibit 19-5).

To select the right approach for your organization, ask these questions:

Exhibit 19-5. Incentive Design Options for Teams.

Design Option		
Individual incentive	+	Team recognition
Individual incentive	+	Team pool
Individual incentive	*with*	Team modifier or hurdle
Individual incentive	+	Team incentive
Team incentive	*with*	Individual modifier or hurdle
Team incentive	+	Individual pool
Team incentive	+	Individual recognition

1. What type of selling team are we using?
     —Cross-functional selling team that shares a customer or customer segment
     —Cross-functional selling team that shares a selling process
     —Regional selling team that shares a destiny
2. What type of team member are we designing incentives for?
     —Core member who is a member of one team as his or her entire job
     —Contributor who is a member of one to four teams and may have individual accountabilities
     —Resource who is a member of more than four teams and probably has individual accountabilities
3. What is our compensation philosophy?
     —More team oriented
     —More individually oriented.

The answers to these questions will help you determine the type of selling team and the level of contribution of each team member. (See Exhibit 19-6).

Using team incentives can generate administrative headaches related to crediting sales performance. One approach is to establish a credit pool that is divided among team members based on the nature and extent of each individual's responsibility for and contri-

(text continues on page 270)

Exhibit 19-6. Team Incentive Design Options by Role.

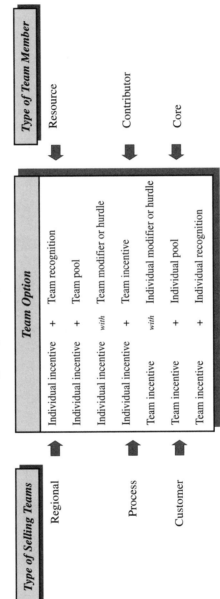

Type of Selling Teams		Team Option			Type of Team Member
Regional	→	Individual incentive	+	Team recognition	Resource
		Individual incentive	+	Team pool	
		Individual incentive	*with*	Team modifier or hurdle	
Process	→	Individual incentive	+	Team incentive	Contributor
		Team incentive	*with*	Individual modifier or hurdle	
Customer	→	Team incentive	+	Individual pool	Core
		Team incentive	+	Individual recognition	

Exhibit 19-7. Cross-Functional Selling Team Sharing a Customer.

Situation

Company Sales Profile—Aerospace Manufacturer

- Long selling cycle
- Complex selling process (many decision makers and influencers)
- Technical, customized products
- High prices
- Critical after-sale service

Type of Team

Cross-functional team (with sales, manufacturing, engineering, purchasing, customer service, field service personnel) with different backgrounds and perspectives, focusing on sales to key customers

Type of Team Members

Core, contributor, resource

Compensation Philosophy

Team oriented

Why Team Selling Is Appropriate

- The need for a more integrated customer sales strategy
- Vendor's lack of value-added solutions that address customer's specific short-term and long-term objectives
- To decrease component production costs by involving manufacturing and engineering in the sales process

Performance Measurement

- Specific sales goals by customer or account, reflecting achievement of revenue and selling milestones (e.g., products demonstrated to customer engineering team) over designated performance period

Balance Between Individual and Team Incentive Pay

- Eligibility of all team members for incentive pay (expressed as percentage of base salary)
- Differing amounts of pay at risk depending on role (e.g., core member eligible for 25 percent of base, resource member eligible for 10 percent of base)
- Weighted incentive opportunity for each team member, according to how much time and effort is spent on that team

Exhibit 19-8. Cross-Functional Selling Team Sharing a Process.

Situation

Company Sales Profile—Specialty Chemical Manufacturer

- Operations-focused culture moving toward a customer-oriented organization
- Lack of communication between sales reps, on-site chemical process engineers, and customer service
- Customers expect high service level

Type of Team

Cross-functional team (sales, engineering, customer service) that requires close coordination of a hand-off once individual's goal is completed

Type of Team Members

Core, contributor

Compensation Philosophy

Team oriented, with some recognition for individual contribution

Why Team Selling Is Appropriate

- Lack of seamless sales, implementation, and postsales process
- High level of chemical process implementation errors and customer service complaints and low sales rep new account development selling time
- Conflicting operations and sales goals

Performance Measurement

- Individual and team incentive components based on prominence in the sales process
- Goals set for each account recognizing revenue, profit, and strategic sales objectives

Balance Between Individual and Team Incentive Pay

- Team incentive with individual modifier
- Target incentive for contributors based 70 percent on individual goals and 30 percent on team goals
- Target incentive for core members based 30 percent on individual goals and 70 percent on team goals

---

Exhibit 19-9. Regional Selling Team Sharing a Destiny.

Situation

Company Sales Profile—High-Tech Company

- Entrepreneurial culture orientation
- Primary sales channel through distributors
- Still adding region managers, sales reps, and applications engineers across the country

Type of Team

All employees wear many hats, as is typical in new, unstructured, fast-growth businesses. Strong shared-destiny management style or philosophy

Type of Team Members

Core, contributor, resource

Compensation Philosophy

Team oriented

Why Team Selling Is Appropriate

- Culture does not foster sharing best practices, coaching, and mentoring
- Team selling is a major strategic initiative
- Inaccurate sales forecasting at the region and sales rep level, due to fast growth

Performance Measurement

- Overall company performance as measured by sales and profits
- Region performance as measured by sales and profits

Balance Between Individual and Team Incentive Pay

- Core, contributor, and resource members eligible for incentive based on achievement of target level of company profits. All eligible for same percentage of base pay.
- Core and contributor members directly involved in sales process eligible for incentive based on region performance. Their opportunity differs in amount at risk, depending on role.

---

bution to the final results. Another option is to provide varying levels of dual credit to team members. Whatever approach is used, it's critical to define and communicate clear rules and follow them rigorously to avoid the kind of counterproductive negotiations that can derail an otherwise well-designed program.

19.5 Examples

Exhibits 19-7 through 19-9 show three types of selling teams: a cross-functional team that shares a customer, a cross-functional team that shares a process, and a regional selling team that shares a destiny. Although these real-world examples are neither exhaustive nor mutually exclusive, they spotlight some of the ways measurement and pay systems can encourage sales reps to work together smoothly in support of an organization's broader business goals. The examples also highlight the importance of a customized approach to measuring and rewarding sales teams.

20

Compensating the Sales Manager

The role of the first-line sales manager requires active, hands-on management style. Sales managers need to set direction, mentor and coach reps, and lead by example. They need to keep in close contact with their field sales force, discussing problems, modifying goals, evaluating performance, and providing help. Hence, they need first-rate leadership, communication, and management skills, buttressed by a clear understanding of the company's selling strategy and how that strategy links to both the compensation and recognition programs. As such, a sales manager pay plan should communicate sales and strategic priorities and reward appropriate selling behavior but without distracting incumbents from their managerial duties. In fact, a good sales manager pay plan rewards those who manage well.

The sales manager, by the very nature of the job, has significant direct influence on the success or failure of the sales incentive compensation program. Strangely, many companies ignore this crucial fact when designing incentive plans. Some even measure and pay their sales managers in a manner that conflicts with the very salespeople they supervise or, on occasion, neglect to link sales management pay to measures they can directly influence. For example, many companies pay sales managers for performance against corporate or divisional goals—inappropriate for all but the most senior sales management professionals, since most sales managers' influence and focus is limited to a specific geographic district or region.

20.1 Approaching the Issue of Sales Manager Pay

For sales managers, the process by which companies design the incentive plan should be linked to the design of the incentive plan for the sales force. This ensures that management performance measures do not conflict with sales rep measures and helps plan designers create the appropriate pay structure. When redesigning pay plans for both reps and managers, it is important to design the sales reps' plan first and then craft a plan for sales management. This is critical to ensuring that the managerial plan supports fully the roles of front-line sellers and reinforces both effective leadership and sales behavior. Of course, changes to both the rep plan and the management plan should be rolled out simultaneously.

As with plans for sales reps, the first issue to consider is eligibility. Should all sales managers be eligible for incentive compensation? To answer this and many other questions regarding sales management incentives, plan designers should look first at how they plan to pay the sales force. Generally if sales reps are eligible for incentives, their managers should also be eligible.

The next issue is pay mix. As with salespeople, prominence, or the degree of influence on the sale, is a key driver of pay mix. The greater the influence on the sale, the greater the mix; that is, jobs with high prominence should have relatively low base salaries and relatively high incentive opportunity. Since sales managers are generally one step removed from the sale, the pay mix for most managers is usually less variable than the mix for the salespeople they supervise. For example, if a sales manager is supervising a group of sellers whose pay mix is 50 percent base salary and 50 percent incentive pay, the sales manager's mix might be 60 percent base salary and 40 percent incentive pay, with the exact pay mix depending on the nature of the sales management job and its influence on the sale.

A possible exception to this rule occurs in the case of the manager with direct selling responsibility. Some sales managers are responsible for sales to specific accounts or territories in addition to their managerial duties. For these jobs, it is important to examine carefully the desired balance between managerial and sales activities along with the manager's prominence on both direct selling and sales through his salespeople.

20.2   A Perspective on Performance Measures

There are three schools of thought on the best performance measures for sales management. The first approach, called the *alignment approach*, says that sales managers should be measured and paid on exactly the same things as the salespeople they supervise. Advocates of this approach argue that it helps management and salespeople cooperate because they share common goals.

The second approach, called the *top-down approach*, says that managers should be held accountable for corporate or divisional goals such as return on assets (ROA), earnings before interest and taxes (EBIT), or other indicators of corporate or divisional performance. Advocates of this approach argue that since many managers in nonsales positions are held accountable for these measures, sales managers should be too.

The alignment approach ignores the fact that those who move higher in the sales force management structure eventually encounter jobs that are responsible for cost, profitability, pricing, and setting goals for the sales force. These important duties, when appropriate, should be reflected in the compensation plan. Conversely, the top-down approach measures and rewards sales managers for results that are almost entirely out of their control; first- and second-level sales managers normally have little direct influence on the overall profitability or earnings of the company.

Therefore, the third and best approach (which has no name) merely states that performance measures should reflect the nature and responsibilities of the job role and that measures should be tightly linked to results that the sales manager can directly influence.

20.3   Typical Performance Measures

There are almost as many ways to measure and pay a sales manager as there are for sales reps. Rather than provide an exhaustive list, we will instead discuss some of the most effective management performance measures and the reasons for their use.

Overrides

The simplest sales management performance measure is an *override*, a percentage of subordinates' aggregate earnings *or* sales. Examples include 0.1 percent of sales revenue or 10 percent of all assigned sales reps' earnings. It is called an override because companies pay this percentage over and above the payment made to the sales force. The override is *not* deducted from sales force pay.

Overrides are generally used in start-up or fast-growth companies or in those with sales reps who receive most or all of their pay in the form of commission. By their very nature overrides reward volume selling and align management and sales rep objectives; but they do not distinguish between profitable and unprofitable sales, nor do they reflect the achievement of specified volume objectives.

Profit

Profit (or gross margin) is another popular sales management performance measure that is often used by more mature organizations selling into developed markets. Its primary purpose is to focus sales managers on deciding when to approve discounts and to focus their salespeople on the best products and accounts. An important challenge when measuring profit is obtaining good performance data. In addition, some companies shy away from releasing profitability data to the field organization for fear that the information will leak to competitors and customers. This problem can be circumvented by defining a surrogate for actual profit; proxies include discounts from list price, product mix, and weighted revenue.

Management Effectiveness

This is an innovative measure used by many organizations that are concerned with fair goal allocation and sales rep training and development. This performance measure rewards sales managers for increasing the number (or percentage) of their direct reports who achieve quota. This focuses managers on assigning quotas to their salespeople that are realistic and attainable. In addition, it does not reward them for cultivating a few star performers (as does the override measure) but instead pays them for effective coaching and development of all of their direct reports. Management effectiveness is best used by mature organizations with large sales forces that link sales force pay to quota achievement.

20.4   Types of Sales Managers

A sales manager's role is best defined by the characteristics of the sales representatives he or she supervises. There are two basic categories of sales representatives: the *account representative*, who primarily services and sells to an assigned group of accounts that are loyal to the company rather than to the individual representative, and the *entrepreneur*, who acquires and, in effect, controls her own accounts. The entrepreneur generally prefers such industries as life insurance, real estate, and financial services, while the account representative usually gravitates to manufacturing and consumer products. Exhibit 20-1 sets out further distinctions between these two categories. The techniques and skills needed to manage these two types of sales reps

Exhibit 20-1. Distinctions Between Two Categories of Sales Representatives.

Account Representative	Entrepreneur
▪ Services and sells to an assigned group of accounts.	▪ Sells to a diverse customer base who must constantly be convinced of the product or service need.
▪ Customers are loyal to the company rather than to the individual representative.	▪ Customers are at least as loyal to the representative as to the company represented.
▪ Represents the breadth of supplier services in a marketplace where the supplier is well known and offers numerous linkages into the customer.	▪ Often sells products and services that are essentially undifferentiated, have significant competition, or are priced uncompetitively.
▪ Sells in accordance with company policy, procedures, and culture.	▪ Employs a high degree of initiative and creative approaches.

Exhibit 20-2. Responsibilities of the Two Types of Sales Managers.

Account Rep Sales Manager	Entrepreneur Rep Sales Manager
▪ Manage existing resources to achieve company objectives.	▪ Attract new producers to provide company with new account base.
▪ Train current representatives in account retention and penetration.	▪ Train current representatives in prospecting and business development.
▪ Deploy reps efficiently among accounts and prospects.	▪ Inspire productive representatives to higher levels.

are very different. Exhibit 20-2 contrasts the responsibilities of the account rep and entrepreneur rep sales managers.

The sales manager in charge of account reps is typically expected to increase overall sales volume, although sometimes her goals encompass other strategic objectives, such as broadening product mix or increasing gross margin on a specific product. Generally senior management has imposed the sales organizational structure and marketing plan. This manager is dealing with a fixed resource (number of territories) and can increase its value only by getting the most out of every producer.

Most companies compensate entrepreneur reps with straight commission and low (if any) out-of-pocket expense reimbursement.

As a result, the companies usually profit from the business of even their lowest producers. The sales manager of an entrepreneur sales force is therefore charged with boosting gross productivity. He can accomplish this by effectively training current reps, retaining productive ones, and attracting new producers who will bring additional accounts with them. Because it is the individual rep, not the company, who controls the customer, this sales manager is not bound by a fixed (territorial) resource and may hire or fire reps as necessary.

Compensation Approach for Account Rep Sales Managers

The account rep sales manager's task is to maximize the return on a fixed resource. Therefore, her compensation plan should serve to hold her accountable for the results she achieves through her management of the field force. Usually the best way for the company to accomplish this is by measuring the collective efforts of the sales reps. Such accumulated results are most often expressed in terms of the aggregate volume of territories supervised. However, volume need not be the only measure. For example, in a highly competitive market, market share gains may be more important than absolute volume. Therefore, the reps' plan should include some incentive to increase market share, and the sales manager's plan should measure the cumulative result or market share gain.

Ideally, the sales manager's and sales reps' incentive plans should complement each other. Although one plan need not mirror the other exactly, a high degree of synergy is desirable, thereby supporting the company's sales goals at both field sales levels. But it is important to avoid holding the sales manager responsible for account-specific objectives that can be controlled only by an individual sales rep. For example, the company may require reps to sell more of product X than Y because X is more profitable. The only way the reps can achieve this is through their ongoing customer contact. The sales manager, however, cannot directly influence each rep's performance, but she *can* be measured according to the aggregate result.

Measuring the sales manager in this way makes her goals compatible with the reps' efforts to sell more of X. A simple equation translates accumulated results into compensation:

100 percent achievement of results
    = 100 percent incentive payment
    = 100 percent achievement of target total compensation.

If results fall short, the sales manager receives no bonus (or less than the target incentive), and her total compensation remains below the target level. If results exceed the objective, she is paid a higher bonus, bringing her total compensation above the targeted level.

The sales manager's challenge is to improve the company's return (sales volume or profit) on a fixed investment (a number of territories with a specified number of selling hours to be utilized). In doing this, she will effectively increase the average productivity of her sales reps. Because the sales manager can control district or region volume through her management of territorial resources, her compensation can be closely linked to that volume.

Given a volume objective to achieve, it is up to the sales manager to parcel out sales rep territory quotas in a manner that will best help her meet her own goals. Clearly the easiest way to achieve this is to follow the "80/20 rule": expect the top 20 percent of her reps to produce about 80 percent of her region's objective. She then divides the remainder of the objective among the average or below-average producers. If the company seeks to develop average and below-average reps, a compensation plan that holds the sales manager accountable for individual territory results as well as overall performance will require her to concentrate at least some energy on developing less productive reps.

There are two ways to construct such a plan:

1. Pay target compensation only when *both* aggregate and individual territory quotas are achieved.
2. Pay full target compensation upon achievement of aggregate objectives, with extra bonuses based on individual territory performance quotas.

Plans that incorporate individual territory results into the sales manager's goals place a greater burden on the sales manager, but ultimately everyone benefits. The sales manager increases her current income and potential for future bonuses by developing a better sales force. The sales reps improve their productivity, motivational level, and income. And the company enjoys a greater return from its sales organization.

Compensation Approach for Entrepreneur Rep Sales Managers

The entrepreneur rep sales manager, concerned with maximizing productivity, must ensure that competitors don't lure away his high producers because the resulting loss of accounts will cause a corresponding drop in overall productivity. In addition, because very few reps walk into the company with pockets full of accounts, the manager also spends a good portion of his time training and motivating low to average performers. Finally, the sales manager must recruit and train new reps to replace any who do not succeed. In the light of the scope of his responsibilities, the sales manager's performance is best evaluated by his effectiveness in training current reps, ability to attract new producers who can provide the company with additional accounts, and skill in retaining productive reps. These measures of sales management are all reflected in the aggregate productivity of the sales manager's subordinates.

Because entrepreneur reps are generally paid largely by straight commission, their income is directly linked to productivity. The aggregate earnings of the sales force therefore is an appropriate gauge of the sales manager's success. It follows that a bonus based on a percentage of his subordinates' aggregate earnings or sales—the so-called override approach—is the most effective incentive compensation for this type of sales manager.

20.5   How Much Should Sales Managers Make?

One of the most common questions asked when designing sales incentive plans is whether sales reps should be able to make more than sales managers. The answer is yes, absolutely. The *best* salespeople should make more than their sales manager (if the reps' goals are set properly!). Some might argue that the best sales reps should make more than the president of the company (and some do). But generally sales managers should make more than sales reps at target levels of performance. That is, if a sales rep and a sales manager both exactly achieve their goals, then the sales manager should earn more than the salesperson. This provides an incentive for salespeople to develop their management skills and also ensures that managers don't leave their jobs and return to the field.

An example pay curve illustrating the differences between sales manager and sales rep pay progression is shown in Exhibit 20-3. The pay curves shown are identical below goal, but above goal the rep's pay increases much more rapidly than the manager's pay. This ensures that the rep (who has more control over the sale than the manager) is rewarded handsomely for achieving above-target results. It also ensures that while the sales manager is rewarded for above-

Exhibit 20-3. Comparison of Sales Manager and Sales Representative Compensation.

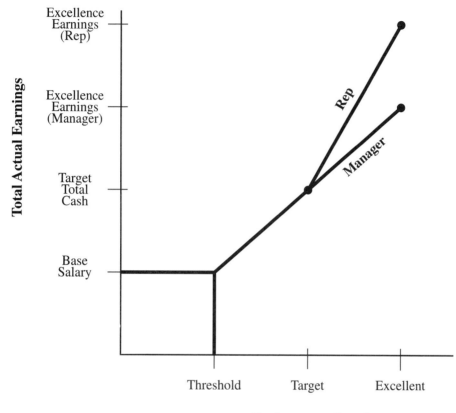

target performance, he is not distracted from his management and business responsibilities.

If nonsales managers outside the executive ranks participate in nonsales bonus plans, companies should carefully consider whether to include sales managers in those programs. Many companies choose to exclude sales managers from nonsales bonus programs that are designed to reward the achievement of individual objectives (under the assumption that the sales compensation plan rewards the sales manager's personal contribution). However, some plans also have a small component reserved for company-wide or division-wide goals, and many include sales managers in this part of the corporate plan.

20.6   When to Use the Executive Compensation Plan

Top sales executives and top sales and marketing executives are often considered part of the executive team. If peers of the top sales or sales and marketing executives are eligible for participation in an executive bonus and stock option plan, then the sales executives should also be included. Although a separate sales incentive plan might be better suited for sales executives, excluding them from the plan covering other executives may convey the message that the sales executives are less important to the organization than their peers.

If the sales executive participates in the same bonus plan as do his nonsales peers, the plan should have some provision for pay based on the achievement of individual objectives. That would allow the plan to contain field sales goals among its personal objectives. Since many companies make the individual portion of executive plans relatively small, management must select one, or at most two, measures of individual performance to ensure the appropriate focus for the sales executive.

21

Total Rewards Package

21.1 A Broad Perspective for the 1990s

As the millenium nears, corporations worldwide are taking a broad view of rewards. Just as the sophistication of customers is growing, employees too are seeking more tailored, multifaceted solutions to their needs. As a result, sales incentive compensation is no longer looked upon as a discrete reward.

Today employees—including even the most independent of salespeople—believe their "contract" with their companies encompasses more than just pay. Corporate executives are responding with total reward packages that now include a broad array of features that extend well beyond traditional cash compensation. Such additional features include various forms of benefits and reimbursements, personal development initiatives, and work environment factors. Exhibit 21-1 lists the more common components found in contemporary reward packages.

The previous chapters of this book concentrated heavily on cash compensation. Since modern total reward packages include much more, this chapter explores in some detail other reward forms that fit into the pay and benefits components.

21.2 Contests

A trucking carrier recently introduced international freight services to its customers. As a result of the complexity of the service and the long sales cycle, domestic account managers continued to sell the less time-consuming national services and placed minimal emphasis on international services.

The carrier had never implemented an incentive program for the sales force. But slow sales prompted management to create a three-month contest to motivate the sales force to sell international freight services, increase their knowledge about the service, and strategically drive sales on a regular basis. All account managers

Exhibit 21-1. Total Rewards Package Components.

Component	Sample Forms
Pay or compensation	Base salary Short-term cash incentive compensation Contests and spot awards Long-term incentives Recognition awards
Benefits or reimbursements	Health care Retirement and savings Paid time off Reimbursements Death and disability insurance Elder and child day care
Personal development	Technical training Leadership development Coaching and mentoring Career development and career paths Full-circle feedback and performance management
Work environment	Accountability Communications Flexibility Performance standards Fairness, teamwork, and integritiy

who sold international services would receive points to purchase valuable catalog prizes like furniture, crystal, and electronics.

Management perceived the three-month contest to be a success. International freight sales increased dramatically during the quarter, and account managers were more knowledgeable about the service. The sales force, however, was less excited about the contest. Less than 50 percent of the account managers accumulated enough points to purchase prizes; the majority of their territories did not have a high potential for international sales, which inadvertently excluded them from the contest. In addition, the Canadian account managers had to pay significant duty as well as income taxes on their prizes. Morale plummeted, and most of the account managers reverted to selling national services. Management realized contests are a powerful tool to drive behavior—if the program's details are well thought out.

This example illustrates the pros and cons of contests, which are common incentive tools. Such events entail short-term effort on the part of a sales force to maximize results for a particular nonrecurring purpose. The company offers cash, merchandise, travel, or recognition to the salespersons who achieve the highest sales volume (or other measure) within a specified period of time.

Sales contests serve a useful purpose in the right arena. In their most common form, they are designed to produce a single or a few winners who qualify for the prize over a short period, usually three months or less. (The contest duration could be as short as a week.) In some contests, there may be several winners: the leading salesperson in each of several sales districts, for example. And there are contests in which all sales employees can participate, with some winning more valuable prizes than others.

As peripheral elements of the reward system, sales contests can be powerful enhancements if used correctly, and they can be beneficial for both the company and the salespersons because they:

1. Recognize the efforts of the better-performing sales reps.

2. Can improve morale and team effort toward the achievement of a common goal.

3. Focus attention on specific near-term tactical sales events that might otherwise garner insufficient attention. Without a contest to fill the last fifty berths on a cruise liner, for example, the ship might sail with some or all of the berths unfilled.

A sales contest is also a relatively inexpensive way to create greater sales effort. Because the prize values are usually small, they constitute only a small percentage of an individual's annual total cash compensation. And given the relatively small number of winners, the aggregate costs are small compared to the incremental volume a contest can generate.

Although contests serve many useful functions, they should never be viewed as a substitute for incentive pay or as a remedy for inadequate or incomplete compensation programs. Contest earnings differ from other forms of incentive compensation because there is usually only one or a few winners. Further, contests often focus competition internally, toward other members of the sales force, rather than externally, toward the competition or the customer. Also, contest winnings are inconsistent, and the random nature of contests does not provide enough incremental compensation to offset uncompetitive earnings levels.

Before you implement contests at your company, remember that they have some distinct dangers:

▪ They displace sales volume from one time period to another. Aggregate sales volume might not increase; instead, sales volume normally captured in one time period will be moved to another period. (In essence, the salespersons are manipulating orders to maximize performance during the contest period.) Such behavior has negative implications for production planning and revenue forecasting. Production may be strained in the attempt to reach desired product flows during the contest period. Further, it is difficult to estimate future revenue when volume is cannibalized from those periods.

▪ Contests are often designed to focus attention on a specific product or product line. This may be dysfunctional from a strategic perspective. A short-term emphasis may undermine ongoing sales management processes (and the attention of the sales force) to encourage attention on products of greater strategic interest to the company over the long term. There are many examples of contest winners who fail to achieve their annual volume or product line volume goals because their attention was diverted in midyear.

▪ Certain sales reps may have a natural advantage because of the composition of their territories.

▪ Invariably, the top-performing salesperson wins the contest time after time. This will have a negative effect on the attitudes of recurring nonwinners or those who have only a marginal probability of winning.

21.3   Recognition Programs

Reaching into her mailbox, the wife of one of the computer company's seventy sales reps retrieved a brightly colored envelope addressed to her. "Tahiti First Class, the Only Way to Go" read the text on the back. The envelope didn't contain the standard advertisement for the local travel agent; instead, it contained the first of many mailings targeted specifically at spouses of the company's sales force. Each subsequent monthly note would provide an update on the planned trips. But not every salesperson could go to Tahiti—only those who achieved established annual sales targets. Management assumed that the spouses would provide moral support to encourage the sales reps to attain the highly desirable trip.

Interviews with the sales force revealed that the Tahiti trip was on everyone's mind and had been so for months. Sales management had aggressively promoted the two-week trip and its first-class amenities. Because of this unrelenting advertising, the recognition program had become a cause celebre among the salespersons and their spouses. Nothing could stop those who had a chance to reach the threshold for attendance. Clearly, management had gotten the attention of the sales force, whose members were working hard to join the elite "performance club."

The management of a large regional bank was looking for a tool to increase its tellers' morale and commitment. Management wanted to recognize the quality of service the tellers provided, but it also wanted to remind tellers of a tactical sales objective to increase the number of Visa credit card holders. To achieve these ends, the bank's branch supervisors selected a four-inch-tall clear Plexiglas pyramid; embedded in the center was a small gold token indicating that the teller was an award recipient. Management also created and published objective criteria for winning the Teller of the Quarter award. This recognition tool turned out to be one of the most popular in the bank's history. Why? Winners were permitted to display the unusual award at the front of their teller cages, and customers invariably inquired about its origin. This gave the winning tellers many opportunities during the workday to discuss their achievement, which provided constant reinforcement.

These examples illustrate the value of corporate sales recognition programs. In many companies, such programs have a greater impact on morale and motivation than do cash incentive programs. Their principal objective is to affirm that the company values the efforts of its better personnel. This is usually accomplished by highlighting the achievements of these employees before peers, management, or perhaps customers. Such programs can be a powerful inducement to continuing high performance.

In general, recognition programs entail defined criteria that, when met, entitle the salesperson (and possibly the sales manager and others supporting the selling function) to a trip, participation in a select group, or some form of material recognition. To attain maximum value, management promotes the program strenuously and publicizes the names of those whose performance warrants recognition.

The Pros and Cons

At the heart of such programs is the need to instill a sense of pride. For a relatively modest cost, a company can use a recognition program to let employees know they are doing a good job. Even when the awards are financial, many managers feel that the real value is symbolic: status, pride, and a sense of value can have more impact than regular compensation does.

As is the case with contests, managers should be wary of using recognition awards incorrectly; they can have some very negative ramifications. Here are some points to consider:

- Employees may feel that favoritism is a criterion for selection. Management must take special care to develop and fully communicate the criteria or goals to be achieved to earn recognition.
- All employees must believe that they can win; otherwise, marginal performers will not try.
- Awards must be promoted internally if employees are to be fully recognized by their peers.

Not all recognition programs will work effectively in all sales forces. The selling situation can greatly affect the success of the program. For instance, commission salespersons are essentially self-directing and may have little or no actual involvement with field management. They set their own day-to-day schedules and have minimal interaction with other company employees, including their supervisors, during the work week. Because of this isolation, high-prominence (commission) salespeople have different recognition needs. They lack the close supervisory environment in which frequent face-to-face encouragement is possible. Thus, recognition programs take on greater importance.

Peer recognition among such sales reps becomes highly symbolic and reflects the company's sense of the salesperson's value. Recognition programs for these employees are usually quite frequent, and travel incentive clubs focus on individual recognition. Clubs and sales meetings present opportunities to gather the salespeople at one location and celebrate achievement.

Conversely, recognition programs for salaried salespersons (with lower prominence than that of commission salespersons) tend to focus on face-to-face acknowledgment, commendations, and other forms of direct encouragement. Large-scale programs may take on less importance, because the lower-prominence salespersons have more opportunity for daily interaction with their supervisors.

Measuring Performance

All employees presumably have an equal chance to earn recognition. This is a key issue, but building fairness and equity into recognition programs can be difficult. Some measures that work perfectly for one part of the sales force (like market share) may not work for another (market share usually favors small territories). To avoid any perception of inequity, management should consider having several winners. For example, a company might use a common recognition measure across several sales territories, with a winner in each. Another technique is to use a range of measures that gives several salespersons in a given territory the opportunity to qualify—salespeople with more than 15 percent sales growth over the previous period, for example.

Most companies use recognition programs to highlight above-average sales performance, but some directly recognize less successful employees for their weak performances. Posting the results of all sales reps' efforts is usually enough to highlight the less-than-stellar performers. More direct recognition, such as "crying towel" awards, can be humiliating and may create anger. These forms of negative recognition should be avoided.

Many companies are now expanding eligibility for the recognition programs to sales support and customer care positions. In some forward-thinking high-technology companies, top applications engineers and customer service people are also eligible to attend; these technical positions have daily interaction with the salesperson's accounts to ensure that purchased equipment meets the customer's needs and continues to operate efficiently. Although these specialized support persons participate in many of the same recognition activities as do the sales reps, special recognition events are also scheduled to highlight their achievements among their peers. Participation in such recognition programs by technical support or customer service personnel encourages teamwork in the selling process while recognizing the importance of individual achievement.

Sales performance aside, recognition programs can also be used to acknowledge longevity through some material award. Jeweled pins, rings, plaques, merchandise, and even cash are common awards. Longevity recognition programs are typically used for all employees and are not restricted to sales or service personnel.

Forms of Recognition

Recognition can take a wide variety of forms and can be either short or long term. Most recognition awards are nonmonetary, although cash awards can be used. In fact, many new employees and those at the lower end of the organizational ladder tend to prefer cash. But experience suggests that a combination of some form of cash incentive and nonmonetary recognition can be the most effective motivator. The selling situation is a key factor in determining the form of recognition and the relative degree of emphasis.

Short-term recognition programs acknowledge an employee's achievement, but the award itself may not have lasting value. Common examples include:

- Small, on-the-spot cash bonuses for exemplary achievements.
- Small awards of stock or other forms of equity.
- Plaques, pins, certificates of achievement, and travel or trip vouchers.
- Personal encouragement from a direct supervisor or senior management.
- Letters and telephone calls of commendation from senior or sales management.
- Group activities (such as lunches or small parties) to recognize the achievement of team goals.
- Honorary job titles.

An incentive travel award program for the top-performing sales reps is a highly successful short-term tool. As illustrated in the Tahiti trip example, these trips can be powerful motivators. In a typical travel award program, a portion of the sales force will become eligible to participate in the annual "club," with the achievement celebrated in an exotic resort locale. Eligibility is usually based on meeting a specified sales target or attaining a specified percentage of quota. Although these trips include some minor training and business meetings, their principal purpose is recreational.

It is common for a salesperson's spouse or "significant other" to attend as well. This prevents the inevitable concerns about the lone spouse's activity and provides an important benefit: creation of a "home cheerleader" to encourage more selling effort. Aside from their obvious value in recognizing performance, these annual gatherings allow the best and the brightest of the sales force to learn from one another and to build mutually beneficial alliances.

There are some interesting variations on the club concept to consider. In some companies, the top-performing salesperson receives extra recognition during the club event, flying first class while the other participants fly coach, for example. Other extras may include a rental car, an upgraded room, special side trips, or extra time. Of course, allowing extra time away from the territory has its obvious opportunity costs.

Another interesting variation involves special consideration for salespeople who have attended the club for several years. One company provides increasingly larger and more prestigious awards for each subsequent year of attendance. If a year is missed, the award sequence begins again. In this way, continuous performance over the years receives special attention.

Some recognition programs can have longer-term implications for sales and specialized support personnel—for example:

- Advancement to a new position, perhaps with different, unusual or special responsibilities.
- Special education or training opportunities to improve existing skills or build new ones.
- The opportunity to serve in a specialized training capacity for the benefit of other (not necessarily more junior) salespersons.
- Special work assignments where new techniques, selling methods, or tools can be developed and tested.

These and similar efforts have significant longer-range benefits for employees who develop faster, learn new skills, and transfer knowledge to other, less-skilled sales personnel. Obviously the company benefits as well.

21.4   Expense Reimbursement

A leading producer and marketer of premium wine encourages its salespeople to entertain customers in top restaurants. A dinner for four at New York's Four Seasons or Chicago's Charlie Trotter's will cost the winery well over $3,000. Of course, only the best wines, including some from competitors, are consumed. Is the expenditure worth it? The winery thinks so. Aside from introducing its products to the sales rep's invited guests, the expenditure further cements the relationship with the restaurant owner, who has the winery's products on the wine list. The winery, the restaurateur, the salesperson, and the invited guests all benefit.

By way of contrast, the perennially top-performing salesperson with a major insurance company, who has total cash earnings well into six figures, is not reimbursed for his business expenses. He is responsible for paying travel, automobile, and entertainment costs. Does this make sense? The insurance company and probably the salesperson will say it does.

In both cases, the company's expense reimbursement policy has taken into consideration the selling environment, the influence (or prominence) of the salesperson, and the corporate tax situation. Because the selling environment and the influence of the salesperson differ greatly from one company to another, it is not surprising that expense reimbursement policies also differ. In fact, expense reimbursement practices run the gamut from full to no payment. In some cases, companies partially reimburse specified categories of expenses; in others, companies impose an upper limit on business-related expenditures.

The principal factor that determines the extent of reimbursement is the nature of the selling job. To state it a different way, the prominence of the sales personnel in the company's marketing mix should dictate the extent to which expenses are reimbursed.

Expenses should not be reimbursed when a sales rep's job entails significant self-direction and the probability of failure is high. Here, "failure" means that sales to most customers will not be consummated on the first try; several visits will be necessary. Furthermore, most potential customers will not buy, so the salesperson must do a lot of prospecting. In such situations, a small percentage of the total sales force develops a large portion of the sales volume. These salespeople are normally paid strictly on commission (as in the insurance case example); travel and entertainment expenses, company cars, and automobile allowances are not usually provided. Such an apparently stringent policy makes sense for several reasons:

- The company will not subsidize weak performers. By paying expenses, the company incurs overhead to maintain a marginally productive salesperson in the field. By not paying these costs, the company can redeploy its limited dollars into incentives for the stellar performers.
- The company minimizes its fixed costs. Because the cost of maintaining the selling effort is borne by the salesperson, the company avoids costs that may not be offset by revenues.
- By reimbursing expenses and automobile costs, the company provides a sense of comfort that may encourage weak sales reps to remain in its employ. By contrast, the stringent policy will encourage turnover among marginally performing sales staff.
- Outstanding performers can readily afford their own automobiles and expenses. In fact, commission rates are often set to provide a special cushion of dollars to fund such expenditures; thus, the company does not incur these costs unless actual sales are made. Furthermore, the most successful salespersons will be able to buy more desirable automobiles than those normally offered to the sales force.

In selling situations other than the one just described, companies usually use the same expense policy for salespeople as for other employees. This is particularly important where the size of the territory requires considerable travel and related expenses. A company that does not reimburse sales reps for their costs runs the risk of discouraging selling activity, because salespeople will be reluctant to spend their own money to maximize the number of calls or to take the extra trip.

Many companies pursue a middle ground between the two expense reimbursement extremes. Some aerospace companies, for example, partially offset expenses by paying a flat allowance (say $2,000 per month) or by providing a per diem—a flat number of expense dollars for each day of travel. In both cases, employees are able to spend as they wish, but the company's financial exposure is limited.

It is also common for companies to reimburse some expenses fully. For example, salespeople with large territories will be eligible for airfare and overnight lodging reimbursement, but salespersons in very small territories that can be covered by automobile will not.

A sales rep may need to spend money on a wide variety of services and products in pursuit of sales. A typical corporate expense reimbursement policy might cover as many as thirty expense categories, which can be broadly grouped into eight classifications:

1. Travel
2. Entertainment
3. Promotion
4. Automobile
5. Telephone and communications
6. Office and home office
7. Automation
8. Miscellaneous

These classifications encompass diverse selling expenses that may or may not be reimbursed depending on company culture and policy, the selling situation, and federal tax law. Exhibit 21-2 subdivides each of the eight classifications to illustrate the breadth of service and product expenses that might be reimbursed.

The selling environment and the associated compensation plan are key determinants of whether particular expense categories are reimbursed. Commission sales forces (high-prominence salespeople) are eligible for some reimbursement of a few expense categories,

Exhibit 21-2. Checklist of Reimbursable Selling Expenses.

Classification	Expense Item
Travel	Airfare Ground transportation Lodging Meals Automobile rental Airline clubs Parking and tolls Incidentals (e.g., dry cleaning)
Entertainment	Meals Refreshments Theater and sporting events
Promotion	Advertising Trade show expenses Samples Audiovisual equipment Meeting rooms
Automobile	Auto club expenses Fuel Maintenance Insurance License tag
Telephone and communications	Usage and line charges Cellular service fees and per-call charges Equipment rental or lease Answering service
Office and home office	Space lease costs Clerical staff Personal computers Equipment Specialized books and periodicals Supplies
Automation	Computer supplies Software Specialized telephone line charges Database usage fees On-line services
Miscellaneous	Credit card fees Personal insurance

where salaried salespeople typically receive a more comprehensive reimbursement.

The most commonly reimbursed selling expenses relate to travel and entertainment. Most companies offset fares for commercial airlines, ground transportation (including some form of automobile expenses), lodging, meals, and customer entertainment.

Automobile policies vary greatly. Although many senior executives receive automobiles as perquisites, companies are encouraging salespeople to use their own cars and accept some form of reimbursement for relevant expenses, typically paid as a predetermined allowance, a payment for each mile driven, or a combination of the two. In some cases, the company pays all relevant operating expenses, including fuel, maintenance, and insurance.

Becoming more prevalent is reimbursement of sales expenditures associated with the home office. The high cost of office locations, highway congestion, and lengthening travel time are encouraging many companies to reimburse home office costs. These might include equipment rental, lease, or purchase (such as facsimile machine, copier, or computer hardware); telephone and supplies; and furniture. In some industry segments, such as insurance sales, the company may establish small remote offices and reimburse the salesperson for some (but not all) associated expenses, such as clerical services and equipment. These remote offices might be found in the salesperson's home or in a nearby office complex.

21.5   Employee Benefits

A specialty drill manufacturer's salespeople make frequent helicopter trips to offshore oil rigs. Company products are used primarily to drill for natural gas pockets located deep in the sea bed, dangerous work because of the possibility of ignition of the flammable gas. It is common for sales reps to work directly with the roughnecks who attach drill tips to the thirty-foot pipe sections and to stay overnight at the platforms. Because of the dangers associated with the on-site work and the possibility of helicopter accidents, all company salespeople are provided with special life and medical insurance coverage—specifically, higher dollar limits on life insurance policies and broader and more valuable disability coverage than that provided to other company employees.

Specialized benefit programs are designed to reflect the nature of the selling task, business strategy, and the overall role and influence of the sales force. Aside from direct compensation (base salary and some form of incentive) and expense reimbursement, the total rewards package commonly includes various forms of indirect compensation. Indirect compensation is designed to protect sales reps and their families and to build financial security for the future. Benefit programs might include some or all of the following coverages:

- Comprehensive health insurance, which may include hospital and related services, outpatient psychiatric care, vision, and dental coverages
- Disability insurance, including both short- and long-term coverage, and accidental death and dismemberment benefits
- Survivor benefits, such as group life insurance and surviving spouse's coverage
- Retirement programs
- Profit-sharing or productivity gain-sharing programs
- Child day care
- Financial planning
- Capital accumulation programs, such 401(k) plans
- Stock grants or stock purchase plans

In principle, sales personnel should receive the same benefit coverages as do their peers in other company functions (that is, employees of stature approximately equal to their own). Thus, benefit coverages for salespersons at certain total cash compensation levels (salary plus incentive pay) should match those provided to other employees with similar compensation.

In reality, there will probably be some variation, particularly in establishing survivor and retirement coverages. The key issue is the earnings base for calculating coverages. For example, the amount of life insurance available under the company's group policy is usually expressed as a percentage of annual compensation. For salaried sales personnel and other employees, this calculation is straightforward. But it becomes more complex for salespeople whose compensation comprises both salary and variable compensation that can change significantly from year to year. This issue may be addressed by excluding all incentive earnings and determining benefit coverages on the basis of salary only, using total earnings in the most recent full year as the earnings base, or calculating coverage on current salary plus a moving average of several recent years' incentive payments.

The first option—excluding incentives—is viable only if incentive awards do not constitute a large part of total earnings, say 20 percent of salary at most. It is unduly discriminatory to ignore the incentive earnings of those salespersons who depend on variable compensation as their principal source of income. The second option—using most recent total earnings—may also create inequities. Benefit coverages could be reduced if incentive payments decline because of changing market conditions (outside the salesperson's control) or a one-time slump in personal performance. Given these caveats, the third option—using a moving average to calculate benefit coverages—is an appropriate compromise.

A sales rep's role in the marketing mix is the principal determinant of benefit coverage, assuming basic benefits are generally comparable to those given to other employees. The situation is analogous to the reimbursement of selling expenses: Representatives in high-prominence selling roles, where high turnover is likely, are not generally provided with the more costly benefit coverages.

Finally, by minimizing benefits (and possibly reimbursed expenses), a company will not run the risk of encouraging marginal performers to stay with the company. Generous benefit and payment programs provide extra comfort to weak salespeople who need the security.

22

Managing the Other Drivers of Sales Performance

Although pay and benefits frequently represent the largest monetary costs associated with salespeople, the opportunities to manage performance and the return on those investments extend well beyond the sales compensation plan.

Ask yourself if the following statements describe your sales operations:

"We attract and retain talented employees who give our company an edge over the competition."

"Turnover and the costs related to it are where they should be."

"We know what our customers want and our sales, service, and technical personnel are well trained to meet those needs."

"Our sales reps are focused, are motivated, and create a positive buying experience for our customers."

"Our sales managers are driving key results and serving as effective role models."

"Our middle and senior sales managers demonstrate exemplary leadership qualities."

"Our 'bench strength' enables us to keep key positions staffed with very capable people."

"Our sales reps and managers are clear about how best to execute our sales and operations strategies."

If you answered no or maybe to any of the above statements, there is a good chance that your organization needs attention. The good news is that the problems may be addressed fully or partially by improving your sales force management programs.

Exhibit 22-1. Spectrum of Performance Management Programs.

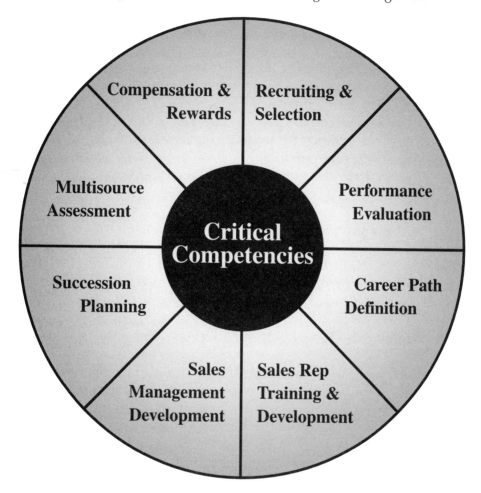

To improve sales rep performance, you must consider the "ho-listic view" taken by many employees for whom pay is only part of the picture. To unlock extra discretionary effort you must consider the full range of sales force management programs illustrated in Exhibit 22-1.

The level of excitement and commitment exhibited by your employees will be directly affected by the quality and integration of the following programs:

- *Recruitment and selection initiatives* screen candidates for critical competencies and clearly communicate the company's culture and personal success factors.
- *Performance evaluation programs* deliver ongoing, frequent feedback that is accurate, fair, and useful.

- *Defined career paths* provide clear opportunities for personal growth if they are well communicated.
- *Training and development opportunities* increase sales rep and sales manager capabilities and competencies, which enhances their value in both the internal and external marketplaces.
- *Succession planning* and promotion criteria recognize company capability requirements.
- *Multisource assessment programs* provide more credible and diverse performance feedback to reps than do supervisor-only assessment programs.
- *Compensation and reward programs* recognize appropriate sales results, desired behaviors, and competencies.

Painting the entire picture entails developing or improving performance management programs to help salespeople acquire the critical competencies they'll need to succeed and to ensure that your company has the capabilities required to win in the marketplace.

22.1 Building the Foundation for Successful Program Design

As with the process for sales compensation design, when designing performance management programs you first must consider the three drivers of an effective sales system that we introduced in Chapter 1:

1. *Well-defined market opportunities*—understanding what customers need and value.
2. *Clear strategy*—setting selling strategic and tactical goals and deciding how to go to market to accomplish them.
3. *Understanding of the company's capabilities*—assessing the collective abilities of the company to execute its strategy and win in the marketplace with the purpose of identifying gaps and surpluses.

As illustrated in Exhibit 22-2, these three drivers can form the foundation of a well-constructed program for performance management. One of the main objectives of such a program is to help close a company's capability gaps. The trick in making any investment in such performance management is to focus on closing the most important gaps. Through a variety of analytical techniques, you can identify the capabilities required, rank each capability according to its importance, and assign it a score that denotes your company's perfor-

Exhibit 22-2. Performance Management Program Design Process.

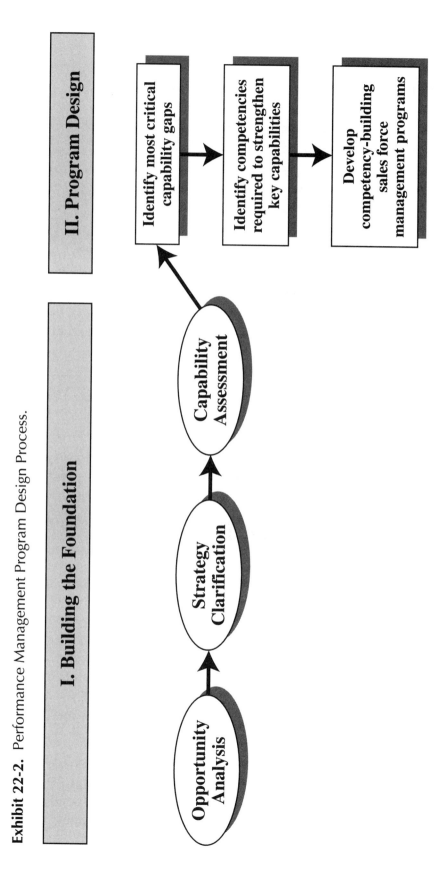

I. Building the Foundation

II. Program Design

Opportunity Analysis

Strategy Clarification

Capability Assessment

Identify most critical capability gaps

Identify competencies required to strengthen key capabilities

Develop competency-building sales force management programs

Exhibit 22-3. Example Company Capability Analysis.

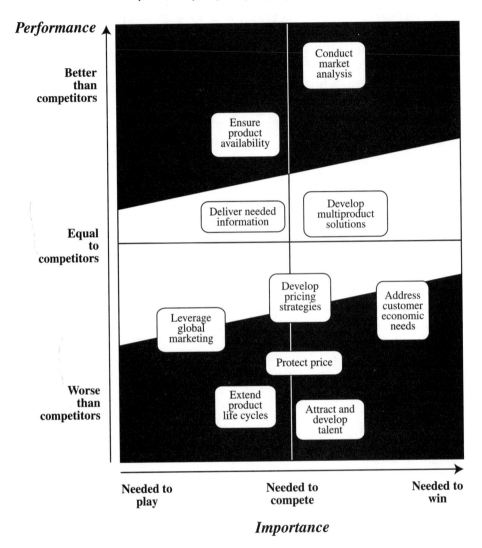

mance. Graphing each required capability (as illustrated in Exhibit 22-3) pinpoints where your company is performing better than, the same as, or worse than its competitors. It also shows where it may be over- or underinvesting and which capability gaps require the most immediate attention.

For example, the company depicted in Exhibit 22-3 is overinvesting in market analysis and underinvesting in attracting and developing sales talent and addressing customer economic needs (among other things). Properly designed sales force management programs can help a company acquire, develop, and reward employee competencies that collectively will improve its performance on key capabilities and effectively "close the gap."

It may seem obvious that successful sales strategy execution depends on the collective capabilities of your sales organization, which in large part stem from the specific competencies of your salespeople. Determining which competencies are most important, where performance is weak, and how to strengthen critical competencies is quite another matter. Taking a disciplined approach to identifying the drivers of sales force effectiveness and critical sales force capability gaps will help you decide where to direct your investment in performance improvement programs.

22.2 Competencies: Building Blocks of High Performance

Competency-based sales force management programs can help close your company's capability gaps. Did you ever wonder what life would be like if you could clone your best performers? What your team could accomplish if it consisted entirely of superstars? What it would take to capture your top salespeople's "magic" and replicate it across the sales force? A competency-based approach to performance management offers a way to answer these questions.

Competencies are the observable skills, knowledge, and behaviors underlying organizational success and personal performance. Broadly speaking, there are two types of competencies. Enabling and domain competencies are defined below:

Enabling competencies are:	*Domain competencies* are:
• Essential to implementing business strategy or values	• Required for success in a particular job family
• Typically critical behaviors and skills	• Typically involve demonstrated knowledge in a technical, professional, or process area
• Generally relevant to all employees	• Behaviors needed in a particular role or function but not in the company as a whole
For example:	For example:
• Adaptability	• Product application knowledge
• Teamwork	• Negotiation
• Communication	• Directing others

Competencies that help close capability gaps are identified by answering such questions as the following:

- What key activities make up this capability and what behaviors are required to successfully perform these activities?
- If we were strong in this capability, what would we be doing, what would we know, or what skills would we have that we don't today?
- What do people who are really effective know or do that distinguishes them from others?

Exhibit 22-4 illustrates how to identify groups of competencies that support the development of organization capabilities. For example, to strengthen your sales force you first must determine which competencies should be acquired and which should be developed in-house. This will help you decide which programs to develop first (e.g., recruiting/selection versus training/development and performance evaluation).

The competencies that you use to develop sales force management programs should have the following characteristics:

- Be linked to the company's strategic business challenges, and thus ensure impact.
- Directly support organization success factors, and thus provide competitive advantage.
- Represent current and future requirements—to address tomorrow's as well as today's challenges.
- Be derived from a rigorous methodology, and thus be robust and accurate.
- Be specific, concrete, and behavioral, and thus be observable.
- Reflect superior (not just good) performance.
- Be simple to understand—to enhance credibility and user acceptance.

Let's review an example of how competencies can be used to improve sales force performance. Consider a company whose goal is to become a top-tier supplier to managed care organizations. It discovers that a "needed-to-win" capability is promoting and selling the economic benefits of a bundled, multiproduct customer solution—not just the superior features and reliability of its individual products. On investigation, the company discovers that although its account executives are product application experts, few are capable of selling on the basis of economic value. Thus, to better execute its

Exhibit 22-4. Capabilities vs. Competencies Matrix.

Identifying Required Competencies

Organization Capabilities	Competencies						
	Accountability	Partnership and Teamwork	Customer-Focused Actions	Innovation and Creativity	Communication	Business Knowledge	Functional Knowledge
Quality service		✔	✔				
Customer relations			✔		✔		
External communication					✔	✔	
Ownership behaviors	✔	✔					✔
Speed and agility	✔			✔			
Market segmentation		✔	✔			✔	✔
Market driver					✔		
Information access							✔

Exhibit 22-5. Example Competency Model for a Managed Care Account Executive.

	Core Category	
Professionalism	*Solutions Orientation*	*Personal Effectiveness*
Business savvy	Consultative skills	Adaptability
Customer service orientation	Influence	Results orientation
Organizational expertise	Innovation	Self-confidence
		Teamwork

sales strategy, this company could develop a competency model for this position that emphasizes business savvy, a competency critical to success of the business. All account executives then would be assessed against each required competency, and performance management programs would focus on closing individual competency gaps.

Further, competencies can be organized into core categories. For example, a competency model for this managed care account executive might focus on three competency categories: professionalism, solutions orientation, and personal effectiveness. Within each core category are the specific personal competencies that the account executive must possess. The categories and the specific personal competencies for this account executive are listed in Exhibit 22-5.

Each identified personal competency should be accompanied by a clear definition of the required skills, knowledge, and proficiency. Using that definition you can determine the behaviors and actions to be exhibited by the account executive. Exhibit 22-6 lists these attributes for two of the competencies required of the account executive.

To close the "business savvy" capability gap (and other capability gaps) this supplier should begin to incorporate these role-specific competencies into some core performance management programs, starting with recruitment and selection, performance evaluation, training and development, and then career path definition and promotion criteria. The goal is to begin to operationalize or institutionalize competency development, measurement, and recognition.

22.3 Applying Competencies to Performance Management Programs

Competencies can be applied to a wide range of performance management programs, including recruiting and selection, performance evaluation, career path definition, training and development, succession planning, multisource assessment, and compensation and rewards.

Recruiting and Selection

Weaving competencies into recruitment advertising, recruiting profiles and selection criteria, interview techniques, and internal and external recruiter training funnels into the recruitment stream those prospects who are most likely to succeed. That is, they are most likely to execute sales strategy, drive the achievement of performance goals, and create competitive advantage for the hiring company.

Incorporating competencies into recruiting and selection programs will yield the following benefits:

Exhibit 22-6. Sample Competencies and Their Associated Behaviors.

Competency	Definition	Sample Behaviors and Actions
Business savvy	• Having a broadly based understanding of key business fundamentals, and applying that acumen to health care management • Knowing how business gets done and how decisions get made, and striving to develop financially prudent partnerships • Demonstrating a clear grasp of the drivers of the customer's and company's business success and stability in the short and long term	• Discusses health economic issues and thinks in terms of cost-effectiveness and patient outcomes. • Develops financial analyses and business cases to support economic value of recommendations. • Develops market and account plans that target best prospects or highly influential managed care organizations. • Studies the history and patterns of managed care organizations to determine profit potential and account strategy. • Leverages information technology and other sales managerial tools to ensure that the best information is readily available. • Has a return on investment bent, and recognizes that efforts must ultimately lead to product movement and market penetration.

(continues)

Exhibit 22-6. (*continued*)

Competency	Definition	Sample Behaviors and Actions
Customer service orientation	• Concentrating efforts on discovering and meeting the customer's short and long-term needs • Understanding the multiplicity and diversity of customers, and addressing their unique needs • Showing a commitment to, and a sense of urgency about, helping the customer gain and sustain a competitive advantage	• Constantly asks, "What value is my customer getting from my actions?" and thinks of that value from the customer's perspective. • Keeps commitments: does what he or she says he or she is going to do, and follows up to be certain it was done to the customer's satisfaction. • Makes it a priority to listen to, understand, and respond to different customer needs and goals within as well as across managed care organizations. • Serves as an advocate of customers and gets them quickly connected to valuable resources and solutions inside and outside the company. • Is sensitive to time constraints on customers and ensures own interactions and information are of the highest possible quality and value. • Tailors approach to customers to be sensitive to their particular needs and to make it as easy as possible to do business.

- A better fit between the requirements of the job and the personal characteristics of the reps you hire (which also results in higher job performance and job satisfaction).
- Potentially the shortest route to direct, visible impact on your organization.
- The opportunity to screen for the "deeper" competencies that are difficult to build through training, such as flexibility.

Performance Evaluation and Feedback

Here we measure total employee performance by defining it in terms of both "the what" (results) and "the how" (competencies). This provides a framework for answering sales rep questions such as:

- What did I accomplish, and did I use the appropriate methods?
- Where do I stand in relation to my peers, and where am I going?
- What can I do to develop my skills and progress more rapidly?

Incorporating competencies into performance evaluation and feedback programs provides a common, job-relevant framework for your sales managers and reps to use when discussing the behavioral side of performance.

Career Path Definition

Competencies and proficiency levels required for each position are identified and communicated throughout the organization; the multiple career tracks open to the sales rep are delineated as well. Incorporating competencies into career path programs provides reps with a more detailed road map, including the specific competencies that they will have to develop to progress in their careers.

Training and Development

Competencies that are "trainable" are identified and then incorporated into needs assessments, to compare where reps are versus where they should be. Arising from this evaluation are various training options such as classroom-based training; self-paced written, audio, and video materials; job assignments; and mentoring programs.

Incorporating competencies into training and development programs ensures a direct "line of sight" between the development opportunities sales reps are offered and the competencies that are critical to your organization's success.

Succession Planning

Identifying key jobs and their competency requirements enables you to assess possible successor candidates and to develop replacement charts. Building competencies into your succession process increases the rigor with which you can assess candidates by providing detailed information on candidate competencies that supplements the review of past performance and accomplishments.

Multisource Assessment

This performance evaluation process allows for direct feedback from individuals judged to be in the best position to observe the rep's performance. Those providing input might include the rep being evaluated and the sales manager, co-workers, subordinates, or customers. Incorporating competencies into a multisource assessment program greatly improves the credibility and richness of the feedback provided to the sales rep.

Compensation and Rewards

In addition to recognizing results (as discussed in earlier chapters), these programs can be used to reinforce competency demonstration and development. Paying for and rewarding competency development demonstrates your organization's commitment to competencies as a valued part of employee performance.

Glossary

accelerating incentive rate   An incentive rate that increases after a certain level of performance is achieved.

at the margin   The point at which sales reps make active trade-offs among various priorities.

barrier to entry   Credentials that a candidate must possess to be considered for a particular position.

barrier to exit   The combination of cash compensation, noncash awards, and career opportunities designed to retain qualified employees.

bonus   An opportunity to earn a percentage of salary or a set dollar amount or range in exchange for attaining specified results.

cap   Maximum earnings realizable from an incentive plan.

combination rate plan   A plan that uses two or more incentive rates to compensate sales reps.

commission   A predetermined proportionate sharing of revenue arising from a discrete unit of sales.

cost-of-sales ratio   Sales costs divided by sales volume.

decelerating incentive rate   An incentive rate that decreases after a certain level of performance is achieved.

direct compensation   Compensation in the form of cash or cash equivalents, including salary, bonus, and commission.

disguised base salary   Level of income above base salary that is highly likely to be earned regardless of the individual's effectiveness.

distribution channel   The conduit by which a commodity is marketed or merchandised.

draw   Cash advanced against future income.

draw, nonrecoverable   Minimum level of income guaranteed for a specific period of time regardless of sales results.

draw, recoverable   Strict cash advance for which a sales rep must forfeit any portion not covered by calculated incentive earnings.

end user   The ultimate consumer of a finished product.

event-driven approach   Incentive whose payment is made at the date of accomplishment rather than at chronological intervals.

experience approach   Same as maturity ladder approach.

high-risk compensation   Income that the sales rep may receive none of, unless warranted by results.

house accounts   Customers buying very large volumes who are managed, serviced, and "sold" by management rather than by the field sales rep.

implicit quota   Unspecified patterns of performance that create high income for the sales rep.

incentive compensation   Payment received to reward current productivity (may be commission, bonus, or combination).

leverage   The proportion of the pay package that is represented by high-risk compensation.

line-of-credit approach   Program in which part or all of the sales rep's salary is treated as an advance against future incentive earnings.

lone ranger   Sales rep whose only concern is maximizing the number of sales and who is not responsible for customer care.

longevity approach   Base salary increases as years of internal sales experience increase.

low-risk compensation   Compensation a sales rep is virtually assured of receiving, regardless of effectiveness.

market segments   Groupings of accounts whose buying characteristics are similar.

marketing strategy   A statement of the focus and priorities of a company's business.

maturity ladder approach   Base salary increases as years of sales experience increase.

moderate-risk compensation   A package that combines assured income with high-risk compensation.

percentile   Measure of location in a distribution of numbers that defines the value below which a given percentage of the data fall.

perforated cap   Restrictions on maximum incentive plan earnings that allow partial credit for a windfall sale.

perquisite   A benefit tied to a specific key or management-level job (e.g., a company car).

principle of sufficient difference   The difference in economic return sufficient to make a sales rep actively pursue one course of action over another.

progressive commission rate   A commission rate that increases in steps after certain levels of performance are achieved.

prominence   Degree of the sales rep's influence on the buying decision.

quota   Expected or planned level of performance assigned to a sales rep.

quota "kicker"   Increase in commission rate resulting from quota attainment in each product line.

recognition program   Program that provides material recognition to employees for meeting defined criteria.

regressive commission rate   A commission rate that decreases after a certain level of performance is achieved.

RFP   Request for proposal issued by an organization soliciting bids for a project.

risk-averse   Incentive compensation with little true variability based on sales results.

risk compensation   Income that a sales rep may not receive.

sales contest   Event entailing short-term sales effort to maximize results for a nonrecurring purpose in an effort to win a prize.

sales information system   Formal compilation of the collective knowledge of the markets, together with systems for disseminating the information.

single rate base salary   All sales reps receive the same base salary.

split credits   Sharing of sales credit between two or more sales reps.

stack ranking   Salary increases are taken out of an allotted budget based on the ranking of each sales rep's performance.

tenure approach   Same as *longevity approach.*

threshold   Performance level at which an incentive plan payout begins.

validation factor   That part of a sales rep's guaranteed income that must be covered by computed incentive earnings before incentive is paid.

variable pay   Nonguaranteed portion of total compensation.

windfall   A sale created by fortuitous conditions beyond the influence of the sales rep.

Index

[Page numbers in italics refer to exhibits.]

About the Editor

Stockton B. Colt, Jr., has 20 years of experience in sales management consulting with international corporations involved in selling to other businesses and to the consumer. Aside from his focus on employee rewards and recognition, he councils his clients on sales strategy, organization of sales and service staffs, sales role design and competencies, sales and service force deployment, and personnel performance management. His work has encompassed both direct and indirect sales forces, telesales, and the customer service functions in a variety of industries.

In addition to his personal consulting, Mr. Colt leads Towers Perrin's global sales management consulting practice, which help clients implement customer-centered sales and marketing strategies by effectively managing people resources. In this role he is responsible for the work of consultants worldwide as well as the development of consulting concepts relating to customer management. He is a principal of the firm.

Mr. Colt is a frequent speaker on sales productivity and incentive compensation. He has conducted courses on the topic of sales incentive design for the American Compensation Association for over five years, and he also creates and presents training classes for clients, trade groups, and professional associations. Mr. Colt has published numerous articles in a broad range of professional and business periodicals, including *Sales and Marketing Management Magazine.* He wrote sections of the first edition of *The Sales Compensation Handbook* as well as managed the contributions of others.

Mr. Colt has a B.A. in languages from Auburn University and an M.B.A. in marketing and international management from UCLA. Prior to his career in industry, Mr. Colt was a naval aviator. He currently resides in Santa Fe, New Mexico.

Contributors

Twenty-five business consultants contributed their expertise and knowledge to this book. Their decades of collective sales management experience provide a pragmatic perspective on the issues of sales incentive compensation. Shown below, the handbook's contributors served diverse clients in a variety of industries as consultants with Towers Perrin, a global consulting firm that provides an array of integrated human resources and general management services. Towers Perrin helps clients improve their competitive position and implement strategy through the cost-effective management of their investments in people. Sales incentive compensation is one tool to achieve this goal.

Ronald G. Burke
Gordon Canning, Jr.
Stockton B. Colt, Jr.
J. Mark Davis
Philip B. Davis
James R. Deach
Frank X. Dowd III
Mark T. Flavin
Marla J. Forbes
Edward A. Francisco
Robert J. Freedman
Steven H. Grossman
Kevin R. Hummel
Mark R. Hurwich
Jay C. Knoll
Gary R. Lawrence
Christopher M. Lewallyn
Gary M. Locke
John K. Moynahan
Michelle A. Rogers
Michael V. Savage
Eric L. Sawyer
David N. Swinford
Timothy W. Weiler
Timothy J. Weizer